PRODUCING THE PAST

REINTERPRETING CLASSICISM
Culture, Reaction and Appropriation
Series Editor: Caroline van Eck, Vrije Universiteit, Amsterdam
Published with the assistance of the Getty Grant Program

Sir John Soane and the Country Estate
Ptolemy Dean

Allan Ramsay and the Search for Horace's Villa
Iain Gordon Brown, John Dixon Hunt, Bernard D. Frischer,
Patricia R. Andrew
Forthcoming 2000

*Germain Boffrand's Traité d'architecture concernant les principes
généraux de cet art*
A Critical Edition
Caroline van Eck
Forthcoming 2000

*The Built Surface: Volume I: Architecture and Pictures from
Antiquity to the Enlightenment*
*The Built Surface: Volume II: Architecture and Pictures from
Romanticism to the Millennium*
Edited by Christy Anderson and Karen Koehler
Forthcoming 2000

Producing the Past

Aspects of Antiquarian Culture and Practice
1700–1850

Edited by Martin Myrone and Lucy Peltz

ASHGATE

Published by   Ashgate Publishing Company
Ashgate Publishing Limited   Old Post Road
Gower House   Brookfield
Croft Road   Vermont 05036–9704
Aldershot   USA
Hants GU11 3HR
England

British Library Cataloguing-in-Publication data

Producing the past: aspects of antiquarian culture and
    practice 1700–1850
    1. Historiography – Social aspects   2. Antiquarians – Great
    Britain – History   3. Great Britain – Historiography   4. Great
    Britain – Civilization – 18th century   5. Great Britain –
    Civilization – 19th century
    I. Myrone, Martin   II. Peltz, Lucy
    941'.0072

Library of Congress Cataloging-in-Publication data

Producing the past: aspects of antiquarian culture and practice,
    1700–1850 / edited by Martin Myrone and Lucy Peltz.
        p.   cm.
    Includes bibliographical references and index.
    ISBN 1–84014–275–8 (hardback)
    1. Museums–Historiography.   2. Historical museums–History.
    3. Museum techniques–Historiography.   4. Historiography–History.
    5. Antiquarians–Historiography.   6. Archaeology and history.
    7. Material culture.   8. Antiquities.
I. Myrone, Martin   II. Peltz, Lucy
AM7.P76   1999
069'.09–dc21   98–53016
                                                                                 CIP

ISBN 1 84014 275 8
Printed on acid-free paper

Typeset in Palatino by IML Typographers, Chester
Printed in Great Britain at the University Press, Cambridge

[10580]

Contents

List of illustrations

from the Thomas Monro estate, 1806.
© The British Museum

10   Science and sensibility: architectural antiquarianism in the early nineteenth century

10.1   *The 'Willow Cathedral' built under the direction of Sir James Hall*, etching, W. & D. Lizars, published in Sir James Hall, *An Essay on the Origin, History and Progress of Gothic Architecture* (1813), frontispiece. By permission of the British Library, 434.i.22

10.2   Reconstructions of the Great Paleothere from its fossilized skeleton, wood engraving, after an illustration by C. Laurillard from *Recherches sur les Ossemens Fossiles* (1821–4), published in R. Owen, *A History of British Fossil Mammals and Birds* (1846), fig.109, p.316. University of London Library

10.3   Edmund Sharpe's reconstruction of the east window of Tintern Abbey, wood engraving, G. B. S., published in E. Sharpe, *Illustrations of Decorated Windows* (1849), pl.12. By permission of the Syndics of Cambridge University Library, 1268. C.45(2)

10.4   Robert Willis's tabulation of the stylistic sequences proposed by earlier scholars, Add. MS 5029, f.62, Cambridge University Library. By permission of the Syndics of Cambridge University Library

10.5   Henry de la Beche's tabulation of the geological systems proposed by earlier scholars, published in H. T. de la Beche, *A Geological Manual* (1831), pp.38–9. University of London Library

10.6   Robert Willis's historical plan of Canterbury Cathedral, wood engraving, drawn by R. Willis, engraved by Delamotte and Heaviside, 1843, published in R. Willis, *The Architectural History of Canterbury Cathedral* (1845), figs. 5–6. Author's collection

11   Story, history and the passionate collector

11.1   Ferdinand Franz Wallraf sitting among his collection like a dragon in his lair, chalk drawing, Nicolas Salm, *c.*1820. Rheinisches Bildarchiv, Köln

11.2   Hans von Aufsess living in and amidst his collection of medieval artefacts, n.d., photograph. Germanisches Nationalmuseum, Nürnberg

11.3   'The Knight', Hans von Aufsess, does battle with the foes of historical preservation, pen & ink – illustration in the guestbook of Castle Aufsess, Wilhelm von Kaulbach, 1865. Archiv Familie Aufsess

List of contributors

STEPHEN BANN is Professor of Modern Cultural Studies at the University of Kent. He is the author of several books on the history of historical representation, including *The Clothing of Clio* (Cambridge, 1984), *The Inventions of History* (Manchester, 1990), *Under the Sign: John Bargrave as Collector, Traveller, and Witness* (Ann Arbor, 1994) and *Romanticism and the Rise of History* (New York, 1995). His most recent publication is *Paul Delaroche: History Painted* (London and Princeton, 1997) and he is currently working on the culture of reproduction in nineteenth-century France.

STEPHEN BENDING is a lecturer in the Department of English, University of Southampton. He is the author of a number of articles on the politics of eighteenth-century garden design, the co-editor of the forthcoming anthology, *The Writing of Rural England, 1500–1800,* and is completing a study of gardens and polite culture. His research interests include popular aesthetics and travel, antiquarianism, garden history, and eighteenth-century fiction.

ALEXANDRINA BUCHANAN is an archivist at Lambeth Palace Library. Her PhD was entitled 'Robert Willis – and the Rise of Architectural History' and she continues to research and publish on the subject of medieval architecture and its interpretation.

SUSAN A. CRANE is Assistant Professor in Modern European History at the University of Arizona. She has lectured on the history of collecting and issues of historical memory. Her recent publications include 'Loss vs Preservation: The Differences Between Historical Memory and Collective Memory', *American Historical Review*, 102:5 (1997) and 'Memory, Distortion and History in the Museum', *History and Theory*, theme issue 36 (1997). She is a contributing editor for the volume *Museums and Memory* (Stanford, California, forthcoming).

DAVID HAYCOCK read Modern History at St John's College, Oxford, and Art History at the University of Sussex. He has recently completed a doctoral thesis at Birkbeck College, University of London, entitled: 'Dr William Stukeley (1687–1765): antiquarianism and Newtonianism in eighteenth-century England.' He is currently a junior fellow at Wolfson College, Oxford.

MARIA GRAZIA LOLLA has recently completed her PhD ' "Monuments" and "Texts": Antiquarianism and Literature in Eighteenth- and early Nineteenth-century Britain', at the University of Cambridge. Her publications include articles on eighteenth-century literary forgeries and Caribbean literature in English. She is currently working on a project entitled 'Rivers Unknown to Song', which treats antiquarian explorations of the East and West Indies. She completed this article when she was senior fellow at the Center for the Humanities at the Wesleyan University.

HEATHER MACLENNAN is lecturer in Fine Art and Cultural Studies at Cheltenham and Gloucester College of Higher Education. She is currently completing her PhD, 'Antiquarianism, Master Prints and the Aesthetic in the New Collecting Culture of the Early Nineteenth Century', at Birkbeck College, University of London . She has also written on aspects of art education.

MARTIN MYRONE is Programme Curator British Art pre-1900, at the Tate Gallery of British Art. His main area of research addresses masculinity and academic art in late eighteenth-century Britain and he is also currently preparing an article on the career of George Vertue for publication in the *Walpole Society*.

LUCY PELTZ is Assistant Curator of Prints, Drawings and Paintings at the Museum of London. She is currently preparing a book on the history of extra-illustration with the assistance of a post-doctoral fellowship from the Paul Mellon Centre for Studies in British Art.

ANNEGRET PELZ currently holds a Lise-Meitner-Scholarship at the Universität GH Paderborn, where her field is Literary and Cultural Studies. She has given lectures at the universities of Hamburg, Oldenburg, Osnabrück, Tübingen (Germany) and Klagenfurt (Austria). Her recent publications include: 'The Invention of Europe: Its Mapping Recollected', in Thomas Wägenbaur (ed.), *The Poetics of Memory* (Tübingen, Stauffenburg, 1998); *Frauen reisen. Ein bibliographisches Verzeichnis deutschsprachiger Frauenreisen 1700–1810* (co-authored with Wolfgang Griep) (Bremen, Edition Temmen, 1995); 'Karten als Lesefiguren literarischer Räume', *German Studies Review*, ed. Gerald Kleinfeld, 18:1 (February 1995), pp. 115–29; *Reisen durch die eigene Fremde* (Köln, Weimar, Wien, Böhlau, 1993). Her next book will be on writing and space.

JOHANN REUSCH is Assistant Professor in the Department of Fine and Performing Arts, Baruch College, City University of New York. He has written extensively on art and culture from the eighteenth century to the present day and curated numerous exhibitions.

SAM SMILES is Principal Lecturer in the History of Art at the University of Plymouth. He has published extensively on landscape painting and the history of antiquarian illustration. His most recent works include: *The Image of Antiquity* (New Haven and London, 1994), *The Perfection of England: Artist Visitors to Devon c. 1750–1870* (Exeter, 1995) and *Two-Way Traffic: British and Italian Art c. 1880–1980* (Exeter, 1996).

Acknowledgements

The idea for this book was first formulated at a session of the Association of Art Historians' annual conference, held at the Courtauld Institute of Art, in April 1997. It was there that we realized the extent to which antiquarianism has been neglected as an area of cultural history. It was also in preparing that session, and at the conference itself, that we observed the wide-ranging potential as well as the complex, interdisciplinary debates and vibrant new work that antiquarianism could generate. We would like to thank all the contributors to that session, many of whose work is represented in this volume. Especial thanks go to Stephen Bann, for taking an interest in our project and for providing us with a stimulating and incisive preface. Also to Marcia Pointon for her ongoing support and to Anne Puetz for her translation of Annegret Pelz's essay. Finally we are indebted to our editors, Pamela Edwardes and Sue Moore.

Preface

Stephen Bann

In the opening chapter of *The Old Curiosity Shop*, first published in serial form in April 1840, Charles Dickens describes in a wonderfully dense and suggestive paragraph the setting which gives the novel its name:

> The place through which he made his way at leisure, was one of those receptacles for old and curious things which seem to crouch in odd corners of this town, and to hide their musty treasures from the public eye in jealousy and disgust. There were suits of mail standing like ghosts in armour, here and there; fantastic carving brought from monkish cloisters; rusty weapons of various kinds; distorted figures in china, and wood, and iron, and ivory; tapestry, and strange furniture that might have been designed in dreams. The haggard aspect of the little old man was wonderfully suited to the place; he might have groped among old churches, and tombs, and deserted houses, and gathered all the spoils with his own hands. There was nothing in the whole collection but was in keeping with himself; nothing that looked older or more worn than he.[1]

Dating as it does from the last decade of the period covered by this collective study, the text conflates the 'old man' with his milieu and produces what could almost be called a hieroglyph of antiquarianism: a short exercise in the grotesque which is evocative of so many earlier literary presentations, just as the accompanying illustrations draw on a well-established iconography of the antiquarian in his overcrowded study. But for Dickens, it is not simply a matter of providing verbal (and visual) vignettes to establish the narrative. The mouldering milieu which initially sets off the fresh and innocent figure of Little Nell also serves as an intradiegetic metaphor of the gloomy experiences that she will undergo, surrounded by 'associates as strange and uncongenial as the grim objects that are about her bed when her history is first foreshadowed'.[2]

Dickens has no scruples about using the antiquarian context as a mere foil to the saintly and vulnerable figure of his tiny heroine. Whereas Sir Walter Scott, in *The Antiquary*, had established an affectionately ironic distance between the eponymous Jonathan Oldbuck and the authorial voice, Dickens can only castigate Nell's improvident grandfather. He is revealed to be a compulsive gambler and, as a result of his addiction, the whole elaborate decor of the 'Curiosity Shop' has to be demolished and sold off before Nell's adventure starts. However both Scott and Dickens present us with a problem of method which clearly relates to the present study. How do we get behind the stereotypes of antiquarianism, as they have been powerfully reinforced by visual and literary traditions? Is it too much to hope that Little Nell, after all her peregrinations, might have opted to return home and open up the 'Curiosity Shop' for business?

Let me say in response to these rhetorical questions that the young scholars contributing to this study do indeed enable us to see the phenomenon of antiquarian culture with fresh eyes. What is more, this is a cumulative effect, arising from the remarkable variety of the chapters as well as their intrinsic quality of openness and lack of prejudice before the materials. Historians have certainly not neglected the study of antiquarianism in recent years. Yet all too often the nature of the enquiry has been largely defined by the evident wish to distinguish good from bad historiographic practice, according to contemporary lights. It is as if Dr Jekyll had written his autobiography and carefully set a distance between his own eminent career and the disreputable doings of a certain Mr Hyde. Whilst Scott as a nineteenth-century novelist could resourcefully explore his own complex investment in the past by manipulating the fictional persona of the Antiquary, the historian of our own century has not infrequently tried to project a disciplinary superego on to past masters who are ill equipped for such a burden.

As Maria Grazia Lolla argues in the survey of antiquarian aesthetics which opens this collection, this has resulted in what could be termed, with reference to Herbert Butterfield's iconoclastic attack on Macaulay and his successors, 'the Whig interpretation of historiography'. Arnaldo Momigliano deserves the ambivalent credit of having taken the antiquarians seriously, and having at the same time determined the serious part of their enterprise to be a flattering mirror-image of the profile of the twentieth-century historian. In a recent lecture commemorating the achievement of William Camden, the Tudor historian Patrick Collinson has neatly transposed this debate into the very heartland of English antiquarianism by asking if the author of *Britannia* can be considered 'one of us'.[3] The Thatcherite refrain reminds us that there is inevitably a political agenda involved when a historian attempts to assess his predecessors according to their respect for the 'documents'. As Collinson himself demonstrated, the respect for the 'archive' in Tudor historiography derived from the view that historical agents such as princes and their ministers were closest to events, and would ideally be their own historians. To consult documents was therefore to get as close as possible to the sources of historical action, rather than to vindicate a rule of unbiased objectivity.

To be reminded of this kind of point is also to be aware of how recently it would have gone against the grain of professional opinion. Even such recent and justly acclaimed studies as the collection of essays edited by Eric Hobsbawm and Terence Ranger, *The Invention of Tradition* (1983), can be accused of favouring far too clean a division between the false history conveyed by insecurely based 'traditions' and the true history which authenticates itself precisely by relegating such things to the penumbra. In so far as many of the 'traditions' instanced in this work were fostered and revived by antiquarians, we might view even so fruitful and influential an enquiry as helping to perpetuate the Whig interpretation of historiography.

I detect a different spirit in all the contributors – Italian, German and American as well as British – to this study. They do not appear to be intimidated by the notion of an absolute disciplinary ideal which is the ultimate guarantee of value. They are off the gold standard. But this makes them all the more qualified to look at the bewilderingly rich range of practices which make up the spectrum of antiquarian activity in the one and a half centuries under review. In particular, they are attuned to the extraordinary diversity of non-verbal media through which the antiquarian community defined its attitude to the past: from landscape gardening to extra-illustration, from the detailed documentation of historical costume to the storing of 'curios' in a writer's desk. Yet it is not simply a matter of broadening the spectrum in order to take in so many diverse types of activity. A more fundamental point about method emerges, and this should be taken into account.

All of these contributors are aware of the many useful tools of analysis, bearing particularly on visual materials, that have become available over the past thirty years. In his chapter, Sam Smiles lists some of the most important: Barthes's concept of the 'reality effect', which directs attention to the energizing role of the supernumerary detail: Derrida's notion of the 'supplement', which suggests novel ways of approaching the practice of illustration; and in general, the positing of 'Word & Image' as correlated semiotic systems, which has enabled a spate of useful studies, not least in the journal which bears that particular name. But arguably more important than any of these, in the antiquarian context, has been the liberating effect of Foucault's 'archaeological' method which, by establishing as a first principle the discontinuity of epistemological systems, dealt Whig interpretations a fatal blow. Foucault indeed insisted that the map of knowledge at any one time had to be reconstituted structurally and synchronically, rather than through the lazy and untested assumption that intellectual practices evolved uninterruptedly from age to age.

Foucault's shift in method meant, incidentally, that the antiquarian way of thinking suddenly acquired an avant-garde patina, compared with the nine-teenth-century diachronic historiography which had preserved its hegemony for so long. In *The Archaeology of Knowledge* (1969), historians were being urged to do precisely what the antiquarians had been stigmatized for – the diligent rearrangement of fragments which did not aspire to the resurrection of the life of the past. But, on a more practical level, Foucault encouraged us to examine the ways in which antiquarian discourses permeated all areas of culture, stretching out their capillaries through the fields of the arts and sciences. Although Foucault himself did not directly address antiquarian culture, there is good reason to see in the pioneering works of Krzysztof Pomian both a reflection and an elaboration of the basic features of this method. Pomian's seminal writings, brought together in the English edition of *Collectors and Curiosities* (1990), cultivated the Nietzschean side of Foucault's method in directing attention first and foremost to the historical etymology of the key terms involved in the discourse of collectors and antiquarians. For the first time, perhaps, it was possible to observe the term 'curiosity' itself being taken off the shelf and dusted down, the better to observe its intricate and unexpected patterning.

Yet both Foucault's archaeological approach, and Pomian's virtuoso analy-sis of concepts, ran the danger of what I would call the excluded middle: that is to say, the positing of a middle term (such as the originally quite derogatory 'Middle Ages') which is conceived simply as a bridge or transition between two more substantial points of reference. I detect even in so indispensable and early an aid to antiquarian scholarship as Stuart Piggott's biography of William Stukeley a hint of this tendency. As Piggott phrases it: 'Stukeley is a link between two worlds.'[4] His attempt to position Stukeley between the 'scientific and scholarly traditions of the late seventeenth century' and the age in which history is 'in the hands of the dilettanti' makes a great deal of sense. But it has the inevitable effect of depreciating the specific interest of Stukeley's practice. To an even greater extent, Pomian's concern to position curiosity in relation to the seemingly more stable epistemological regimes which preceded and followed it runs the risk of relegating it to a mere 'interim' existence. As he himself phrases it: 'Curiosity … enjoyed a temporary spell in power, an interim rule between those of theology and science.'[5] Such an assertion can at least be taken as clearing a space for the specific acknowledgement of curiosity in contradistinction to 'theology' and 'science'. But it implies the exclusion of 'curiosity', even as a subversive counter-discourse, from the so-called period of scientific hegemony.

As my own initial quotation from *The Old Curiosity Shop* implies, I would be by no means satisfied with this implication. I believe that in the seventeenth century it was perfectly possible for an object to serve both as a 'curiosity' and as a vehicle for scientific demonstration. Indeed the 'very artificial anatomy of a human eye' which John Bargrave purchased in Venice and later installed in his cabinet clearly satisfied both purposes.[6] Equally, the way in which Dickens ostensibly conflates 'curiosity' with objects of primarily antiquarian interest is an interesting pointer to the conceptual economy which existed at the end of the period covered by this study. In the mid-seventeenth century, one might say, both antiquities (*antiqua*) and rare objects (*rara*), though distinct categories, came together under the general designation of 'curiosity'. Dickens, for his avowed rhetorical purposes, historicizes 'curiosity' and gives it anthropomorphic form in the person of a hoarder of antiquities who is also a compulsive gambler. But he cannot obviate the fact that, in the immediately ensuing period, the conflict between the 'enlightened' motivations of the educator and the compulsive attachments of the collector was to be played out on an increasingly public stage: for example, in the divided allegiances to the display of useful objects and the accumulation of 'treasures' which were to mark the early years of the Victoria and Albert Museum.[7]

The contributors to this study invariably allow for this kind of conceptual heterogeneity with regard to the interpretation of the diverse practices of antiquarianism. They are attentive to etymologies, where crucial terms like 'monument' (or '*denkmal*') are concerned. They delve into the specific histories of technical practices where these are relevant: a series of chapters deals with the absorbing history of printmaking and print collection, which has rarely been so resourcefully harnessed to this theme before. In general, one might say that the shift from a dogmatically Foucauldian position can be measured by the fact that history appears throughout as being *foliated*: that is to say, instead of inviting interpretation in terms of large synchronic units, it offers an endless field of differences, both synchronically and diachronically. This is perhaps the Nietzschean perspective overhauling the Hegelian, within the broad disciplinary overview that Foucault opened up.

Two particular instances of difference are worth singling out, and the fact that they overlap in some respects is also significant. The image of the antiquarian as it developed over the period of this study is overwhelmingly male, though (as Martin Myrone points out) it is a maleness qualified by connotations of dryness rather than fecundity. It is almost as difficult to credit the keeper of the Old Curiosity Shop with the biological role of being Little Nell's grandfather as it is to imagine the diminutive heroine taking over the collection! Nevertheless, this hegemonic maleness needs to be qualified. Lucy Peltz ascertains that women contributed significantly to the practice of 'extra-illustration', though their collaborations with male family members were not always openly acknowledged. Annegret Pelz, however, locates a fascinating genre of writing which is more distinctively female: the compilation of texts which take as their basis the contents of the writer's own desk (*Schreibtisch*). Undoubtedly this practice suggests comparisons, however nuanced, with the collecting and cataloguing of curiosities, and this is not necessarily an anachronistic parallel. In Germany, at any rate, curiosity survived as a pastime remarkably akin (at first sight) to its original form until well after 1850, if we can accept as evidence the remarkable collection probably put together by the Countess von Wendelstadt.[8]

The relation of British to German antiquarianism is the other structuring difference which stands out in this study. No claim is being made, by implication, of the absence of comparable practices in countries such as Italy and France. It would certainly be futile to hope for a pan-European approach within the boundaries of a single volume such as this. Nonetheless, the approach which has been taken can be justified on other grounds than pure expediency. For if Britain was undoubtedly precocious in developing an antiquarian culture of considerable depth and diversity, Germany was late in the field. As Johann Reusch explains, Britain had established a distinct difference between classical archaeology and national antiquarianism by the end of the eighteenth century, whereas this was far from being the case in Germany. British antiquarianism could therefore provide models for the new German investment of sites and buildings, through printed genres such as the illustrated tour. But if Germany followed in this respect, it drew special advantages from its latecoming, and from the fact that practices such as curiosity and emblematics persisted into the eighteenth century and beyond. Britain, being an island, could take stock of its uniqueness more easily than Germany, which was a medley of discordant states struggling to assert itself. But the effort required from the latter-day German antiquarians was proportionately more considerable, resulting equally in Caspar David Friedrich's sublime transcendence of the conventions of topographic painting, and in the heroic personal mission of Hans von Aufsess to establish a German National Museum. For the latter – a close contemporary of Dickens whose career is evoked in Susan A. Crane's closing chapter – antiquarianism could still be a matter of life and death.

Notes

1. Charles Dickens, *The Old Curiosity Shop* (Oxford University Press, 1951), pp. 4–5.

2. *Ibid.*, p. xii.

3. Patrick Collinson, 'The Rutherford Renaissance Lecture' (1998), Wednesday 13 May 1998 (unpublished).

4. Stuart Piggott, *William Stukeley: An Eighteenth-Century Antiquary*, 2nd edn (London, Thames and Hudson, 1985), p.15.

5. Krzysztof Pomian, *Collectors and Curiosities*, trans. Elizabeth Wiles-Portier (Cambridge, Polity Press, 1990), p.64.

6. Stephen Bann, *Under the Sign: John Bargrave as Collector, Traveler, and Witness* (Ann Arbor, University of Michigan Press, 1994), p.15.

7.   See Malcolm Baker and Brenda Richardson (eds), *A Grand Design: The Art of the Victoria and Albert Museum* (London, V&A Publications with the Baltimore Museum of Art, 1997), esp. pp.107–16 and 149–60.

8.   The collection passed into the hands of the Swiss artist Daniel Spoerri in the early 1980s, and is now exhibited with the contemporary art collection of the Château d'Oiron in Poitou. See Daniel Spoerri, *La Collection de Mama W.* (Châtellerault, Château d'Oiron, 1993).

Introduction:
'Mine are the subjects rejected by the historian': antiquarianism, history and the making of modern culture[1]

Lucy Peltz and Martin Myrone

On 2 May 1772, after a two year wait, a delegation from the London Society of Antiquaries gathered expectantly at Westminster Abbey for the exhumation and opening of the tomb of King Edward I.[2] Since their foundation in 1717, when they pledged to investigate 'whatever may properly belong to the History of Bryttish Antiquitys', and following the grant of a Royal Charter in 1751, the Society had progressively styled itself as the representatives of 'a nation not afraid of penetrating into the remotest periods of their origin'.[3] Further promoting the study of antiquity as 'commendable and useful, not only to improve the minds of men, but also to incite them to virtuous and noble actions', the Society of Antiquaries were confident in the belief that their discoveries would be of distinct social and cultural benefit.[4] With the hope of establishing a clearer picture of both medieval burial rituals and the veneration of Edward I, the Fellows of the Society of Antiquaries approached this excavation with their habitual mixture of rigorous enquiry and enthusiastic curiosity. In line with the former, their findings were recorded on site, then presented to the Fellows at an unusually crowded meeting ten days later, and eventually published in the Society's journal *Archaeologia* (1775) for any interested party to read.[5] But there, in the comparatively public medium of print, Joseph Ayloffe had no qualms about admitting their collective curiosity in the corpse's 'state of preservation' and, rather more morbidly, in its level of 'putrefaction'.[6] He not only described the King's burial vestments and regalia but, in graphic and repulsive detail, he also lingered over 'some globular substance, possibly the fleshy part of the eyeballs, [which] was moveable in their sockets' and the wasted flesh which had attained a 'dark-brown, or chocolate colour, approaching black'.[7]

Careful to take everything into account, what the Society failed to notice was the troubling, even macabre, nature of this investigation; a fact which certainly left them open to criticism for many years to come. Thomas

Rowlandson's sketch of *Death and the Antiquaries* (*c.*1795) (Figure 0.1) reminds us that one of the greatest vehicles for antiquarian publicity – or, perhaps, more accurately, *notoriety* – came in the form of graphic and literary satire. Published as part of his *English Dance of Death* (1815–16), and accompanied by William Combe's explanatory verses, Rowlandson's composition tapped into many of the stock themes of antiquarian satire.[8] A typically motley crew of deformed and deficient antiquarians, who 'love to poke among the dead', strain to catch sight of their ghoulish subject.[9] Such is their engrossment in the strangely pristine figure of Edward I, that they do not recognize the social impropriety of their actions – a point which is drawn by the juxtaposed expressions of horror and bewilderment on the faces of the clergyman and labourers. Nor do they heed the quintessential irony – that of their own personal antiquity and their own imminent demise, here signalled by the skeletal figure of Death waiting to wreak vengeance on any member for disrupting the sanctity of the tomb. The necromantic and idolatrous mythology of this event continued to proliferate. The unfounded rumour that one of the antiquarians present had snapped off the corpse's ring finger, as an impromptu quasi-religious relic, was intimated in Rowlandson's design and had previously been expounded in a satirical article, in the *Town & Country Magazine* (1790), in which the narrator marvels: 'such was the intrepidity of my antiquarian friend, that he would have attempted the head, instead of a pitiful finger, as he had on a large Watchman's coat for the purpose'.[10]

In the vocabulary of satire, then, antiquarians emerge as distinctive and grotesque characters. From Robert Burton's *The Anatomy of Melancholy* (1621) to Sir Walter Scott's *The Antiquary* (1816), antiquarians were ridiculed for their fascination with dirty and recondite objects, their creation of cabinets filled with 'rotten and stinking' relics 'the better for being mouldy and worme-eaten', in short, for being polluted by the fragments that they studied, collected and fetishized.[11] Like the recurrent motif of the chamber-pot, mistaken for a 'sarcophagus, or Roman urn', the satiric response to antiquarian tomb openings was a particularly evocative one which afforded different critics ample ammunition for ridicule.[12] As early as 1628, in his essay on the antiquarian, John Earle had drawn the conclusion that his 'grave does not fright him, for he has bene used to sepulchers, and he likes death the better, because it gathers him to his fathers'.[13] But rather than presenting an honorific picture of a figure in some sort of harmony with his forebears, the antiquarian was more commonly represented revelling in some overly-materialist, self-indulgent and pointless twilight zone between this life and the next. The tension surrounding the antiquarian attitude towards historical evidence is neatly expressed in one early satire where the pointedly-named 'Veterano' insists that fragments, relics and ruins 'are the Registers, the Chronicles of the age they were made in, and speak the truth of History, better than a hundred of your printed Commentaries'.[14] In reality, of course, this bias towards tangible evidence and the desire to witness history first-hand did not prevent antiquarians from writing and publishing myriad tomes on their research and speculations. And though Richard Gough, later a Director of the Society of Antiquaries, launched a vehement attack upon the quality of this literature, the increasing scale and refinement of antiquarian publishing, often embellished with numerous high-quality illustrations, suggests that these volumes became objects of desire in their own right.[15] The level of commercial investment commensurate with such publishing projects also provides evidence of the size, and social diversity, of the market for antiquarian publications, which extended far beyond the limits of the Society itself.

The frequent occurrence of antiquarian satire, by the late eighteenth century, points to the same conclusion. It affords evidence of the comparative degree of awareness, familiarity, even sympathy, that antiquarianism enjoyed within contemporary society: 'to be target for wit acknowledges a common subject in every day conversation ... to ensure that the point of jest is seen'.[16] Not deterred by this risible stereotype, antiquarian interest became increasingly apparent within all sectors of polite, and specifically literate, society. Marked by this breadth of compass, the early image of antiquarianism has less to do with any of the several formalized societies that were instituted by the end of the eighteenth century, than with the existence of numerous amateur and leisured clergymen, gentlemen or landowners all in the pursuit of the genealogy, provenance or conditions of their own property, family or region. And while aspects of such local and personal projects occur throughout the antiquarian tradition, as the concept of national heritage became increasingly conjoined with a patriotic rhetoric it was widely promoted as having direct bearing on the 'publick spirit'.[17] With the improved mobility afforded by advancements in transportation during this period, this was not necessarily a passive, bookish knowledge. Instead, it evolved in tandem with the rise of domestic and international tourism where travellers were especially encouraged to 'take notice of monuments of Antiquity'.[18] Arguably, it was the very accessibility of the more immediate vestiges of antiquity that underpinned both the popularization of antiquarianism and much of the criticism its protagonists suffered. As genteel society became attuned to viewing architecture, ruins and monuments in terms of antiquarian records, more determined antiquarians went to ever greater lengths to counteract the invisibility of the past.

Another exhumation, which occurred in 1790, brings us back to the image of the antiquarian operating at the boundaries of social acceptability. On opening up the tomb of King Edward IV, in St George's Chapel, Windsor, the assembled Society members were not satisfied with the limited access that the Dean of Westminster Abbey had stipulated in the case of Edward I. What had previously only been manifest in the satirists' imagination, was now acted upon in reality: the antiquarians' desire to get their hands on the body of the king. Finding the skeleton immersed in a dark brown 'liquor' with an appearance 'very much like that of walnut-pickle', they removed a 'phial' for analysis.[19] Buried beneath a legitimizing veneer of scientific enquiry, the published description of this strange 'liquor' as 'inodorous and tasteless, excepting a small degree of ... astringency', and the conclusion that this was 'produced by the dissolution of the body itself', highlights the antiquarians' characteristic craving, even hunger, to engage with the past on an intimate and sensual level. Horrific as this morbid sampling now appears, it neatly captures the specificity of the antiquarian approach to historical evidence and how remote that approach is from the sanitized and institutionalized disciplines we know as history.

For modern scholars, perhaps no less than for the satirists of an earlier age, the antiquarian persists as a figure whose desires and interests appear, at best, marginal, at worst, irrelevant. While unlikely to provoke the vehement response of eighteenth- and nineteenth-century critics, the antiquarian remains subject to indifference, or, as here in the words of the most influential historian of antiquarianism, Arnaldo Momigliano, to self-conscious nostalgia:

Nowadays the pure antiquarian is rarely met with. To find him one must go into the provinces of Italy or France and be prepared to listen to lengthy explanations by old men in uncomfortably cold, dark rooms. As soon as the antiquarian leaves his shabby palace which preserves something of the eighteenth century and enters modern life, he becomes the great collector, he is bound to specialise, and he may well end up as the founder of an institution of fine arts or of comparative anthropology. The time-honoured antiquarian has fallen victim to an age of specialisation. He is now worse than out-dated: he has himself become a historical problem to be studied against the backdrop of crosscurrents of thought and of changing 'weltanschauungen' – the very things he wanted to avoid.[20]

Like Momigliano, here quoted from his lecture 'The Rise of Antiquarian Research' originally written in 1961–2, the contributors to the present volume recognize the antiquarian and antiquarianism as a 'historical problem' of considerable interest.[21] Though antiquarians may seem alien to us in terms of their historical priorities and methods, arguably much that is central to the cultural representation of history in the modern era, as organized by scholars, curators and patrons, is anticipated and even informed by their activities. The sense of alienation should not, though, be underestimated; like the Italian historiographer, our contributors find the antiquarian hidden in his 'shabby palace' a distant, even amusing, curiosity. Moreover, this shabbiness perhaps extends to the distinctive products of antiquarianism. The antiquarian products considered in this collection, whether visual or textual representations of the monuments, persons or events from the past (especially the national past), can appear, by our standards, as insufficient forms of historical

documentation as they are wanting in aesthetic value. Yet, each of our contributors has considered these as worthwhile objects of enquiry and starting
points for a wide range of histories.

It should be no surprise, then, to find a number of our contributors citing
Momigliano. In a series of publications, starting for the English speaking
world with his now classic 'Ancient History and the Antiquarian' (1950),
Momigliano provided important guidelines for the historical understanding
of antiquarian practice.[22] His characterization of the antiquarians and their
methods – their preference for systematic or structural analysis over chronological narrative, their investment of equal value in both visual and textual
evidence, their insistent perhaps obsessive concern with details – remains
persuasive. Yet as this book shows, the contribution of the antiquarians to
modern culture remains a potentially rich area of enquiry. The antiquarian is
still a historical problem, but not a problem to be analysed only from the perspective of historiography and the history of ideas, however valuable that may
be. There are crucial links between the antiquarians of the eighteenth and early
nineteenth century and the collectors and academics of the present age. There
are also defining relationships between the collecting habits and historical
methods of the antiquarians and those of the professionals that displaced
them. As this collection as a whole makes clear, these links are not simply
intellectual, but social, imaginative and political. In tracing these points of difference and lines of continuity in their rich variety, the essays in this volume
introduce the antiquarian as existing in complex relationships with the society
he or she inhabits. Antiquarians are here considered as the producers of
objects and texts that raise significant questions of the dialectic between text
and image, the status of historical truth and the nature of aesthetic quality.

Arguably, we are in a better position than ever to understand the peculiar
contribution of the antiquarian to modern scholarship and culture. We now
have a number of important studies that directly address antiquarianism as an
historical activity. Equally, the documentation and analysis of collecting
habits has emerged as a field of wide-reaching interest, as history of the
preservation, restoration and reappraisal of the material traces of the canoni-
cal cultures of Antiquity touches upon key issues of élite self-definition in the
early modern period.[23] Of particular interest in the context of the present
volume are the numerous interpretative studies of late eighteenth-century
Classical scholarship, specifically works on Johann Joachim Winckelmann, the
Baron d'Hancarville and Richard Payne Knight. Far from being recondite or
simply rarefied, these figures' antiquarianism has been proved to be vitally
engaged with key cultural transformations. In each case antiquarian activities
have been revealed as a means of engaging with, and even refuting,
hegemonic social, sexual and political discourse. The writings of d'Hancarville
and Payne Knight have been shown as vigorous, heterodoxical, and perhaps

in the latter case self-destructive, attempts to re-imagine Antiquity in throughly sexualized terms at a key moment in the history of sexuality.[24] And as Alex Potts has shown, Winckelmann's own sexual and political stance towards the Classical past was enormously influential. The German scholar's impassioned and politicized engagement with the Classical past, an engagement which could not be contained within the traditional methods of antiquarian studies, effectively brought about a crucial shift toward a more visually orientated analysis of the past, toward, that is, art history in its modern manifestation.[25] Starting from the premises of antiquarianism, Winckelmann appeared in the process of his scholarly development to have 'devalued the narrow methods of antiquarians' and heroically to have forged a role as the founding father of art history and archaeology.[26] Both the philosophical and historical analysis of the aesthetic, as we understand it, and empiricist archaeological methods were, therefore, demonstrably the product of an antiquarian auto-criticism. In that respect, the contribution of Classical antiquarianism to the shaping of modern culture has been shown to be crucial.

The essays in the present volume address the more neglected field of parochial antiquarianism, which has been variously the bed-fellow of Classical scholarship, or a radical alternative – its 'Other'. As a whole, this book shows that there is still much to be found out about the relationships and tensions between national antiquarianism and the issues of cultural self-definition, historical representation, and the discipline of history and art history. Yet there has already been some important work that has engaged with these forms of antiquarian activity in its own terms, and in relation to emerging scholarly disciplines, and also in the context of broader cultural activities. In the work of Joan Evans, Stuart Piggott and others, the Society of Antiquaries and its associates were subject to extensive documentation which adds considerably to our knowledge of their activities while suggesting further areas of study.[27] More recent studies have concentrated, for example, on aspects of antiquarianism as a commercial enterprise within the field of ballad publishing, on the matter of antiquarian forgeries, and on the complex institutional and personal relationships between antiquaries, scientists, archaeologists and historians.[28] In the latter category Phillipa Levine's study of the overlapping operations of amateurs and professionals at the crucial moment in the development of History as an academic discipline has been especially pertinent.[29] Antiquarians have also featured prominently in recent histories of collecting, where they emerge as key figures in the shaping of museum culture, from the *kunstkammern* of the seventeenth through to the great institutions of the nineteenth century, encompassing the subtly shifting and contested definitions of 'taste' and legitimate collecting practices so brilliantly analysed by Krzystof Pomian.[30] The intensive interest in the history of gardening in recent decades has thrown much new light on the distinctive role of antiquarian interests in shaping the landscape, especially a nationalist and romantic landscape.[31] From the perspective of the history of art, Michael McCarthy, Clive Wainwright and, most notably, Francis Haskell have shown the profound influence antiquarian concerns exercised over architecture, design and representation in the late eighteenth and early nineteenth centuries.[32] More generally, political and cultural histories have alerted us to the intricacies of historical writing in the period and to their contribution to the production of national identities.[33] As the title of this volume suggests, we are now crucially aware that to write or visualize the past is never simply to record but to produce, and to produce from motivations variously conservative or radical, reactionary or progressive.[34]

As Stephen Bann has highlighted in his preface to this volume, the same period has seen profound shifts within the discipline of history itself. With the boundaries in the academic discourse of history – boundaries between social, political, economic and cultural history – now very much in question, and with the very notion of historical 'truth' subject to intensive and self-referential interrogation, the way is here opened to a productive reappraisal of antiquarianism as a set of activities that raise precisely these issues. When, in his 'Rise of Antiquarian Research', Momigliano observed a perhaps surprising similarity between antiquarian research and the, then new, methods of historical analysis he identified as 'structuralism' he could hardly have predicted the extraordinary questioning of historical methods, and of history itself, that followed.[35] Yet his evocative portrayal of the antiquarian must surely continue to strike a note:

> The antiquarians loved disparate and obscure facts. But behind the individual, seemingly unrelated items there was Antiquity, mysterious and august. Implicitly every antiquarian knew he was supposed to add to the picture of Antiquity. In practice that meant that the individual facts were collected and set aside with a view to a future general survey of those institutions, customs, cults, for which coins and inscriptions were regarded as the most important evidence. The antiquarian's mind truly wandered to and fro between single facts and general surveys. The survey, if it ever came (not very often), would never be an ordinary book of history. Antiquity was static: it called for systematic descriptions of ancient institutions, religion, law, finances.[36]

This concern with material as well as textual evidence, the obsession with detail – almost as a means of stalling the conclusive historical text – the fixation on the disjecta and marginalia of the past, the willingness to extract meaning from the most trivial and neglected of things are all strangely typical of modern historical studies. In particular, they are characteristics of the new (as Bann points out, post-Foucauldian) historical analysis, analysis which refuses to predict grand historical narratives and rather concerns itself with the minute manifestations of power apparent in the anecdotal and trivial, and in the material traces of history. Like antiquarian studies themselves, the essays presented here largely resist ready classification. Drawing variously on the conventions of literary and semiotic analysis, biography, deconstructive criticism and art history, the essays in this volume expand upon the boundaries of traditional historical writing, and retrieve from antiquarian activities meanings which are not limited to their accordance with tidy historical narratives defined by the academic disciplines. The 'age of specialization' is, perhaps, now over, or at least the relationships between the disciplines sufficiently relaxed to admit a productive reappraisal of antiquarianism. The instability we identify in the methods and modes of attention of the antiquarian may prove to be in line with the interdisciplinary approaches of the modern historian. The eighteenth-century historian struggled to produce a sense of fixity and permanence despite or, perhaps because of, the uncertainty of his position, caught between (or straddling) the private and the public, the commercial and the genteel, the intimacies of subjective experience, and the proposal of an all-encompassing national identity.

The application of such methods to antiquarianism is especially valuable for a number of reasons. Firstly, as John Bender has indicated, this is a period traditionally considered on its own terms as an age of Enlightenment.[37] Historians have long struggled to find ways beyond the terminology that emerged in this period for conceptualizing the self, society, nation and history. In that respect, antiquarianism itself is of special interest as a marginalized 'defining other' to mainstream Enlightenment historiography and social discourse. As the anecdotal evidence presented above should indicate, the antiquarians' apparent willingness to transgress normative boundaries (of social behaviour, of the body, of intellectual disciplines) is useful in highlighting the very existence and the very artificiality of those boundaries. Antiquarianism in the eighteenth and early nineteenth centuries largely lacked the discursive coherence and self-confidence bred by an institutional framework. The source of its power, and of its instabilities, was its emergence in multiple spheres of activity: the private spaces of the study and the library; the middle-ground of the club, and the public sphere of the metropolitan market for the printed word and image. All the spaces of genteel and of mercantile life, which have been so much under consideration in recent historical writing, are equally the spaces of antiquarianism. Antiquarianism also allowed for occasional interventions on the part of women, who are often thought to have been excluded from such cultural activities. As demonstrated by Lucy Peltz, in her analysis of extra-illustration, and Annegret Pelz, in her consideration of the theme of the desk in antiquarian self-imagining, antiquarianism was both public and private – potentially feminine and masculine. And if we can identify, in the revived Society of Antiquaries, a formal institution with professed public functions, antiquarian instincts elsewhere functioned to shape highly subjective and emotional responses to the landscape and the past. Johann Reusch shows this in his study of the influence of antiquarian conventions in the work of that most Romantic of painters, Caspar David Friedrich. Yet again, as Stephen Bending and David Haycock argue, the national landscape could equally constitute the foundations of a common culture rich in political and personal associations. Antiquarian motivations and methods existed across a range of social spaces, and they encompassed both textual and visual representations and the most refined and the most prosaic cultural productions. Increasingly in the eighteenth century antiquarianism came to occupy an ambiguous position between a closed sector of élite culture potentially removed from social currency by its self-obsession, and the larger marketplace which sustained and disseminated the antiquarian project. As Martin Myrone suggests, in his study of the engraver George Vertue, antiquarian activities generated graphic products whose meanings were complex, not least because they answered the diverse needs of genteel scholarship and commercial factors. In each of these contributions we encounter a phenomenon typified by contradictions that lead us far away from the neat genealogies of intellectual progress so long typical in histories of the period.

The present-day historian is equipped with methodological techniques that here prove especially fruitful given the distinctive nature of antiquarian artifacts. Antiquarian products are susceptible to an uncritical reading that would posit them as neutral or untainted by social and political desires. The distinctive antiquarian text is a list or catalogue, organized apparently without logic or reason, at once wholly impersonal and devoid of social content. Equally, the antiquarian image is descriptive, deliberately bland and characteristically lacking any aesthetic ambition. Again, it is through Foucault's legacy that we may reapproach such artefacts with new eyes – eyes trained to perceive in the most apparently neutral modes of representation the embodiment of specific constructions of power and authority. This collection shows that such products do indeed embody social meaning despite, or rather because of, their apparent utilitarian purpose. Moreover, through the book as a whole we may begin to sense a highly defined and distinctly powerful aesthetic at work in these otherwise neglected images. As Sam Smiles and Maria Grazia Lolla show, antiquarian imagery can support highly sophisticated visual analysis, and each reveals a perhaps surprising depth in their subjects. Far from being simply prosaic, the graphic work of antiquarians emerges as richly layered in meanings.

Given the points made above, it should be clear that this collection of essays does not pretend to offer even the outline of a comprehensive history of antiquarianism in the eighteenth and nineteenth centuries. Nor, clearly, would such a history now be desirable. Yet neither is this simply a collection of fragments. Antiquarianism is shown as having a role in many of the key cultural changes which were wrought during the period. Discussing aspects of the antiquarian response to monuments in the landscape, David Haycock, Stephen Bending and Johann Reusch all demonstrate how antiquarians participated in the growing sense of a national culture so crucial in Northern Europe from the late eighteenth century. And as many of our contributors stress, antiquarians were frequently far from being the pathologically retentive figures given in satire. Instead, they were deeply involved in the processes of modernization as they found expression variously in commercial enterprise, urbanization and intellectual activity. This book offers evidence that shows antiquarianism provided incentives to self-analysis, and towards the documentation and recreation of modernity itself. Indeed, antiquarianism here emerges as an attempt to manage the rapidly changing social reality of the period. The final essays in this collection offer insights into the disintegration or transformation of antiquarianism at the end of our period. The history of antiquarianism, as expounded by modern antiquarians and archaeologists (Stuart Piggott most prominent among them), has long accounted for its decline with direct reference to its popularization and diffusion. In contrast, our contributors point to areas of overlapping interest and new beginnings. For Heather MacLennan, it is antiquarian concerns that helped shape the modern print collection in the early years of the nineteenth century, contributing to the remodelling of 'taste' into something resembling art history. Alexandrina Buchanan explores the intricate and vital relationships between developing scientific procedures and the foundations of architectural history as a scholarly discipline in the same period. In the last essay in this volume, Susan A. Crane considers the idiosyncratic yet proto-museological collecting activities of Hans von Aufsess in mid-nineteenth-century Germany. There, as we return to the lambasted and comic figure of the antiquarian, we are invited to review him not simply as marginal but as an initiator of our own, more programmatic, processes of historical representation.

Notes

1. Richard Gough, *Sepulchral Monuments of Great Britain*, 2 vols (London, J. Nichols, 1786), 1, p.4.

2. The idea was first suggested to the Society on 25 January 1770 by Daines Barrington, but met with initial objections from the Dean of Westminster Abbey. For a discussion of this incident see Joan Evans, *A History of the Society of Antiquaries* (Oxford University Press, 1956), pp.154–8.

3. *Society of Antiquaries in London, Minute Book*, 1 January 1718, 1, p.3 [Richard Gough], 'Introduction Containing an Historical Account of the Origin and Establishment of the Society of Antiquaries', *Archaeologia: or, Miscellaneous Tracts Relating to Antiquity*, 1 (1770), pp.i-xliii, p.ii. The Society's definitive history is Evans, *A History of the Society of Antiquaries*.

4. Joseph Ayloffe, 'An Account of the Body of King Edward, as it Appeared on Opening his Tomb', *Archaeologia*, 3 (1775), pp.376–413, p.376.

5. *Ibid.*

6. *Ibid.*, p.377.

7. *Ibid.*, p.383.

8. *The English Dance of Death*, 2 vols (London, R. Ackermann, 1815–16), 2, facing p.271.

9. William Combe, 'Death and the Antiquaries', *ibid.*, pp.271–4, p.272.

10. 'Character of a would be Antiquarian supposed to be written by himself', *The Town & Country Magazine, or, Universal Repository*, 22 (August, 1790), p.375. As a result of the strict guidelines laid down by the Dean of Westminster Abbey, the Society were not allowed to disrupt the coffin's contents – they were not even supposed to touch the corpse.

11. John Earle, 'An antiquary', *Micro-cosmographie; or, a Piece of the World Discovered in Essayes and Characters*, ed., I.G. (rpt, 1628, London, J.M. Dent, 1899), pp.14–15 (p.14). For an interesting discussion of the relationship between dirt, death and social pollution see Mary Douglas, *Purity and Danger: An Analysis of the Concepts of Pollution and Taboo* (rpt, 1966, London, Boston, Melbourne and Henley, Ark Paperbacks, 1984), esp. p.176.

12. Samuel Foote, *The Nabob* (London, Mr Colman, 1772), p.54.

13. Earle, *Micro-Cosmographie*, p.15.

14. Shackerly Mermion, *The Antiquary. A Comedy* (London, I. W. & F. E., 1641), act 2, n.p.

15. Richard Gough, *Anecdotes of British Topography* (London: W. Richardson, 1768), pp. xviii–xix. Gough was appointed Director in 1771.

16. Stuart Piggott, *Ancient Britons and the Antiquarian Imagination* (London, Thames and Hudson, 1989), p.15.

17. [Francis Brokeby], *A Letter of Advice to a Young Gentleman at the University* (rpt, 1701, London, n.p., 1701), pp.12–13.

18. *Ibid.*, p.12.

19. Mr Emlyn, 'The Vault, Body, and Monument, of Edward IV, in St. George's Chapel at Windsor' (1790), *Vetusta Monumenta*, **3**, pp.1–4, pp.1, 2 and 3.

20. Arnaldo Momigliano, 'The Rise of Antiquarian Research', in *The Classical Foundations of Modern Historiography* (Berkeley and Oxford, University of California Press, 1990), pp.54–79, p.54.

21. 'The Rise of Antiquarian Research' was first written as a lecture in 1961–2, and was revised by its author in the mid-1970s.

22. See his 'Ancient History and the Antiquarian', *Journal of the Warburg and Courtauld Institutes*, **13** (1950), pp.285–315; this was republished in his *Studies in Historiography* (London, Weidenfeld & Nicholson, 1966).

23. The outstanding work in this respect is Francis Haskell and Nicholas Penny, *Taste and the Antique* (New Haven and London, Yale University Press, 1981).

24. Michael Clark and Nicholas Penny, eds, *The Arrogant Connoisseur: Richard Payne Knight* (Manchester University Press, 1982); G.S. Rousseau, 'The Sorrows of Priapus: Anticlericalism, Homosocial Desire, and Richard Payne Knight' in G.S. Rousseau and Roy Porter, eds, *Sexual Underworlds of the Enlightenment* (Manchester University Press, 1987), pp.101–53; Randolph Trumbach, 'Erotic Fantasy and Male Libertinism in Enlightenment England', in Lynn Hunt, ed., *The Invention of Pornography: Obscenity and the Origins of Modernity* (New York, Zone Books, 1993), pp.253–82; and Andrew Ballatyne, *Architecture, Landscape and Liberty: Richard Payne Knight and the Picturesque* (Cambridge University Press, 1997), pp.86–109. See also Matthew Craske, *Art in Europe 1700–1830: A History of the Visual Arts in an Era of Unprecedented Urban Economic Change* (Oxford and New York, Oxford University Press, 1997), pp.239–50.

25. Alex Potts, *Flesh and the Ideal: Winckelmann and the Origins of Art History* (New Haven and London, Yale University Press, 1994).

26. Quatremère de Quincy, *Éloge Historique de M. Visconti* (1820), quoted and discussed in Potts, *Flesh and the Ideal*, p.14.

27. See Evans, *A History of the Society of Antiquaries* and Stuart Piggott's *Ruins in a Landscape* (Edinburgh University Press, 1976) and *William Stukeley: an Eighteenth-Century Antiquary*, 2nd edn (London, Thames and Hudson, 1985); Joseph M. Levine, *Dr Woodward's Shield: History, Science and Satire in Augustan England* (Berkeley and London, University of California Press, 1977).

28. See Dianne Dugaw, 'The Popular Marketing of "Old Ballads": The Ballad Revival and Eighteenth-Century Antiquarianism Reconsidered', *Eighteenth-Century Studies*, 21:1 (1987), pp.71–90; Paul Baines, ' "Our Annius": Antiquaries and Fraud in the Eighteenth Century', *British Journal of*

Eighteenth-Century Studies, **20** (1997), pp.33-51. Two studies that do not address antiquarianism directly but which shed much light on its intellectual and social contexts are: Michael Hunter, *Science and Society in Restoration England* (Aldershot, Gregg Revivals, 1992) and N. Jardine, J.A. Secord and E.C. Sparry (eds), *The Cultures of Natural History* (Cambridge University Press, 1995).

29.   Phillipa Levine, *The Amateur and the Professional: Antiquarians, Historians and Archaeologists in Victorian England, 1838–1886* (Cambridge University Press, 1986).

30.   See O.R. Impey and A. MacGregor, *The Origins of Museums: The Cabinet of Curiosities in 16th–17th Century Europe* (London, Oxford University Press, 1985); Arthur MacGregor, 'Collectors and Collections of Rarities in the Sixteenth and Seventeenth Centuries', in Arthur MacGregor (ed.), *Tradescant's Rarities: Essays on the Foundation of the Ashmolean Museum, 1683* (Oxford, Clarendon Press, 1983); Antony Griffiths, *Landmarks in Print Collecting: Connoisseurs and Donors at the British Museum since 1753* (London, British Museum Press, 1996) and Krzystof Pomian, *Collectors and Curiosities: Paris and Venice, 1500–1800*, trans. Elizabeth Wiles-Portier (London, Polity Press, 1990).

31.   See, for example, John Dixon Hunt and Peter Willis, *The Genius of the Place: The English Landscape Garden, 1620–1820* (London, MIT Press, 1988) and Catherine Levesque, *Journey Through Landscape in Seventeenth-Century Holland: The Haarlem Print Series and Dutch Identity* (Pennsylvania University Press, 1994).

32.   Clive Wainwright, *The Romantic Interior: The British Collector at Home, 1750–1850* (New Haven and London, Yale University Press, 1989); Michael McCarthy, *The Origins of the Gothic Revival* (New Haven and London, Yale University Press, 1987) and Francis Haskell, *History and its Images: Art and the Interpretation of the Past* (New Haven and London, Yale University Press, 1993).

33.   See, especially, J.G.A. Pocock, *Virtue, Commerce and History: Essays on Political Thought and History, Chiefly in the Eighteenth Century* (Cambridge University Press, 1985).

34.   On the status of history as a form of representation see Roland Barthes, 'The Discourse of History', in *The Rustle of Language*, trans. Richard Howard (London, Basil Blackwell, 1986), pp.127–40, also Hayden White, *The Content of Form: Narrative Discourse and Historical Representation* (Baltimore and London, Johns Hopkins University Press, 1987).

35.   Momigliano, 'Rise of Antiquarian Research', pp.78–9.

36.   *Ibid.*, p.58.

37.   John Bender, 'A New History of the Enlightenment?', in Leo Damrosch (ed.), *The Profession of Eighteenth-Century Literature: Reflections on an Institution* (Madison and London, Wisconsin University Press, 1992), pp.62–83.

0.1 Thomas Rowlandson, *Death and the Antiquaries*, c.1795, pen and ink

1

Ceci n'est pas un monument:
Vetusta Monumenta and antiquarian aesthetics

Maria Grazia Lolla

Tout, au monde, existe pour aboutir à un livre.
(Stéphane Mallarmé)

In his ground-breaking essay 'Ancient History and the Antiquarian' Arnaldo Momigliano challenged centuries of received wisdom by taking the antiquaries seriously. Having dismissed as 'conventional' the view that the major feature of 'the Age of the Antiquaries' was a simple revolution in taste – the spread of Grecian, Celtic and Gothic revivals – Momigliano initiated what can be termed the Whig interpretation of antiquarianism. Though they were 'not quite' historians, he argued, eighteenth-century antiquaries laid the foundations of modern historiography. According to Momigliano antiquaries were to be credited for ushering in the distinction between original and derivative authorities, using non-literary evidence, and pioneering the study of subjects normally outside the province of the political historian, such as customs, institutions, art and religion. Whereas the 'conventional' view of antiquarianism as agent in a revolution in taste has rarely been expanded, antiquarianism is now conventionally understood as some sort of history.[1]

Often characterized as passive catalysts of a revolution in taste, antiquaries themselves have seldom – if ever – been associated with (eighteenth-century) taste and even less with (nineteenth-century) art. Quite the contrary: the antiquary is, almost by definition, he who is irremediably devoid of taste, the very antonym of the critic, the poet, the fiction-writer or the artist. Horace Walpole, whose collected correspondence has indexed entries such as 'Antiquaries, Society of: H W's contempt for' and 'Antiquary; antiquaries: always turn into fools'; 'ridiculed for recovering trifles', articulated *ad nauseam* the widespread view that antiquaries were indiscriminately acquisitive, impenetrable to taste, 'ridiculous', and doomed to be 'dry and dull' for centuries to come.[2] In the

'Discours préliminaire' of the *Encyclopédie* the antiquary was immortalized as the inveterate enemy of both the poet and the historian, while Walter Scott created in Dr Dryasdust, Fellow of the Antiquarian Society, an antiquary whose predilection for a cadaverous past and commitment to empirical research rendered him constitutionally incapable of writing fiction.[3] As to figurative arts, William Gilpin's evaluation of George Vertue as 'an excellent antiquarian; but no artist' indicates that antiquary and artist were more likely to be mutually exclusive identities than not.[4]

In the following essay I will pursue Stephen Bann's suggestion that antiquarianism was something other than 'an imperfect approximation to … the maturity of scientific, professionalised historiography', without necessarily invoking an undifferentiated notion of taste.[5] I will do so not by focusing on the illustrious example of Johann Joachim Winckelmann who 'began by searching for ollas and ended up studying the Apollo, the Laocoon … and writing the history of the art of design',[6] nor that of Giovan Battista Piranesi, whose artistry was celebrated *despite* his proficiency in antiquities, nor even the work of those, like Jean Barbault, who claimed to redeem antiquarianism from its dullness by producing 'views of the most beautiful remains of antiquity'.[7] Instead, I will analyse the work of those who 'just' published monuments – indefinitely and indiscriminately – as did the Society of Antiquaries in the first 100 years following their revival in the first decade of the eighteenth century. I will argue that, as well as challenging stereotypes of the antiquary as acquisitive and backward-looking, the quintessentially antiquarian activity of publishing monuments had a considerable bearing on aesthetics. Even though publishing monuments was advertised as an act of preservation, the monuments themselves were reproduced as artistic objects. More importantly, by issuing previously unpublished monuments antiquaries contributed to expanding the category of the artistic in ways that can be either explained by analogy with the catholicity of the Romantic concept of the poetic or viewed as the articulation of a novel aesthetics.[8]

From the beginning of the Renaissance, monuments – either collected in museums, or unearthed in recent excavations – had been published by both individuals and learned societies in an unending succession of volumes. Monuments were published by the thousands for a variety of reasons: as a tribute to their owners; to enhance the value of originals and to advertise private collections; to improve taste in the arts or to provide models for kitchenware; to further scientific discussion, or just to make a living. Rarely published to prove the shortcomings of philology, as Winckelmann had done by publishing his *Monumenti antichi inediti* (1767), and still less often 'to hasten their ruin', which is what Richard Gough feared the French Revolutionaries were going to do, monuments were published in many cases as an act of preservation.[9] From the beginning of the Renaissance, that is, monuments had been published in anticipation of the objects' disappearance, or in the wake of the distress for their progressive destruction, or even after the originals had been lost. When this was the case, publication was a highly emotional transaction, invariably described with a sense of urgency.

Where Winckelmann published monuments to show off his brilliant insights into the literature of the ancients, his predecessors in the post of Prefect to the Vatican antiquities, Pietro Santi Bartoli and Raphael, 'just' published monuments out of anxiety at their disappearance. Running the risk of disappointing the learned, Bartoli published monuments in a hurry and without written explanations because the 'love' and the 'transfixing pain' caused by 'seeing the beloved thing perish' 'compelled' him to draw the remains of antiquity 'with the utmost exactitude'.[10] Like Bartoli, Raphael, confronted with the daily despoliation of ruins that had provoked the famous epigram 'quod non fecerunt barbari, fecerunt Barberini', communicated to Pope Leo X his 'extreme pain' at seeing the 'cadaver of this once noble city' as well as his commitment 'to keeping alive some image, or else, shadow' of the city – it was not long after those resolutions that Rome underwent its worst sack.[11] Similarly in England, John Aubrey, spurred on by the painful memory of the fire of London, commissioned drawings of the ruins of the Abbey of Osney (soon after demolished) and recommended the publication of views of Wiltshire houses which:

> would remaine to Posterity, when their Families are *gonne* and their Buildings ruind by Time, or Fire: as we have seen that Stupendous Fabrick of Pauls church not a stone left on a stone, and lives now only in Mr Hollars Etching in Sir William Dugdales History of Pauls. . . .[12]

Knowing that all that remained of a monument was a drawing often made publishing more urgent than providing the world with learned lucubrations. It also made it almost impossible to publish monuments without committing oneself at the same time to the cause of preservation. William Stukeley's overdetermined 'intent' in publishing *Stonehenge* (1740) was '(besides preserving the memory of these extraordinary monuments . . .) to promote . . . the knowledge and practice of ancient and true Religion'.[13] Likewise, Richard Gough trusted that by publishing his *Sepulchral Monuments* (1786–96) he would have 'administered to the amusement of an idle hour' as well as 'preserved so many antient memorials of art' in his native country.[14] Even when the stated principal goal was to provide portable 'elegant views' of 'the most interesting objects of curiosity in Great Britain', as was the case of James Storer's *Antiquarian and Topographical Cabinet* (1807–11), it was noted that engravings would 'be hastening to preserve the lineaments of the most venerable remains of antiquity which time is incessantly whittling away by nearly imperceptible atoms'.[15]

The same (unavoidable) concern for preservation that had motivated innumerable antiquarians to publish monuments is apparent in *Vetusta Monumenta* (1747–1906), the first (and for a long time only) publication sponsored by the London Society of Antiquaries. As its title page proclaimed, this publication was intended to 'preserve the memory of British things', a commitment continuously pledged by the Fellows of the Society since its supposed foundation during the reign of Elizabeth I. When, shortly before her death, a group of antiquaries petitioned the Queen for the establishment of a Library and an Academy of Antiquaries, they emphasized that the library was 'to p[re]serve divers old Books concerning Matter of history of this Realme, Original Charters and Monuments', while the academy would have provided 'Publick & Safe Custody' for 'diverse and Sundry Monuments'.[16] To root their case in history they reminded the Queen of 'the Care which her Ma.[ties] progenitors have had for the preservation of such antient Monuments' and pointed out that Edward I in particular, had needed and cared for the 'preservation of such antient Monuments'.[17] Similarly, when the Society was revived for the first time in 1707, Humphrey Wanley drew attention to the 'many most excellent Monuments' which 'for want of due Care, go more and more to decay and Ruin.'[18] When the Society was revived again in 1717, the proposed constitution advertised the 'Study of antiquitys', as, among other things, 'preserving the Venerable Remains of our Ancestors', while the Society itself embraced the purpose of ensuring that the knowledge of antiquities would 'be preserv'd and transmitted to futurity'.[19] Stukeley clearly brought to the fore commitment to preservation by proposing a 'lion crowned rampant' for the arms of the Society, explaining that 'the lyon intimates that generous nature and noble ardour which preserves & restores from the injury of time'.[20]

Although, quite often, as Joan Evans has pointed out, 'recording was but a prelude to destruction', the plates collected in *Vetusta Monumenta* should be viewed as complementing the Society's commitment to the preservation of endangered monuments.[21] Some of the plates represented monuments which would soon be demolished. This was the case with George Vertue's *King street Gate, Westminster* (1725) with the inscriptions 'North Front of King's Street Gate in Westminster, which was taken down in 1723' (Figure 2.5).[22] Comparable was *Glocester Cross* (1751), the drawing for which 'was made in the year 1750, in order to preserve its memory', after Parliament had approved the decision to pull it down.[23] Others offered a precious, exclusive glimpse, of monuments which had been only momentarily disclosed to view, perhaps never to be seen again. This was the case, for example, with the three stalls of Chatham Church (1790), accidentally discovered in 1785, seen by 'Very few persons', but almost immediately 'hid from the eye by being plaistered over', and then 'again brought to view' in 1788, when David Wells 'fortunately got there in time to make a drawing of them'.[24] Equally, a number of plates were reproductions of monuments which had already been destroyed, such as the letter of the English Nobility addressed to Pope Boniface VIII in 1300, 'drawn & Engrav'd from two authentick Transcripts taken from the Original … That Original not being now to be found'; or the series of drawings in the possession of the Duchy office of Lancaster, bearing captions such as 'totally demolished in 1648, is thus transmitted to Posterity by the Society of Antiquaries, London, 1734', or 'long since demolish'd, but from an Old Draught now remaining in the Dutchy Office, this plate was Engrav'd'.[25] Some engravings were even imaginary reconstructions of pre-existing sites, such as Stukeley's detailed plan of the Roman settlement of Verulanium, 'sketched to prevent the destruction of its very ashes.'[26]

Dedicated to monuments just discovered, restored, about to be destroyed, or long disappeared, the plates collected in *Vetusta Monumenta* are, undeniably, a testimony of the Society's concern for preservation. Both their lettering and composition well represent the Society's anxiety at the feared disappearance of monuments. If the oft-repeated captions 'Quod Reliquum est', 'Societas Antiq. Lond ita conservari curavit', 'is thus transmitted to Posterity by the Society of Antiquaries' hint perhaps at the inadequacy of the chosen method, the format – of the first volume, in particular – seems to signal the urgency of the endeavour.[27] Only in the second volume did *Vetusta Monumenta* begin to include textual explanations, and only in the third was every monument rigorously accompanied by a dissertation of some sort. However, in the first volume, where texts do appear, they seem to have to accommodate themselves to the needs of the illustration; thus texts variously fill in the spaces left void by the objects or disguise themselves as monuments, in order to justify their presence in the same plate.

There is no reason to doubt the sincerity of the Fellows' commitment to preservation nor their confidence that engraving was an effective agent of preservation. It was not just Richard Gough, the Director of the Society of Antiquaries, who boasted that it was to the founding Fellows' dedication to publishing monuments that 'we owe the preservation of many valuable Monuments in our own country'.[28] Audiences well beyond the Society put pressure on the Fellows to continue publishing monuments as a speedy conservationist intervention.[29] Indeed, it is in the criticism that the 'art of engraving' was actually responsible for the destruction of monuments that we find some evidence that the Society pursued publishing as the best technology of preservation.[30]

Despite the encouragement the public gave to preserving monuments by means of engravings, and the zeal with which monuments were engraved and then destroyed – despite, in other words, the literal-mindedness with which antiquaries preserved monuments within the pages of a book – it was not just the monument that was published. What was published was a lot less and a lot more – a great deal other – than the given monument.[31]

Although the concern over the impending disappearance of relics led antiquaries to publish the unpublishable – a three-dimensional object – the third dimension is generally not particularly well represented in *Vetusta Monumenta*. The selection of monuments published shows a marked predilection for drawings, paintings, maps, plans, manuscripts, and almost two-dimensional objects, such as coins, seals, and pavements. Moreover the specific representational choices contribute to rendering the objects as immaterial. In fact, the only object consistently reproduced as three-dimensional is paper – which is almost invariably represented as being rolled, or folded, displaying creases and casting shadows on the background. Otherwise, hardly any attempt is made at reproducing the individual monument. The plate depicting Waltham Cross (Figure 1.1), for instance, shows a monumental cross set against a landscape.[32] Although a gentleman contemplates the cross, as if to reinforce the impression of a real monument, three statues ornamenting the cross and a ground-plan of the structure are placed in what should be the sky. Across two views of the Abbey Gatehouse of St Bennet's in Norfolk the section of the building is 'pinned' on a rolled parchment (Figure 1.2).[33] In 'the sky' and 'lawn', a few coats of arms are hanging. On the plate representing the tomb of Robart Colles (Figure 1.3), the letters engraved on the sepulchral monument are placed around the coffin to form a decorative frame.[34] In several plates, the space of the monument is interrupted by inscriptions, captions, cartouches and other pieces of texts, or by 'footnotes', which magnify details or demonstrate layouts.

At the same time as the plates celebrated paper as the ultimate technology of preservation they also drew attention to their being 'just' representations of the objects depicted. An improvement, perhaps, on written descriptions, the plates in *Vetusta Monumenta* do not seek to seduce the viewer into a *trompe l'œil* effect. Instead, by functioning as suggestive souvenirs of lost monuments they were self-consciously constructed as triggers to the imagination and aids to the memory. Arguably, such artful compositions approximated a ritual of preservation. They celebrated the monuments; they were monuments to the monuments, but not the monuments themselves. Like Magritte's 'pipe', at each step they make clear that they are *not* the objects they represent. Perhaps they invoke the object simply to highlight the fragility of the chosen form of preservation and the failure of art to render the richness of the original experience. Perhaps they revel in their failure to replace the object and their willingness to take full advantage of their not being that object: to be better and more pleasing, than the monument itself; to include elements other than the object. If 'this' is not a monument, the plates seem to cry out, still less are the cupids, festoons, tendrils, decorative frames which clutter these plates. If 'this' is a representation, those are decorations. These are not monuments but aesthetically pleasing objects. In short, they are works of art.

Considering the antiquarian's notorious lack of taste and propriety this recourse to playful, elegant decorations can be read as a desperate attempt to win antiquities over to taste. Even a curmudgeon like Walpole could not find fault with *Vetusta Monumenta*; in the middle of a deeply unflattering letter concerning the London Society of Antiquaries he admitted that 'the best merit of the Society lies in their prints'.[35] Indeed, as a conscious effort to infuse taste into antiquities or even as an inert part of the stock-in-trade of the engraver's art, the insistence on the representational nature of the engravings and the recourse to decorative devices unmistakably locates the plates of *Vetusta Monumenta* in an aesthetic/artistic order.

Compared to other antiquarian illustrations, the plates of *Vetusta Monumenta* seem remarkably restrained. Those drawn and (in most cases) engraved by Jan Goerre for Johannes Graevius's *Thesaurus Antiquitatum Romanarum* (1694–9) (Figure 1.4) and Jacobus Gronovius's *Thesaurus Graecae Antiquitatis* (1697–1702) are perhaps the most extreme realization of the decorative features which are barely visible in *Vetusta Monumenta* and latent in most representations of antiquities. In Goerre's repertoire there is hardly a single plate in which monuments are not drawn on a rolled, torn, and crumpled parchment and pinned up or set on a marble slab, or framed or hung, lest the viewer should be fooled into believing that on display was a monument, instead of its representation. Besides, the plates seem to be taking full advantage of their freedom to be 'better' than the original monuments. Monuments are arranged into compositions pleasing to the eye, with no respect for scale so, for example, a coin might be as big as a temple. Equally, monuments are also 'improved' by the deployment of decorations. Ornaments occupy a very large portion of the plate, often unashamedly taking up a larger space than that allocated to the monument itself. Sometimes decorations obscure the view of the monument, or are placed at the centre of the composition. Monuments themselves are used as ornaments. In fact, monuments and ornaments fuse to such a degree that quite often they cannot be told apart – in short, it was not possible to distinguish antiquities used as ornaments from 'real' antiquities.

However modest was its deployment of decorations (and without detracting from its scientific and conservationist intent), the value of *Vetusta Monumenta* seems to have been as much artistic as it was documentary. Even though Vertue's work as an engraver was later criticized for its 'painful exactness' and 'dry, disagreeable manner, without force, or freedom', following Roland Barthes' argument we could say that there is not one plate which 'fails to vibrate well beyond its demonstrative intent'.[36] His plates display the same

'gratuitous justification, of an aesthetic or oneiric order' that Barthes discerned
in the plates of the *Encyclopédie*.

In fact, the plates collected in *Vetusta Monumenta* are 'not monuments' in yet
another sense. In addition to their obvious aesthetic excess and the sacrifice of
the third dimension – and sometimes accuracy and scale – to the needs of the
book, the plates far exceed the boundaries of the object. Again, both a lot less
and a lot more than the monuments gets represented, as can be seen in *Waltham
Cross* (Figure 1.1) where the caption proclaims that the Society of Antiquaries
rescued the cross from the injury of time and restored its former splendour.
Together with the gentleman contemplating the monument with obvious
satisfaction these devices indicate that what is here celebrated is both the
monument and the successful restoration of a historic landmark. (In fact this
plate was donated by Stukeley to the Society after he succeeded in obtaining
ten shillings 'for setting down two oak posts to secure Waltham Cross from
injury by Carriages'.)[37] Or take the design for an independent plate of Arthur's
Oven as projected by Baron Clark in a series of letters sent to the Secretary of
the Society, in 1743. Having informed the Fellows of the fact that a certain
Michael Bruce had pulled down a monument and 'made use of all the Stones
for a Mill dam', he urged them to stigmatize the 'Goth' with an 'indelible mark
of Infamy'. 'This,' he suggested, 'may be easily done by their publishing a
good and accurate print of this noble pile while standing … and a short
inscription historicall under it, would not only perpetuate the memory of this
now lost Antiquity, but the name of the Herostratus that ruined it with
ignominy'.[38] The plate as Baron Clark imagined it would have attempted to
represent something even more difficult to keep between the pages of a book
than the third dimension: a mood, a state of mind and, in this instance, a contemporary outrage about the pillage of the past. In other cases, plates represent the act of surveying and measuring sites, as clearly as the sites
themselves. Vertue's commercial engravings of the *Under Chapel of St Thomas
within London Bridge* (Figure 1.5) show gentlemen intent on examining the
inside, checking the view, and measuring different parts of the chapel with a
variety of instruments.[39] Alternatively, the plate dedicated to the Roman
Hypocaust of Lincoln chronicles the act of discovery, the slow unearthing of
sites by showing in the foreground the different layers and the tools used in
the excavation.[40]

Perhaps what the hundreds of pointing, admiring, and palavering figures
who so frequently people antiquarian illustrations represent most clearly is
'admiration' – an even more influential motive for publishing than the concern
for preservation (Figures 1.5 and 1.6). We should not forget that the plates
bound in the first volume of *Vetusta Monumenta* in 1747 had been published
over the course of thirty years and retrospectively assigned the function of
preserving the memory of British things. As they were issued, however, no

mention of preservation was made, nor indeed of any purpose at all. The first *Minute Book* of the Society is extremely laconic in this regard. It opens with the proposal 'to engrave a drawing of Richard II.^{ds} picture in Westminster Abby taken by Mr Talmans direction & agreed to'.[41] For the Society's next meeting, the minutes report that 'Mr Sam Gale Treasurer is authorizd to pay Mr Vertue two guineas toward engraving the font of S^t. James's church. It is proposd for the second time to engrave R. II.^{ds} picture & agr.'[42] In the third week again it was 'proposd and agreed the 3.^{d} time to engrave R:II Picture in Westminster abby' and shortly after: 'It was unanimously orderd that a Drawing of a Horn presented to the Church of York by Ulphus Prince of Deira, in possession of Mr Samuel Gale be printed' (Figure 1.6).[43] Just as the *Minute Book* records nothing more than the proposal and decision to publish prints, the later committee appointed to examine the Society's first minutes reported, on 11 November 1762, that admiration was the main faculty exercised by the Fellows in their initial meetings. 'The chief business there done', the report narrated with some condescension, 'consisted in *Exhibits* ... Much of the entertainment consisted, in handing round the Table the several *Exhibits*; whereby every person present had a proper opportunity of viewing, considering and speaking upon each particular.'[44] Antiquities, that is, provided a spectacle.

Taken as an account of the initial transactions of the Society, the first plates of *Vetusta Monumenta* thus preserved a record of the handling of the heterogeneous selection of objects accounted for in the minutes – objects safe in cabinets rather than imperilled relics awaiting destruction. Independent of concern for preservation, they chronicled the initial compelling, unquestioned, and unexplained impulse to transmit which followed the exhibition of monuments. Even in the absence of figures to enact wonder, these plates reach to capture the original inarticulate awe that accompanied the sight of monuments and prompted their proud display. As such, they encapsulated the quintessential antiquarian response to monuments, one that made antiquarianism both hopelessly unpopular, so novel as an intellectual undertaking, and so unpredictably close to Romanticism.

Rather than simply asserting the self-evident value of the objects represented, the lack of written explanations in *Vetusta Monumenta* often signals the Society's failure to understand or articulate the origin and significance of the objects represented: objects that escaped comprehension yielded themselves only to a searching gaze, to contemplation and reduplication. Alternatively, this lack of written explanation may have sanctioned their status as curiosities: objects whose scholarly value was next to nil and whose function was, essentially, exhausted in their display. In either case, the 'admiration' these plates memorialized appears to be analogous to that childish credulity and ignorance for which antiquaries were notorious.

The very same puerile admiration that was so mercilessly exposed in the dozens of eighteenth-century caricatures of the antiquary was in fact the very foundation of a novel attitude towards the past and its study.[45] Just as the seemingly tautological duplication of monuments made explicit the antiquarian capitulation in the face of the mysterious presence of the past, it also marked the deferral of explanation to others and to future generations. Accurate plates were understood as the most intellectually honest response to inherently opaque monuments – monuments that eluded final explanation just as they incessantly yielded information.[46] Besides, admiration involved an unprecedented respect for the otherness of the past, an attitude that manifested itself in distant contemplation and the desire to preserve intact the difference of the past. In this respect the dumb and increasingly accurate duplication of monuments in *Vetusta Monumenta* closely corresponded to the work of literary antiquarians whose appreciation of the exoticism of the past made them reluctant to modernize, improve or manipulate such ancient literature.

The same antiquarian stupor in the face of the ordinary that was immortalized in *Vetusta Monumenta* unmistakably located antiquarianism at the intersection of aesthetic and intellectual pursuits. Placed halfway between a sensory and an intellectual response, admiration has been described as the beginning (and for some the end) of both the aesthetic and intellectual experience. Joining a tradition stemming from Aristotle, John Aubrey defined admiration as 'the first step to knowledge & Arts', followed by 'Inquisition', and 'Traditio Lampadis, which we call Learning'.[47] By emphasizing admiration, antiquaries made it clear that the past was not just an intellectual construct beyond the reach of the senses but also an aesthetic experience as well – a subjective, emotional and imaginative response. In this respect the antiquarian admiration is reminiscent of both the Romantic wonder and the Romantic understanding of the role of imagination.[48]

A comparison between the plates of *Vetusta Monumenta* and those that appear in Graevius's and Gronovius's separate *Thesauri* of the late seventeenth century can help clarify this point. In Goerre's plates the ubiquitous presence of unidentified mythological figures, far from contributing to the accuracy advertised on the title-page, advances a very specific view of antiquity and its study (Figure 1.4). Engaged in casual conversation, overlooking the monuments, or with their backs to the monuments, these figures foster a sense of casual normality. Theirs is the perspective of timeless mythological figures for whom the monuments of antiquity are commonplace. By contrast in *Vetusta Monumenta* the perspective is that of the contemporary archaeologist or traveller, engaged in the study, measurement and admiration of monuments and struck by the difference and otherworldliness of antiquities. Even in the absence of figures the plates of *Vetusta Monumenta*, magnified to the point of impertinence, immortalize a present engagement with antiquities as they appear to the senses. Antiquarian aesthetics shifted the focus of attention from the past to the present, and from the object to the observer.

There is one last way in which on looking at *Vetusta Monumenta* we should exclaim 'these are not monuments' – a failure that located antiquarianism in close proximity to Romanticism. If by publishing monuments the Fellows of the Society of Antiquaries succeeded in making clear that a monument was to be admired and preserved, their puzzling selection of objects leaves us less sure of *what* they understood a monument to be. *Vetusta Monumenta*, in fact, does contain a fair share of what current English dictionaries define as monuments: 'a building, pillar, etc., built to preserve the memory of a person or event', or 'a very old building or place considered worth preserving for its historic interest or beauty'.[49] But beside showing a predilection for virtually two-dimensional objects which we might no longer think of as monuments, *Vetusta Monumenta* also includes objects which were probably not immediately recognizable as monuments at the time of their publication. We can hardly suppress a cry, 'This is not a monument!'[50] at the sight of the print representing the Horn of Ulphus (Figure 1.6).

In this respect *Vetusta Monumenta* reminds us not only of the now lost complexity of the term 'monument' but also of the contested nature of its etymology. Although in the first English dictionaries 'monument' was mostly listed as a synonym of sepulchral monument, in antiquity and throughout the eighteenth century it covered a wider range of objects. Thomas Elyot's *Latin-English Dictionary* (1538), for instance, explained 'monumentum' as 'a remembrance of some notable acte, as sepulchres, images, pylars, grete stones, inscriptions, bookes, and other lyke: whereby any thinge excellent, concernynge great wittes, kunnynge, enterprise in armes, puyssaunce, or rychesse is remembred' – a list that has been closely reiterated in successive dictionaries. Thus, Johnson's definition of 'monument' is 'Any thing by which the memory of persons or things is preserved; a memorial'; the Della Crusca academicians proposed: 'any thing or sign providing lasting memory . . . of whatever or whomever' and the *Oxford English Dictionary* suggests that it is 'anything that by its survival commemorates a person, action, period, or event'. The dictionary definition of a monument was broad enough to include not only tombs and masterpieces of art, and both monuments and texts, but also *anything* that happened to have survived from the past.

The fact that 'monument' could refer to a tomb, a statue, a text and 'anything' accounts for the diversity of monuments included in the first volume of *Vetusta Monumenta*. It also explains why antiquarianism was such a fissile discipline – one that could accommodate only with some difficulty Winckelmann's reading of the Torso Belvedere and the Fellows of the Society publishing brass trumpets.[51] On the definition of the word 'monument' hinged conflicting interpretations of antiquarianism. To some, the 'anything' of antiquity, its material culture and everyday life, were more exciting than quibbling philological discussions. Where C. G. Heyne hailed Winckelmann as the long-awaited initiator of an antiquarianism that disdained research on 'small meaningless gems, scrap-brass and old keys', D'Hancarville drew attention to the fact that 'Long before Sesac or Sesostris raised those Obelisks still existing, and which are the marks of his Conquests and power ... a Well, an Oak, a Field even ... were the warrants of the History which Fathers taught their Descendents'.[52]

Monuments did not originate necessarily in the literature of the ancients, nor were they the synecdoche of power. Instead, they could be the sole remnants of those who did not have the power to mark their existence with a higher sign. Alternatively, rather than man's effort to perpetuate his memory, monuments could be the by-product of his very existence, the involuntary survivals which Stuart Piggott described as 'unconscious evidence'.[53] Anything could be a monument since what made an object a monument was more the gaze of the antiquary than any intrinsic quality.

There is a striking coincidence between the contested definition of monument and the Romantic challenge to received expectations concerning both the poetic and what was worthy of poetic representation, as was articulated in the thundering Preface to the first edition of the *Lyrical Ballads* (1798):

It is the honourable characteristic of Poetry that its materials are to be found in every subject which can interest the human mind ... Readers accustomed to the gaudiness and inane phraseology of many modern writers, if they persist in reading this book to its conclusion, will perhaps frequently have to struggle with feelings of strangeness and aukwardness: they will look round for poetry, and will be induced to enquire by what species of courtesy these attempts can be permitted to assume that title.[54]

If the authors of the Preface were delusional in their claim to shocking originality, we can be certain that more than one viewer had to 'struggle with feelings of strangeness and aukwardness'[55] when faced with representations of ordinary objects such as horns, bones, shoes and brass-trumpets – increasingly deprived of the gaudiness and inane phraseology of decorative devices. Indeed, the abundance of parodies on the subject is a clear testimony of public shock. By producing representations of ordinary objects, antiquaries were exploding the concept of what was acceptable for representation, just as their literary contemporaries, by publishing previously unpublished texts from ages deemed to be unpoetic, were opening up the canon of English literature and challenging received ideas of the poetic.

Another analogy with the Romantic mode lies in the indefinite commitment to transmission which, besides showing that antiquaries were focused on the future as much as the past, also reveals that antiquarianism was pervaded by a vital dynamism and guided by an intuition of infinity. *Vetusta Monumenta* began publication in 1747 as the *first* of a series of volumes. Publishing monuments only made sense if open-endedly launched into the future, for the ultimate goal was to approximate (asymptotically) antiquity. For the antiquaries as for Goethe, publishing monuments was an 'endless process' just like 'life', not the entertainment of a necrophile:

It is sad when we have to regard our present collections as closed and complete. Armouries, galleries, and museums which acquire nothing new have a funereal and spectral atmosphere. So restricted a range of art has a restricting effect on the mind, for we tend to regard such collections as complete wholes, whereas we ought instead to be reminded by constant acquisitions that, in art as in life, nothing closed and complete can endure, and that all is an endless process.[56]

By drawing attention to the analogies between Romantic poetics and antiquarian wonder, catholic interest in antiquities and organic conception of antiquity I do not intend to replace one misleading brand-name with another. Nevertheless, I do mean to point out that 'the Age of the Antiquaries' extended well beyond the Grecian, the Celtic and the Gothic revivals, and demands that one consider it in relation to aesthetic concepts other than taste. Antiquarianism should be viewed as an aesthetics in its own right and one that defies existing labels.

   Antiquarianism had as much to do with history as with aesthetics and pleasure. We should not lose sight of the fact that, before the professionalization of scholarship, antiquaries pursued research on antiquity in their spare time and for their own entertainment. If they are to be credited with laying the foundations of modern historiography they should also be given credit for having expanded existing notions of pleasure and value. They ushered in what must have appeared as an oxymoron: a 'taste for learning'; they favoured, that is, such art and literature whose pleasure was enhanced (not spoiled) by scholarship. Rather than being passive consumers of artefacts they participated in the creation of their own pleasure, and although they notoriously did not value masterpieces of art and literature or tasteful antiques, they exposed the nature of artistic value. Their predilection for the valueless indicates that for antiquaries value was not inherent in objects, but was, instead, a construct – in this case a scholarly construct – of the observer.

Notes

1. Arnaldo Momigliano, 'Ancient History and the Antiquarian', in *Studies in Historiography* (London, Weidenfeld & Nicolson, 1966), pp.1–39, p.3.

2. Letter from Horace Walpole to Rev. William Cole, 1 September 1778, reproduced in W.S. Lewis (ed.), *The Yale Edition of the Correspondence of Horace Walpole*, 48 vols (New Haven, Yale University Press; Oxford University Press, 1937–83), 2, p.116.

3. *Encyclopédie, ou dictionnaire raisonné des sciences, des arts et des métiers par une société des gens de Lettres*, ed. Denis Diderot and Jean D'Alembert, 17 vols (Paris, Briasson, David, le Breton, Durand, 1751–65), 'Discours préliminaire des editeurs', 1, p. xviii; Walter Scott, *Ivanhoe: a Romance*, 3 vols (Edinburgh and London, A. Constable & Co. and Hurst, Robinson & Co., 1820), 'Dedicatory Epistle to the Rev. Dr Dryasdust, F.A.S. Residing in the Castle Gate, York', 1, pp. xiv–xv and x–xi.

4. William Gilpin, *An Essay upon Prints* (London, printed for J. Robson, 1768), pp.134–5. For a discussion of George Vertue's work as engraver to the Society of Antiquaries, see Chapter 2 in this volume.

5. Stephen Bann, *The Inventions of History: Essays on the Representation of the Past* (Manchester and New York, Manchester University Press, 1990), p.102.

6. Johann Joachim Winckelmann, *Geschichte der Kunst der Alterthums*, 2 vols (Vienna, Akademie der bildenden Kunst, 1776), 1, p. xxxv.

7. See Jean Barbault, *Vues des plus beaux restes des antiquites romaines* (Rome, Bouchard et Gravier, 1775).

8. See for example the preface to William Wordsworth and Samuel Taylor Coleridge, *Lyrical Ballads* (London, J. & A. Arch, 1798).

9. On Winckelmann's *Monumenti antichi inediti* see Chapter 2 of my unpublished PhD thesis, *'Monuments' and 'Texts': Antiquarianism and Literature in Eighteenth- and Early Nineteenth-Century Britain*, Cambridge University, 1997; Richard Gough, *Sepulchral Monuments in Great Britain*, 2 vols (London, J. Nichols, 1786–96), 2, pt.1, Preface, p. 5.

10. Pietro Santi Bartoli, *Gli Antichi Sepolcri* (Rome, Domenico De Rossi, 1704), p. iii.

11. Raphael, 'Lettera di Raffaelle a Leone X sulla pianta di Roma antica' (1519), in *Raffaello* ed. Vincenzo Golzio (Città del Vaticano, 1936), p.82.

12. John Aubrey, 'The Naturall History of Wiltshire, part II', quoted in Michael Hunter, *John Aubrey and the Realm of Learning* (New York, Science History Publications, 1975), p.68.

13. William Stukeley, *Stonehenge a Temple Restor'd to the British Druids* (London, W. Innys & R. Manby, 1740), Preface, sig.aᵛ. For a discussion of Stukeley's work see Chapter 4 of this volume.

14. Gough, *Sepulchral Monuments*, 2, pt. 1, Preface, p.5.

15. James Sargeant Storer and John Greig, *Antiquarian and Topographical Cabinet*, 10 vols (London, W. Clarke, J. Carpenter & H.D. Symonds, 1807–11), 1, Advertisement.

16. Society of Antiquaries, Letters and Papers 1707–42. This document is a copy of British Museum MS Cotton Faustina, E5, which was transcribed by Maurice Johnson in preparation of the new constitution.

17. *Ibid.*

18. Humphrey Wanley, British Museum, Harleian MS, 7055, f.3, quoted in Joan Evans, *A History of the Society of Antiquaries* (Oxford, The Society of Antiquaries, 1956), p.40.

19. Society of Antiquaries, *Minute Book*, 1 January 1718.

20. Society of Antiquaries, Stukeley, Box, 24a, fol. 287 (A+B), 28 March 1754, MS.

21. Evans, *A History of the Society of Antiquaries*, p.73.

22. *Vetusta Monumenta*, 1, pl. 17.

23. *Ibid.*, 2, pl. 8.

24. *Ibid.*, 3, pls. 4–5, 'Descriptions of Stalls Discovered in Chatham Church, Kent', p.1.

25. *Ibid.*, 1, pls.33, 42 and 48.

26. *Ibid.*, 1, pl. 8; see also pls. 39, 46 and 61.

27. *Ibid.*, 1, pls. 6, 35 and 42.

28. Richard Gough, 'An Historical Account of the Origin and Establishment of the Society of Antiquaries', *Archaeologia* 1 (1770), p. xxxviii.

29. See, for instance, *Gentleman's Magazine* 52 (May 1782), p.223.

30. See *Gentleman's Magazine* 58 (August 1788), p.689. See also Giovan Battista Piranesi *Antichità Romane*, 4 vols (Rome, Bouchard & Gravier, 1756), 1, Prefazione agli studiosi di antichità romane, p. 1 and Cristoforo Amaduzzi and Ridolfino Venuti, *Vetera Monumenta quae in Hortis Caelimontanis et in Aedibus Matthaeiorum Adservantur*, 3 vols (Rome, Monaldini, 1776–9), 1, p.ii.

31. Publishing monuments in books was so common in the eighteenth century that 'edition' was defined

by Samuel Johnson as the 'publication of any thing, particularly of a book'; the word 'museum' appears in the Della Crusca dictionary of Italian as the 'title of a book illustrating a museum'. Samuel Johnson, *A Dictionary of the English Language*, 2 vols (London, J. & P. Knapton et al, 1755); *Vocabolario degli Accademici della Crusca*, 5th edn, 11 vols (Florence, Tipografia Galileiana di M. Cellini & Co., 1863–1923).

32. *Vetusta Monumenta*, **1**, pl. 7.

33. *Ibid.*, pls. 13–14.

34. *Ibid.*, pl. 15.

35. Letter from Horace Walpole to Rev. William Cole, 1 September 1778, correspondence of Horace Walpole, 2, p.116.

36. Gilpin, *An Essay upon Prints*, p. 135; Roland Barthes, 'The Plates of the *Encyclopédie*', in *Barthes: Selected Writings*, ed. Susan Sontag (London, Fontana, 1983), pp.218–35, pp.218 and 230.

37. *Vetusta Monumenta*, **1**, pl. 7; *Minute Book*, 12 July 1721. See also *Minute Book*, 8 February 1720/1.

38. Society of Antiquaries, *Minute Book*, 21 July 1743 and 27 October 1743. For Stukeley's description of the site see *Minute Book*, 16 March 1719/20, 17 February 1724/5.

39. These plates were not part of Vertue's commissions for the Society of Antiquaries. They were published by Vertue, from his commercial premises, in 1747, and donated to the Society on 10 March 1747.

40. *Vetusta Monumenta*, 1, pl. 57.

41. Society of Antiquaries, *Minute Book*, 5 February 1717/18.

42. *Ibid.*, 12 February 1717/18.

43. *Ibid.*, 19 February, 23 April 1717/18.

44. Society of Antiquaries, Stukeley's Box, 24A, f. 286.

45. The nature and recurrence of antiquarian satire, during the eighteenth century, is also discussed in this volume by Stephen Bending and Lucy Peltz.

46. This was explicitly the case of the engraving of the Rosetta Stone, published as soon as it reached the Society of Antiquaries and before it was deciphered (*Vetusta Monumenta* (1815), **4**, pls. 5–7).

47. John Aubrey, 'An idea of Education of Young gentlemen', quoted in Hunter, *John Aubrey*, p.37.

48. On wonder see J.V. Cunningham 'Woe or Wonder: The Emotional Effect of Shakespearian Tragedy', in *Tradition and Poetic Structure* (Denver, Swallow, 1960); Stephen Greenblatt, 'Resonance and Wonder', in *Exhibiting Cultures: The Poetics and Politics of Museum Display*, ed. Ivan Karp and Steven D. Lavine (Washington and London, Smithsonian Institutions Press, 1991), pp.42–56.

49. *Longman Dictionary of Contemporary English* (Harlow, Longman, 1987).

50. *Vetusta Monumenta*, **1**, pl. 2.

51. *Ibid.*

52. C.G. Heyne, 'Elogio di Winckelmann', in Winckelmann, *Storia delle arti del disegno presso gli antichi*, ed. Carlo Fea, 3 vols (Rome, Pagliarini, 1783–4), **1**, p. lxxi; D'Hancarville, *Collection of Etruscan, Greek, and Roman Antiquities*, 4 vols (Naples, F. Morelli, 1766–7), **1**, p.116.

53. Stuart Piggott, *Approach to Archaeology* (London, Black, 1959) p.2.

54. Wordsworth and Coleridge, *Lyrical Ballads*, pp.i–ii.

55. Robert D. Mayo, 'The Contemporaneity of the Lyrical Ballads', *PMLA*, 69 (1954), pp.486–522.

56. Goethe, 'Winckelmann' (1805), in *German Aesthetic and Literary Criticism: Winckelmann, Lessing, Hamann, Herder, Schiller, Goethe*, ed. H.B. Nisbet (Cambridge University Press, 1985), pp.236–58, p.249.

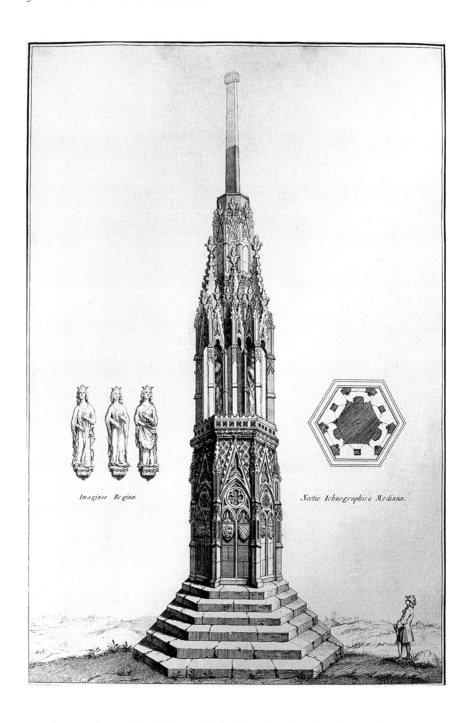

Imagines Reginæ.

Sectio Ichnographica Medianæ.

1.1   [George Vertue after William Stukeley] *Waltham Cross* (1727), engraving

1.2   [George Vertue] *The North West View of the Abby Gatehouse of S*^t*. Bennets in the Holme Norff* (n.d.), engraving

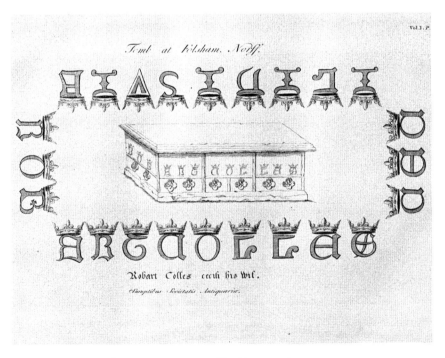

1.3   [George Vertue] *Tomb at Folsham Norff* (n.d.), engraving

1.4   I. Goerre delin., J. Baptiste fecit, *Castellum Aquae Martiae* (1694–9), engraving and etching

1.5   [George Vertue] *The Inside Perspective View of the under Chapel of St Thomas within London Bridge* (1747), engraving

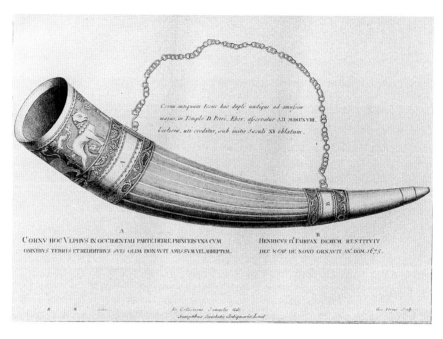

1.6   BM delin., Geor: Vertue Sculp., [Horn of Ulphus] (n.d.), engraving

2

Graphic antiquarianism in eighteenth-century Britain: the career and reputation of George Vertue (1684–1756)

Martin Myrone

In the early eighteenth century, the making, publishing and selling of prints was among the most innovative and vital areas of metropolitan cultural life.[1] Thoughout this period of expansion George Vertue (1684–1756) was one of the most prolific and prominent of the professional engravers working in London. In a long career that stretched from the first years of the century to the last months of his life he executed reproductions of portraits and topographical views and, most distinctively, antiquarian plates, in very large numbers. A manuscript list of his engravings drawn up by the engraver himself includes over five hundred items though it covers only the period between 1709 and 1740.[2] Aside from his engravings, the artist was active as a draftsman and portrait limner, medallist, designer of silver plate, art agent, and dealer in prints, and, of course, he was a scholar, publishing a number of antiquarian texts and amassing notes for a comprehensive history of British art.[3] A member of almost all London's art institutions, a Fellow of the Society of Antiquaries and the Official Engraver to the University of Oxford, his contemporaries reckoned him one of the masters of the art of engraving.[4] Although he never received a knighthood (as the engraver Nicolas Dorigny did in 1720) he was esteemed highly enough to be buried in Westminster Abbey, at which time he received hyperbolic obituaries.[5]

An etched self-portrait executed, as a later inscription tells us, 'within a few years of his Death', presents the artist as supremely confident in his status as craftsman and intellectual (Figure 2.1). Vertue is depicted in half-length in a simple costume. Engraving tools are laid on the table before him, while the device at the head of the print is made up of a compass and a pair of water-colour brushes. Each draws attention to the practice of his trade. However, Vertue's right elbow rests upon a bound volume, which, together with the fact that he is unwigged, indicates his status as a man of learning. It was these twin aspects of scholar and artisan that Vertue imagined would give him a place in posterity. The Latin banner that unfurls across the top of the image can be translated as 'virtue lives beyond the grave'.

This was certainly not the case. Within a few years of his death Vertue's reputation as an engraver and as a scholar declined rapidly, and, it would seem, permanently. The comments of the Reverend William Gilpin in his famous *Essay Upon Prints* (1768) are typical. In his catalogue of engravers' lives, which often tends to sharpness, the Reverend was briefly dismissive of Vertue. His criticism can be quoted in full:

> VERTUE was an excellent antiquarian, but no artist. He copied with painful exactness; in a dry, disagreeable manner, without force, or freedom. In his whole collection of heads, we can scarce pick out half a dozen, which are good.[6]

Thirteen years later, in the third edition of the *Essay*, Gilpin was even less favourable to the artist. Vertue was now only a 'good antiquarian' but a 'worthy man'; nevertheless, he remained 'no artist'.[7] Something can be added to our understanding of Gilpin's criticism if we compare it to his comments on the seventeenth-century artist Wenceslaus Hollar, whom Vertue admired highly and, as we shall see, identified with. Gilpin condemned Hollar in terms reminiscent of those used in reference to Vertue: 'Hollar was an antiquarian, and a draftsman; but seems to have been little acquainted with the principles of painting'.[8] As Gilpin had stated in his introduction, it was precisely the 'principles of painting' that he would use in his assessment of prints.[9] By that standard, Vertue, like Hollar, has been found wanting. Moreover, in their failure to accord to the standards set up by Gilpin, each is identified as an 'antiquarian' rather than an artist proper. It would appear that antiquarianism and artistry are not only incompatible, but perhaps even defined against each other.

There has been no attempt to revise this opinion even in this century. Vertue remains 'of greater interest as an antiquary' than as a practising artist and, despite a number of interesting studies of aspects of his work, there has been no concerted effort to give a comprehensive account of his career.[10] Yet every student of British art knows his name. The fifty or so notebooks he filled with his records of artists, collections and patrons constitute a uniquely detailed record of his own time, and an invaluable source for earlier periods. Their partial publication in their original form by the Walpole Society earlier this century remains one of the achievements of modern art history and transformed the study of eighteenth-century British culture.[11] Until very recently, the *Notebooks* were viewed as a useful source of information, but little else. According to the art historian Ellis Waterhouse, Vertue should be considered only as 'an accumulator of the raw facts of history, and in no sense an historian'.[12] While there are now several attempts to reconsider his voluminous notes on the history of art as richly suggestive historical documents in their own right, Vertue remains valued as, above all, an antiquarian distinguished by a relentless commitment to factual data.[13]

As in the case of his artistic practice, these prejudices emerged soon after Vertue's death. In much altered form, his art-historical notes were published in 1762–71 by Horace Walpole as *Anecdotes of Painting*. In the Preface of the first volume, Walpole explained that as Vertue's notes had 'no order, no connection, no accuracy' nor 'was his style clear enough to be offered to the reader in that unpolished state' he had been forced to rewrite everything.[14] Furthermore, he had attempted to 'enliven' the 'dryness' of Vertue's treatment of the subject with entertaining anecdotes. The wisdom of this was seemingly accepted within Walpole's circle. As Lord Beauchamp wrote in a letter to the author of *Anecdotes of Painting*:

I confess I was at first prejudiced against the subject of your work – it appeared dry, and I doubted even of your ability to render the laborious compilations of an antiquary both amusing and instructive to a common reader.[15]

At the same time, Walpole received a letter from Henry Zouch stating that the subject of the *Anecdotes* was 'dry' and 'uninteresting' but had been made entertaining by its editor.[16] In later years Walpole played up the distance between the 'dry' and antiquarian approach of Vertue and his own, more casual method. The 'faithful and sedulous' Vertue provided him, he claimed, only with 'dates and facts'. He could do nothing but re-cast those notes into a more palatable form, as he could 'not bring [him]self to a habit of minute accuracy about very indifferent points'.[17]

In these comments we might identify the emergence of a distinctively modern notion of the antiquarian as opposed to the legitimate writer of history.[18] The antiquarian is cast as the maker of lists, the accumulator of meaningless data, who can bring neither order nor meaning to the materials he gathers. He is, in consequence, 'dry', where the more imaginative historian is fecund. It should be obvious that this assessment of Vertue's writings resembles the dominant opinions on his graphic works in some important ways. In each case Vertue's failure is identified as a characteristic of the antiquarian. In being an antiquarian, he fails to be either a historian or an artist.

In this essay I hope to restore some sense of the historical richness of Vertue's life, work and ideas, while considering also the motivations behind the transformation of his reputation in the last decades of the eighteenth century. I intend, thereby, to rupture some of the continuities of thought between the late eighteenth century and the modern day and open up questions regarding the relationships between historical knowledge and social relations encompassed by the practice of antiquarianism. The changing fortunes of Vertue's status as a graphic artist and antiquarian, or rather as an artist who seemed to practise antiquarianism via graphic means, illustrate with great

clarity a set of profound and connected shifts in the social history of historical
practice and aesthetics.

Through scattered comments in his notebooks and in his versions of an
autobiography, we can reconstruct quite fully Vertue's proclaimed professional ambitions.[19] In his autobiographies he describes an artist dependent
upon and intimate with a closed network of élite patrons whose generosity
towards their protégé is brought to an end only by their inopportune deaths.[20]
The autobiographical narrative is structured around a series of associations
between the subject and his increasingly select sponsors: first Kneller, the portrait painter, then the two successive Earls of Oxford, the Earl of Winchelsea,
the Duke of Norfolk, and finally the Prince of Wales. Indeed, both versions of
the text end with dramatic notices of his current sponsor's death. The last lines
of the first draft (1741) read:

The death of this great and Noble Collector of arts and encourager [the second Earl of
Oxford] was an unhappy loss to the public but to Mr Vertue most fatal indeed ... from
this loss and time of death Vertue may date – his great decline of friends and interest.[21]

The event proved not as fatal as Vertue claims, for a decade later, at the end of
the second version of his life, he stated:

unhappy day. wensday march 20. 1750 / 1.
about 10 a clock the eveningy dyed. His Royal highness Frederick Prince of Wales at
Leister feilds house – the loss of this prince may I lament ... observations on my   indifferent health and weakness. of sight encreasing – and loss of Noble friends and the
encouragement from them less and less daily – this year – and worse in appearance
begins with 1752.[22]

Thus the deaths of his major patrons provide the opportunity for staging his
own death in a rhetorical sense. In his projection of a total dependence upon
the favours of aristocratic patrons, Vertue was drawing an analogy between
his own life and that of Hollar, on whom he published a monograph in 1745. In
that volume Vertue described how the Bohemian engraver and draftsman
served at court and attached himself to the house of the Earl of Arundel, gain-
ing his patronage and companionship. According to Vertue this ended only
with the Earl's sudden death, when Hollar was 'turn'd adrift' and forced to
work for printsellers, 'no doubt at very low prices'.[23] This, implicitly, is the fate
Vertue projects for himself in 1741, and then again in 1751. He was all too
aware of the dangers presented to the engraver by the open marketplace and
its mercenary commercial printsellers and publishers. The *Notebooks* mourn-
fully record the fate of a whole class of engraver–draftsmen like himself (and
including his pupil Giles King) who were exploited by commercial agents and
died in abject poverty.[24]

Given all we know about the cultural weakness of the court and the general
disinterest shown towards contemporary British art by the aristocracy in

eighteenth-century Britain, Vertue's purported dependence upon high-born patrons appears to be highly unlikely. Rather, it must be read as an attempt to exploit the conventions of artistic biography – as derived from the courtly culture of the Renaissance – to fabricate for himself a self-aggrandizing association with the traditional social élite. In the list of his engravings drawn up by the artist himself, and without it would appear any view to publication, a quite different picture emerges. This shows that from the outset of his independent career he produced very large numbers of engravings, but only rarely for private patrons. In fact, he admitted that the water-colours and drawings generally undertaken for such employers were done 'by stealth as it were' as 'the continuall employment of engravings took his time mostly'.[25] Vertue's list shows that, after training as a silver-engraver with the goldsmith Blaise Gentot and then as a copper engraver with Gerard Vandergucht, he produced ephemeral printed matter for a few years before, in 1709, starting to work for himself. From that date he produced engraved portraits, mainly for publishers, and from the late 1710s antiquarian prints. Although the lists are occasionally interrupted by brief comments that suggest some narrative development – for instance, the note on his engraving of George I that says that this print made his name with the public – there is almost no sense of the substance or range of his work changing over the years. There is certainly no indication of any dramatic turning points around the years highlighted by Vertue in his autobiographies. Rather, once the range of his activities was established (by around 1720) they remained virtually unchanged until his death. Far from being dependent upon a handful of patrons, Vertue maintained his professional engraving activity at a constant level, working variously for himself, for individual patrons, for commercial publishers, and for institutions. Arguably, it was his association with institutions, most significantly the revived Society of Antiquaries of London, that provided the engraver with long-term security.

Vertue's role within the Society of Antiquaries has been detailed quite adequately by Joan Evans in her history and so need not be dealt with at length in the present context.[26] Vertue gained the post at the revival of the Society in 1717, when he was also made a Fellow, and retained it until his death. During that period he was responsible for engraving and publishing almost every print issued by the Society. Coming to be known as *Vetusta Monumenta*, this amounted to sixty-four separate projects, a total of eighty-six plates. The variety of prints was considerable, and included prints of antique objects, reproductions of historical text and paintings, maps, views and architectural plans (Figures 2.2, 2.4 and 2.5). On average the engraver received around £20 worth of work each year, though this figure fluctuated considerably,[27] with the largest sums being received for the production of new prints. Throughout his tenure as Engraver to the Society, Vertue was responsible also for republishing old prints, and acting as an occasional agent, and sometimes he delivered papers at the Society, as well as performing more mundane tasks. From 1727 Vertue combined this post with an appointment as official engraver to the University of Oxford.[28] For around £50 a year he was responsible for the engraving (though not the design or publication) of the University's almanacs. On the basis of the income derived from his institutional posts alone, we can calculate that Vertue received an annual wage of more than the £75 which Robert Campbell, in his vocational guidebook of 1747, reckoned to be the proper reward of a 'tolerable' engraver.[29] Vertue's greater wealth and fame was due, however, to the repercussions of his official status as an antiquarian engraver.

Firstly, the Society brought Vertue into direct contact with the network of aristocratic and gentrified patrons who made up its membership. Fellows issued a number of individual commissions, some substantial.[30] More generally, Vertue's dual role as a professional artist and antiquarian considerably increased his usefulness to longer-term patrons. With the first Earl of Oxford, his most consistent patron in the 1720s and 1730s, he undertook a series of antiquarian tours which he recorded assiduously in manuscript pamphlets, and undertook genealogical research in the form of engraving portraits of the Earl's ancestors.[31] At the same time, he provided gossip from the art world, acted as an agent at auctions, and sold him his own prints.[32] Similarly, for the Prince of Wales, who employed Vertue in the 1740s, he provided watercolours from stock, acted as a copyist, and drew up manuscript lists of the royal collection.[33] On other occasions he deployed his antiquarian skills in a more casual fashion, appearing as an expert witness during the dispute over the Duke of Buckingham's will.[34]

Vertue's status as a graphic antiquarian was useful in the wider realm as well. In his work for commercial publishers, his association with antiquarianism was an essential marketing strategy.[35] By the 1720s Vertue's name was itself a marketing device for prints. Puffs for the 1726 edition of *The Life of Thomas More* noted that it was 'beautifully printed on fine paper, in octavo, with the Effigies of Sir Thomas More, curiously engraved by Mr Vertue from the great painting of Hans Holbein'.[36] Similarly, advertisements for editions of Bacon's *Works* (1730) and Castiglione's *Courtier* (1737) named Vertue's prints as a selling point.[37] Though in the 1720s the engraver had undertaken more general illustrative work, by the 1730s at the latest he was evidently well established as a specialist engraver of historical portraits. For the commercially minded Knaptons, he was the natural choice of engraver for their series of historical heads, produced in the 1730s and early 1740s.[38]

Additionally, the ever-astute Vertue exploited the commercial potential of antiquarian engraving in his capacity as an independent publisher of prints, and would often announce his membership of the Society of Antiquaries on individual prints.[39] More sophisticated marketing strategies appeared in his publication of series of antiquarian prints. The 'Twelve Heads of the Poets' series was a response to the boom in portrait head collecting, but Vertue was so fastidious in ensuring the historical accuracy of the images that it took him three years to complete – and he published the frontispiece to the series in Latin. While published through a subscription scheme, one of the practical innovations of the early eighteenth-century print market, the series was marketed with specific reference to the antiquity of both the subjects and their portraits.[40] The publication of the 'Nine Historical Portraits' (1742–51) was announced by a series of earnest antiquarian pamphlets.[41] Indeed, the first subject, a royal family piece after Holbein (Figure 2.3), had been suggested as a suitable subject for inclusion in the *Vetusta Monumenta* as early as 1719.[42] Yet in producing such an ambitious series of prints, Vertue was following established commercial formulae; they were large scale and uniform in their format, and thematically unified. Furthermore, with their elaborate surrounds and size they were eminently suitable for glazing and use as 'furniture' for hanging on the wall. Vertue did precisely that with one of the series when he presented it as a gift to the Bridewell in 1751.[43]

Vertue's close association with antiquarianism allowed the artist to negotiate between contrasting marketing contexts, each of which provided alternative frameworks for the production and reception of a graphic work. It is an indication of Vertue's celebrity both as an antiquarian and as an entrepreneur that after his death his independently executed antiquarian plates were acquired from his widow by the Society of Antiquaries and re-published for their members, while those plates that were included in the posthumous sale were purchased by leading commercial printsellers, including, for instance, John Boydell.[44] Like his literary counterparts, Vertue worked within a mixed economy of patronage in the process of shifting from the aristocratic and exclusive forms predominant in the seventeenth century to the commercial world of free enterprise which typified the later eighteenth, and encompassing the new sociable institutions of the metropolis.[45] The common point of reference that operated in each of these contexts was Vertue's status as an antiquarian. While in a literal sense this was secured through his official post and Fellowship at the Society of Antiquaries itself, Vertue's peculiar success as a graphic antiquarian rested upon distinctive characteristics of his graphic manner – indeed, the characteristics that later commentators down to the present day have found so hard to value.

The early eighteenth-century antiquarian print can be defined in terms other than its content, that is, the historical artefact or subject it represents. We may distinguish a specific aesthetic at work in its visual organization and significatory mode, an aesthetic most completely expressed through the medium of line engraving.[46] The antiquarian print was prized as a form of document whose power was derived from its capacity to record accurately any given image. In the early eighteenth century it was less an illustration, meant to evoke a given object within a projected context, than a compressed statement of the bare presence of an object as an object. This could mean, alternatively, an extraordinary elaboration of details on objects suspended in a vacuum (Figure 2.4), or the multiple representation of an image within a single frame in order to communicate additional information, for instance by including a plan of a building or a detail to a different scale. In each case the opportunity for imaginative projection on the part of the viewer is very limited, and text plays a significant role in policing the meanings of the image by providing a pre-ordained framework of historical, topographical or biographical reference. There is little effort to place any given object within an illusionistic or narrative setting. Nor is there any effort to dispose the image according to the established priorities of formal beauty or literary content, as was meant to occur in the most distinguished modes of picture making. Rather, the artefact was intended to be the primary, even exclusive, object of attention.

Since the seventeenth century, one of the most prominent claims made for line engraving in art-critical discourse was that the medium had the greatest capacity to evoke surface qualities, the substance of forms, even colours.[47] In its descriptive potential, engraving was clearly suited to the production of antiquarian imagery. More significant, however, are the kinds of authorial presence generated out of the practice of engraving. The engraver worked with a repertoire of lines, dots and lozenges whose forms were dictated by the intractability of the copperplate and by the traditional nature of the tools used to work it. The basic notational unit of the engraver, the slightly swelling incised line, was minute compared to the surface necessarily filled with such marks to create tonal effects that did not intrude upon the representational functions of the print. In other words, where the desired effect was not simply linear, the marks had to be organized with some density so that they did not draw attention to themselves as marks. There are two main points to be made here. Firstly, the visual language of engraving was highly conventionalized and did not have great scope for personal expression. Secondly, the work of the engraver was necessarily very time-consuming and was defined in good part by the simple issue of the size of the plate rather than by the aesthetic or intellectual demands of the subject matter.

The significance of these points can be elaborated through Vertue's own writings on the art of engraving. Of course, his *Notebooks* are littered with remarks on the technique and style of individual masters. However, his unpublished essay 'On Engraving History or Portraiture: a simile' was the most developed of his general statements about engraving.[48] In this he drew an analogy between the reproductive engraver and the literary translator:

an engraver is propperly a translator of an author from one language to another. in portraiture he translates from a modern language to a universal one. as from English to Latin History from Latin verse to prose in Latin.

Vertue went on to stress the 'universal' character of engraving, as the act of reproducing an image could free it from 'particular dialects, manners &c'. By implication, the reproductive engraver takes possession of the image he copies. As the engraver is without personal style (his art is 'universal') he is able to command and adapt the styles of others, eliminate culturally specific mannerisms, and thereby refine and preserve. In fact, he even states that the task is especially difficult when the original author is living, as he will inevitably interfere with the work of the engraver even though he does not understand his task.

Vertue's claim to authorial appropriation through the act of graphic repro-duction was given material form by those complete collections of his own proofs that he put together for James West in 1733, for the Bodleian Library in 1737 and for the second Earl of Oxford and Thomas Frankland in 1740.[49] Such collections did have precedents. Vertue knew of Simon Gribelin's methodi-cally compiled volumes of his own reproductive prints and decorative designs, but these had been put together only for the engraver's use, and may not have acted as anything more than an unusually well-cultivated sample book for potential clients.[50] Also John Smith had put together collections of mezzotints scraped or published by him.[51] By contrast, Vertue's collections were of prints executed, but not necessarily published, by him. They were dis-tinct in that their sole unifying factor was the identity of the executive hand and that they were distinguished compilations for favoured patrons. He con-structed for himself a prestigious œuvre that encompassed commercial ephemera, antiquarian illustrations, and prints after Van Dyck and Holbein.

Vertue's claim that the engraver translated an image into a universal form was closely attuned to the intentions of antiquarians. From the outset the Society of Antiquaries was dedicated to a programme of print publication, issuing reproductions of antiquities 'to the end that the knowledge of them may become more universal, be preserved and transmitted to futurity'.[52] Far from being morbidly preoccupied with the past, the antiquarian project was defined as progressive and forward-looking, and hence part, in fact, of the project of refinement that defined cultural enterprise in this period. In the metaphor of translation was a means of linking cultural production, or rather reproduction, to the progressive dynamic of early eighteenth-century metro-politan culture. And in the sociable aspect of the antiquarian project, the insis-tence that for a print to be of value it had to be reproduced and circulated, came a rationale for commercial innovation on the part of the engraver.[53] Vertue's subscription project for the 'Twelve Heads of the Poets', in particular, marks a meeting point between antiquarian enthusiasms and the new forms of marketing and patronage characteristic of the culture of refinement.[54]

A further element of Vertue's elevated discourse on engraving is his empha-sis on the very laboriousness of the technique. Drawing on a vocabulary developed by John Evelyn in his *Sculptura* (1662), he distinguished line engraving from other forms of printmaking on the basis of the higher level of consumption of the artist's time and physical energy it demanded:

of these works of the Graver cut in, may be properly expressed by the word Burin-Sculpture, Burination. the Burinator, or burinavit, from the Greek word, Burim – or plowing – or plough share. for it is properly and naturally a plowing in brass or metal of any kind – like furrowing – in all degrees necessary.[55]

This he contrasted with etching 'done with the point or needle on grounds and eaten in with Aquafortis ... an invention for Expedition' which takes only half the time of engraving, and to mezzotint, a process of 'scraping on the copper' which takes 'one fourth of time – that the same work and dimension can be as well done by the Burinator'.[56] As the technique becomes more expeditious so it becomes, in terms of Vertue's semiotics of artistic labour, more superficial, from 'plowing' lines, through allowing chemicals to do the work, down to simply 'scraping' superficially. The transformed physical matter of the copperplate itself is presented as the bearer of value, over and above the representational artefact that is derived from it. The plate itself is a form of sculpture.

While the connection between engraving and sculpture was of long standing, and by reference to Biblical precedent had considerable power as a means of establishing the high cultural value of printmaking, Vertue's comments are tied to the market conditions of his time.[57] Elsewhere, he explained the commercial logic of printmaking in more detail:

the necessity of such works being printed on paper. a sheet being of small value – subsequent to be multiplyed. and consequently more in number so each of less value. and allways – appears less worthy of esteem on the paper than on the copper plate it-self.[58]

On the face of it this is a ludicrous statement on the part of a reproductive engraver whose job was, after all, to multiply a given image through the deployment of his skills. In fact, his complaint is not that engravings are, perforce, multiples but that the act of multiplication exposes the engraver himself to the machinations of commercial printsellers. As the mass production of prints meant the reduction in economic value of each unit, so more had to be produced and sold. Given the high levels of labour and time that had to be invested into the working of a plate, most engravers necessarily became dependent on printsellers for support. These commercial middlemen are cast as the villains of the piece by Vertue, for they 'squeeze and screw. trick and abuse ... to raise their own fortunes by devouring that of the Sculpture-Engravers'.[59] Furthermore, the general sale of prints on the free market meant that the engraver was divorced from personal relations with any individual patron: as the engraver's fate is 'every.bodys business so it is nobodys'.[60] Yet as greater honour was attached to line engraving, those artists who turned from it to more commercially viable forms of production were characterized by Vertue as mercenary and disgraced. In practice, Vertue did use etching within his engravings, in particular to accent architectural forms and in the characterization of the staffage in topographical views (Figure 2.5). The relatively fluid and flexible marks possible with the etching needle served well in producing such ornamental accents. His theory of art was, however, pre-occupied with the purity of engraved line.

Vertue's comments fit a developing pattern of anti-commercial discourse on the national school of art. Well into the nineteenth century, this remained significant as a means of proclaiming prestige for the reproductive line engraver in the face of more expedient and commercial, and less skilful, graphic techniques.[61] But in the case of Vertue, these claims were co-ordinated to the desires and expectations of the antiquarians. The distinguishing feature of the antiquarian, as the producer of historical discourse, was his tendency to amass rather than order, his obsessive concern with, as Walpole put it, 'minute accuracy about indifferent parts'.[62] Engraving, as a practice, and certainly as it was imagined by Vertue, demanded such a form of attention. The engraver's persistent refusal to co-ordinate his attention and labour to a hierarchy of subjects ranked according to aesthetic values served to identify him as the antiquarian engraver of his age. For the Society of Antiquaries it was a guarantee of consistent quality; for the purchasers of his prints on the London market, it was a guarantee of cultural authority.

In the culture of early eighteenth-century antiquarianism, Vertue found an exceptional means of professional support. While his proclaimed ideal of the artist being fully protected by élite sponsors was manifestly untenable in the age in which he lived, the Society of Antiquaries formed a sort of replacement. It offered him social prestige, financial support and access to a network of patrons. More significant still, it gave his work an exclusive stamp of authority that was useful in the larger market. His achievement was not to be repeated. In the year after his death, the Society ruled that no subsequent official engraver could also be a Fellow. Rather, the commercial potential of the market for antiquarian prints was to be exploited to the full using independent professional engravers and printsellers.[63] By this means the Society clarified the distinction between the liberal status of the Fellows and the mechanic, subservient role of the engravers they employed. The alignment of commercialism and Vertue's unique brand of graphic antiquarianism was temporary.

Vertue's interventions into antiquarianism were those of a professional with specific skills and forms of knowledge that did not otherwise qualify him for élite social status. The practice of engraving was closely attuned to the investigative, documentary notion of antiquarianism dominant within an élite class little compelled to demonstrate their authority by displays of connoisseurial 'taste' and assured of their public duty as historians. But as the century progressed both the discourse of antiquarianism and the discourse on graphic art were transformed, while the material conditions of the practice of both were increasingly subject to commercial pressures and redefined with reference to a general public of consumers. The antiquarian project was diffused variously as local history, romantic antiquarianism, and, eventually, the modern discipline of history, and the antiquarian and his methods fell into ever greater disrepute. As new notions of authorial originality began to dictate the assessment of the graphic arts in theory and in commercial practice, the reproductive engraver became a more suspect figure. The technical achievements of conventional copperplate engraving were marginalized in comparison with the more abstract properties of 'design' derived from the critical paradigms worked out in relation to the art of painting; properties better expressed through the mediums of aquatint or etching whose graphic vocabularies were subject less to convention than to what was construed as individual authorial will.

Line engraving, the subject of anxious historical and theoretical speculation on the part of Vertue, came to be evoked, nostalgically, as a lost ideal of craftsmanship. Vertue's career should alert us, however, to the fact that the effective commercialization of print production, so often seen as a triumphal aspect of eighteenth-century British culture, brought change not only within the graphic arts as a discrete set of practices. It also displaced the visual artist from an equal place within the community of historians. Vertue's lack of imagination, his disdain for 'design', and his dogged industry, qualified him for a place within élite culture that was never again available. If the changes that rendered each of these qualities marginal within legitimate high culture brought into existence an 'aristocracy of culture' rather than one of inherited status, it also meant that the mechanic and the intellectual, and the artisan and the artist, were effectively divorced.[64]

Notes

1. The fullest study of the print market is now Timothy Clayton, *The English Print, 1688–1802* (New Haven and London, Yale University Press, 1997).

2. 'A Collection of Engraved Prints ... the Works of G. Vertue', original manuscript at the Lewis Walpole Library, Farmington CT; photostat at the archive of the National Portrait Gallery, London.

3. For a brief overview of Vertue's career see my 'George Vertue (1684–1756) and the Graphic Arts in Eighteenth-Century Britain', MA Report, Courtauld Institute of Art, University of London, 1994. Vertue's publications include *A Description of the Works of the Ingenious Delineator and Engraver Wenceslaus Hollar* (London, 1745) and *Medals, Coins and Great Seals from the Elaborate Works of Thomas Simon* (London, 1753). For the history of the *Notebooks*, see Lionel Cust and Arthur Hind, 'Vertue's Notebooks and Manuscripts Relating to the History of Art in England', *Walpole Society*, **13** (1913–14), pp.121–39.

4. See Ilaria Bignamini, 'George Vertue, Art Historian, and Art Institutions in London 1689–1768', *Walpole Society*, 54 (1991) pp.1–148, pp.1–18.

5. See Horace Walpole, 'Life of Mr George Vertue', in *A Catalogue of Engravers* (Twickenham, Strawberry Hill, 1763).

6. William Gilpin, *Essay Upon Prints*, 2nd edn (London, J. Scott, 1768), pp.126–7.

7. William Gilpin, *Essay Upon Prints*, 3rd edn (London, J. Scott, 1781), p.127.

8. *Ibid.*, p.147.

9. *Ibid.*, p.v.

10. The quotation is taken from A. M. Hind, *A Short History of Engraving & Etching* (London, Archibald Constable & Co., 1908), n.2, p.154. For very similar comments, see F. Lippmann, *Engraving and Etching: A Handbook for the Use of Students and Print Collectors*, trans. Martin Hardie (London, H. Grevel & Co., 1906), p.242.

11. George Vertue, *Notebooks*, 6 vols, *Walpole Society*, vols 18, 20, 22, 24, 26, 30 (1930–55). The *Notebooks* are hereafter referred to as Vertue 1–6.

12. Ellis Waterhouse, *Painting in Britain 1520 to 1790*, 4th edn (Harmondsworth, Penguin, 1978), p.164.

13. Vertue's writings are considered in Lawrence Lipking, *The Ordering of the Arts in Eighteenth-Century England* (Princeton University Press, 1970), pp.127–40; Johannes Dobai, *Die Kunstliteratur des Klassizismus und der Romantik in England*, 4 vols (Bern, Benteli, 1974–84), **1**, pp.846–66 and Ilaria Bignamini, 'George Vertue, Art Historian', pp.1–18.

14. Horace Walpole, *Anecdotes of Painting in England*, 4 vols (Twickenham, Strawberry Hill, 1762–71), **1**, p.vii.

15. Letter from Lord Beauchamp to Horace Walpole, 10 March 1762, reproduced in W.S. Lewis (ed.), *The Yale Edition of Horace Walpole's Correspondence*, 48 vols (Oxford and New Haven, Oxford University Press and Yale University Press, 1937–83), 38, pp.150–51, p.151.

16. Letter from Henry Zouch to Horace Walpole, 15 March 1762, reproduced in *ibid.*, 16, pp.45–6.

17. Letter from Horace Walpole to the Rev. William Cole, 15 February 1782, reproduced in *ibid.*, 2, pp.300–3.

18. Arnaldo Momigliano, 'Ancient History and the Antiquarian', *Journal of the Warburg and Courtauld Institutes*, 13 (1950), pp.285–315.

19. The two drafts of his autobiography are published in Vertue 1, pp.1–21.

20. Vertue almost certainly based his approach on the Vasarian model. As Barbara Mitchell has noted, the Italian's autobiography exhibits 'an intended, deliberately contrived continuity sketched' from patron to patron. Barbara Mitchell, 'The Patron of Art in Giorgio Vasari's Lives', PhD thesis, Indiana University, 1975, p.163.

21. Vertue 1, p.21. Vertue's often highly idiosyncratic spelling and punctuation are retained in all quotes.

22. *Ibid.*, p.14.

23. Vertue, *A Description of the Works of . . . Wenceslaus Hollar*, p.127.

24. See Vertue 3, p.131 for his notes on King.

25. Vertue 1, p.17.

26. Joan Evans, *A History of the Society of Antiquaries* (Oxford, Society of Antiquaries, 1956).

27. See 'Treasurer's Account Book 1718–1738', MS, Society of Antiquaries, for a record of payment. All the plates are listed with their dates of publication in John Fenn, *Three Chronological Tables Exhibiting a State of the Society of Antiquaries of London* (London, J. Nichols, 1784), Table 2. During Vertue's tenure as official engraver the Society only issued one print not engraved by him.

28. See Helen Mary Petter, *The Oxford Almanacks* (Oxford University Press, 1974), pp.12–26.

29. Robert Campbell, *The London Tradesman* (London, 1747), p.114.

30. Vertue worked on the publications of the Society sponsored by individual members, for example the *Registrum Honoris de Richmond* (1721) and a number of single plates, listed in Harl.MS 7190, f.303, British Library. He also illustrated works published by members, such as Francis Wise's *Letter to Richard Mead* (London 1737). On occasion, members commissioned private plates from him, such as the 'Gaulish Antiquities' for the Earl of Winchelsea (1735), for which see D.F. Allen, 'The Sark Hoard', *Archaeologia*, 103 (1990), pp.1–31.

31. These tours are recorded in Vertue 2, 4 and 5 and Add.MS 70,437 and Add.MS 70,438, British Library.

32. Vertue's relations with Oxford are documented in a series of letters, Add.MS 70,399, British Library, and in C.E. and R.C. Wright (eds), *The Diary of Humfrey Wanley 1715–26*, 2 vols (London, 1966).

33. See Kimberly Rorschach, 'Frederick Prince of Wales (1707–1751) as a Patron of the Visual Arts', PhD thesis, Yale University, 1985, pp.256–61 and Bignamini, 'George Vertue, Art Historian', pp.12–13.

34. Vertue 5, p. 66.

35. For some stimulating comments on the commercial potential of antiquarianism in the context of music publishing, see Dianne Dugaw, 'The Popular Marketing of "Old Ballads": The Ballad Revival and Eighteenth Century Antiquarianism Reconsidered', *Eighteenth-Century Studies*, 21:1 (1987), pp.71–90.

36. See *The Daily Post*, 16 February 1726, and *The Daily Courant*, 16 February 1726.

37. See *The Daily Post*, 27 January 1730 and *The Daily Advertiser*, 28 June 1737.

38. See Louise Lippincott, *Selling Art in Georgian London: The Rise of Arthur Pond* (New Haven and London, Yale University Press, 1983), pp.149–53.

39. For example, on prints of 'Tessellated pavement discovered at Stunsfield near Woodstock in Oxfordshire' (1725) and 'Antient plan of the City of London, from a draught taken about A° 1560' (1737).

40. The publication of the series was announced in a letter to the Earl of Oxford, 17 March 1726, Add.MS 70,399, British Library. Attached to the letter is a printed sheet detailing the subscription plan and calling for subscribers. The terminal date of the series is given in a letter from Mr Jenner to Vertue, 9 April 1729, Add.MS 70,399, British Library.

41. *A Description of four Antient Paintings* (no publisher stated, 1740) and two untitled and undated pamphlets of continuous pagination.

42. Evans, *A History of the Society of Antiquaries*, p.70.

43. Reported in *The London Evening Post*, 21–3 May 1751.

44. See Fenn, *Three Chronological Tables*, p. 19. Vertue's plates were sold by Ford's, 16–19 and 21–2 March 1757, first day's sale, lots 17–41. An annotated copy of the catalogue is at Box II 94.O, National Art Library, Victoria and Albert Museum.

45. See Paul J. Korshin, 'Types of Eighteenth-Century Literary Patronage', *Eighteenth-Century Studies*, 7:4 (1974), pp.452–73.

46. For a discussion of antiquarian aesthetics and *Vetusta Monumenta* see Chapter 1 in this volume.

47. See Susan Lambert, *The Image Multiplied: Five Centuries of Printed Reproductions of Paintings and Drawings* (New York, Abaris Books, 1987), pp.61–3.

48. George Vertue, 'On Engraving History or Portraiture: a simile', Add.MS 23,082, ff. 7–7v, British Library.

49. See Add.MS 23,076, f. 54, British Library (West and Frankland), *The Daily Post*, 25 January 1737 (Bodleian), and Vertue 1, p.7 (Oxford). One such collection came into the hands of Horace Walpole, and is described in Allen T. Hazen, *A Catalogue of Horace Walpole's Library* (New Haven, Yale University Press, 1969), p.176.

50. See Sheila O'Connell, 'Simon Gribelin (1661–1733), Printmaker and Metal Engraver', *Print Quarterly*, 2 (1985), pp.27–38. Vertue referred to Gribelin's volumes in a letter to the Earl of Oxford, 24 December 1737, Add.MS 70,399, British Library.

51. See Anthony Griffiths, 'Early Mezzotint Publishing in England I: John Smith 1652–1743', *Print Quarterly*, 6:3 (1989), pp.243–57. Vertue refers to such a collection in Vertue 3, p.159.

52. From the Society's first *Minute Book*, quoted in Evans, *A History of the Society of Antiquaries*, p.58.

53. On the emerging notion of property as the object of sociable exchange see J.G.A. Pocock, 'The Mobility of Property and the Rise of Eighteenth-century Sociology' in his *Virtue, Commerce and History: Essays on Political Thought and History, Chiefly in the Eighteenth Century* (Cambridge University Press, 1985), pp.103–23. See also Trevor Ross, 'Copyright and the Invention of Tradition', in Eighteenth-Century Studies, 26:1 (1992), pp.1–28, esp. p. 10.

54. On the role of subscription in redefining cultural enterprise in the early eighteenth century see Susan Staves, 'Pope's Refinement', *The Eighteenth Century: Theory and Interpretation*, 29:2 (1988), pp.145–63.

55. Dobai, *Die Kunstliteratur*, 1, p. 856. Vertue 3, p.147.

56. Vertue 3, p.148.

57. On the connection between engraving and sculpture see Morris Eaves, *The Counter-Arts Conspiracy: Art and Industry in the Age of Blake* (Ithaca and London, Cornell University Press, 1992), pp.117–18.

58. Vertue 3, p.146.

59. *Ibid.*

60. *Ibid.*, p.79.

61. See Eaves, *The Counter-Arts Conspiracy*, pp.219–32.

62. Letter from Horace Walpole to the Rev. William Cole, 15 February 1782.

63. See Evans, *A History of the Society of Antiquaries*, p.129.

64. This term is used in Pierre Bourdieu, *Distinction: A Social Critique of the Judgement of Taste*, trans. Richard Nice (London, Routledge, 1984).

2.1   George Vertue, self-portrait (n.d.), etching

2.2   George Vertue, *Fragmentorum codicis Cottoniani libri Geneseos* (1744), engraving

2.3   George Vertue after Holbein, *Familia Regia* (1740), engraving with etching

2.4   George Vertue after Fr. Bartoli, *Tiara Pontificis Romani* (1719), engraving with etching

2.5   George Vertue, *King Street Gate Westminster* (1725), engraving

3

British antiquity and antiquarian illustration

Sam Smiles

In 1815 Samuel Rush Meyrick and Charles Hamilton Smith published *The Costume of the Inhabitants of the British Islands*, a survey of the historical costumes worn by the peoples inhabiting this territory from the remotest antiquity until the late Middle Ages. The volume was richly embellished with coloured aquatints by Robert Havell based on sketches provided by Charles Hamilton Smith, and it is chiefly some considerations suggested by these illustrations that I wish to discuss. My intention in doing so is to raise questions concerning the relationship of image to text in such publications and from that to draw some conclusions about the production of knowledge, be it discursive, iconic, or a mixture of the two. My approach is not intended to be rigorously theoretical insofar as I make no presumptuous claims to any advance in iconic analysis. However, I will draw upon aspects of extant theoretical considerations of these matters to lend my investigation some insights that seem to me to be profitable and which may indicate possible avenues for further investigation in this field.

In terms of related publications, the years surrounding 1800 had seen the appearance of a number of illustrated surveys of historical and contemporary costume. In the latter category mention can be made of Francis Wheatley's *Cries of London* (1793–7), W.M. Craig's *Traders of London* (1804), W.H. Pyne's *The Costume of Great Britain* (1808), George Walker's *Costume of Yorkshire* (1814), and Thomas Rowlandson's *Characteristic Sketches of the Lower Orders* (1820). One element that needs to be emphasized at the outset is the social function of texts such as these. A large part of the meaning of costume books derives from the growth of a generic class of publications whose physical appearance and modes of presentation of empirical evidence work together to constitute a form of knowledge. All of these books set themselves the task of representing the specific costumes of distinctive social factions with some attendant comments on the cultures of their wearers. A taxonomy of social types was thus constructed that brought working class Britain into an ordered and reasonable pattern for middle class entertainment, education and edifica-tion. Antiquarian studies of costume did not, of course, work to produce that same result in any programmatic way, but it is worth speculating that the patterning of social types in illustrations of archaic, feudal or late medieval peoples might have gratified their readership in a broadly similar manner. What is evident is that the presentation of knowledge in all costume books, whether historic or contemporary in focus, works on structurally similar lines and should be seen as part of the same tradition. It is also true to say that it is with antiquarian costume books that this tradition is inaugurated. Thomas Jefferys' *Collection of the Dresses of Different Nations* (1757 and 1772) is perhaps the beginning of this trend, followed by Joseph Strutt's *Horda Angel-Cynnan* (1774–5), Francis Grose's *Treatise on Ancient Armour and Weapons* (1786), Joseph Cooper Walker's *Dress of the Ancient and Modern Irish* (1788) and Strutt, again, with *A Complete View of the Dress and Habits of the People of England* (1796–9).

Before entering into a particular analysis of antiquarian costume books it is worth examining John Law's and John Whittaker's theoretical considerations regarding the technologies of representation, which are particularly apt in this connection:

> In the creation of representations much is suppressed. Such suppression is necessary if heterogeneous objects distributed through time and space are to be brought together in a conformable space at a particular time. But alongside simplification there is another process that we have called discrimination: new classes of objects are brought into being, objects whose boundaries and properties are clearer than those they have replaced, objects that may more easily be interrelated with one another. These new and relatively docile objects replace their savage cousins, but they also speak on their behalf – they are their representatives for no depiction is able to represent unless it also speaks for something else.[1]

It is precisely these new classes of objects that antiquarian illustration con-structed. It did so by clarifying, or seeming to clarify, a historical picture whose boundaries and properties were anything but clear. Indeed, I would go so far as to assert that antiquarian illustrations of ancient or proto-historic Britain provided iconic illustrations of the past which stood in place of the obscure record with which historians wrestled, that they were constitutive of knowledge rather than representative of it. The epistemological stance of a costume book, to dignify with a critical category what arose as a pragmatic intervention in the world of publishing, is marked by its hybridity. These texts are caught in the tension between discursive and iconic representations of knowledge, and while the relationship between letterpress and image seems to be one of mutual confirmation, there is in fact a dynamic instability in this arrangement and the labile relations between image and text undercut the seeming security of the knowledge they display.

To return to Joseph Strutt's *Horda Angel-Cynnan* (1774–5), it makes a virtue of its accurate representations of dress, a strategy which obliges Strutt to abandon the pre-Roman period:

Every one who is conversant in the early parts of the British History, must be acquainted with the doubtfulness and uncertainty of it; and with how little fairness, much less truth and justice, any of the peculiar customs of the Britons can be truly set forth before the landing of Julius Caesar.[2]

Thirteen years later, in the observations included in the address to Lord Charlemont which opens his *Dress of the Ancient and Modern Irish* (1788), Walker is mindful of the same difficulties: 'However ardent I have been in the pursuit of information, I seldom ventured beyond the Christian Age, awed by the settled gloom that clouded the preceding ages'.[3]

Strutt's and Walker's scruples are reminiscent of those expressed by contemporary historians about the impossibility of avoiding conjecture and fanciful imaginings in researching the culture of Ancient Britain. Both their books seek to base their accuracy of depiction on reliable written, as well as extant material evidence. Although that evidence is necessarily fragmentary early in the historical record, for any literate period it is none the less available for antiquarian research. But for the remote world of pre-Roman Britain no comparable evidence existed, or at least not in sufficient quantity to allow a secure representation to be achieved. The publication of Meyrick and Smith's *Costume of the Original Inhabitants of the British Islands* is thus a landmark insofar as it is the first and most substantial costume book to attempt such a project.

That it appeared at all indicates the extent to which the hesitancies of eighteenth-century historians had been overcome by the early nineteenth century. Increasingly, antiquarians such as William Borlase, proselytizing for the study of Ancient Britain, were arguing for deductions to be made from material evidence rather than insisting on a text-dominated historiography. Writing to the future President of the Society of Antiquaries, Charles Lyttleton, in 1749, Borlase explicitly compares these two registers of knowledge:

The materials, style, measurement and appurtenances of monuments are things not to be new moulded by, or made to comply with every fanciful conjecture, but remaining always the same, will be impartial authorities to appeal to, invariable rules to judge of and decide the customs, rites and principles as well as monuments of the ancients; and therefore it is much to be lamented that all curious travellers and writers in antiquity did not draw, as well as travel and write, it being in my opinion next to an impossibility to convey an adequate idea of the simplest monument by words and numerical figures, or indeed to find out the justness and extravagance of a conjecture without seeing what the monument really is.[4]

For Borlase, then, discriminating attention to visible remains might discipline antiquarian illustration. However, this shift from textual to material evidence would necessarily privilege the visual over the verbal, not simply in respect of elaborating visual taxonomies from extant remains, a task which helped to usher in what we might regard as archaeology proper, but also, and perhaps more importantly, by holding out an invitation to imaginative projection that can be closely tied to antiquarian elements within Romanticism.

What I mean by this is the metonymic trope within Romanticism, where scrutiny of the ruin or fragment engenders meditation on the lost whole, such that the imagination may recover what history has dispersed. Insofar as this activity is essentially creative rather than documentary in any strict sense, we are entitled to think of it in terms of poetics, its fashioning of a world which stands in place of the vanished past it presumes to illustrate. Given the limited historical data relating to Ancient Britain, some scant material remains as brief and scattered descriptions from classical authors, the invitation for each individual reader to envisage that past is pretty open-ended, with little check or calibration of appropriateness. When those same readers become viewers as well, however, examining coloured aquatints on quarto-sized pages, their reading of that data will become conditioned by the power of the image confronting them. The more convincing the image appears to be, the more it will control the imagining of the past. This power of antiquarian images in directing imaginative projection is, in my view, somewhat undervalued at present. When the literary tradition is thin and material remains are the chief relics of antiquity then antiquarian illustration becomes a form of knowledge in itself. It is all the more powerful the more the historic evidence is lacking, because its visualization cannot be gainsaid.

We now know that antiquarian recreations of the past often included a farrago of inaccuracies, archaeologically speaking, but this is beside the point for my purposes. These illustrations should not be judged with reference to modern standards of knowledge; rather, their epistemological position must be assessed according to the genre they constitute, and that genre is essentially a rhetorical performance – almost a form of fictional realism. In making such a seemingly paradoxical claim I mean to invoke Roland Barthes's analysis of the 'reality effect' in prose narratives.[5] Barthes distinguishes verisimilitude in classical, ekphrastic rhetoric from the reality of historical narration. Verisimilitude as a rhetorical device uses descriptive skill to conjure up a world and it depends on public opinion for its success or failure. In contrast, from antiquity onwards, historical narration has been seen as concrete and functional, heedless of oratorical performance and thus beyond public opinion. Conventionally speaking, history is the touchstone of what a realistic narrative should be. Nevertheless, all texts produce their own particular effects, including authenticity and truth, and Barthes goes on to consider the ways in which the reality effect is produced in narrative texts by the inclusion of 'historical' details, structurally superfluous notations whose concreteness denotes 'what took place' and thus guarantees the effect of the real in the overall presentation. To be more specific, for Barthes 'a "concrete detail" is constituted by the *direct* collusion of a referent and a signifier' such that the overall sign loses its signified element and thus ceases to be understood *as* a sign. This produces what Barthes refers to as the 'referential illusion', where certain details in a narrative seem to offer a direct and unmediated meaning, to denote reality in the concreteness of their reference, whereas in fact their very concreteness itself signifies connotatively 'this is reality'. Concrete details thus signify the category 'reality' and the effect of the real is produced by their deployment within the overall narrative structure.

Clearly, with reference to antiquarian recreations of the past this is an important insight, for it allows us to understand how the effect of historical reality is produced. Individual details taken, so the letterpress generally informs us, from classical accounts or material remains. Their presence in an antiquarian illustration, then, seems to act as a concrete visualization of accurate data from which a reliable picture of the remote past can be assembled. But, if Barthes is right, this is in fact a rhetorical illusion and the accoutrements assembled on the page, together with the data underpinning them, produce merely the effect of realism or 'historical accuracy'. Thus, when examining illustrated antiquarian publications, although we seem to be confronted with texts that participate in the realm of history we are instead in a world of verisimilitude, reliant on rhetorical devices for the illusion to hold as well as on public judgement for its success.

As an example of this it is instructive to compare Meyrick and Smith's 'A Briton of the Interior' (1815) (Figure 3.1) with Thomas Jefferys' 'Habit of an antient Britain' (1772) (Figure 3.2). Both figures are presented in a broadly similar pose and both purport to give some visual information about their subject. Evidently, the relative differences between the two images are marked, with the later one seemingly more secure in its historical references and sense of cultural context. But what lies behind this change in presentation? A progressivist account of increasing visual accuracy and antiquarian knowledge will only get us so far. For all their differences, both images are artificial constructs and all we can really learn from them is something about changes in public opinion regarding verisimilitude and antiquarian illustration in the forty years that separate the two publications.

Jefferys' verbal account is sparse, noting merely that the figure is derived from that published in John Speed's *History of Great Britaine* (1611). His authority for most of his images is thus restricted to secondary sources, providing his readers with a convenient four-volume compendium of illustrations culled from a number of travel accounts and histories in different languages.[6] Meyrick and Smith, on the other hand, were publishing for a clientele grown increasingly used to notions of historical accuracy in the visual arts, and they go to considerable lengths to justify their rendition, citing Caesar, eighteenth-century antiquarian writings, excavation details and place-names as evidence.[7] Each part of the Briton's apparel is separately itemized and historically justified, as are the hill fort behind him and the dog at his side. Havell's illustration presents these details with diligent clarity. The vignette shows 'a battle-axe head and ring of the same kind of semi-metal, found at Tadcaster', to justify the idea of ancient British axes being slung from the shoulder. In the main illustration, Havell depicts that same ring again, not as an excavated relic but as a piece of equipment in use. In effect, he is substantiating the hypothesis offered in the text, offering visual corroboration for antiquarian speculation.

In Barthes' terms, it is the concreteness of these details that produces the illusion of reality. Havell's representation of an excavated axe-head as it was presumed to have been worn is precisely 'the *direct* collusion of a referent and a signifier' which Barthes identified within narrative texts. What makes this so is its representation in the vignette as excavated material evidence – as hard fact – whose concreteness then reappears in the fuller context of the Briton's apparel immediately above. In contrast Jefferys' Briton is quite different. He and his accoutrements are constituted as signs, as emblematic tokens of the concept 'Ancient Briton'. It is thus to some extent immaterial that his shield looks suspiciously armorial and his partially obscured and medieval-looking sword is so anachronistic, for 'realism' in the sense that Barthes outlines and as Meyrick and Smith's readers were offered it in 1815, is not on the agenda in 1772.

Barthes was primarily concerned with verbal texts and although his insights are penetrating, his account leaves the verbal-visual problem to one side. Here, therefore, I would like to introduce some insights from the Tartu School of Semiotics, as outlined chiefly by Boris Uspenskij and Jurij Lotman.[8] They are concerned to analyse 'the functional correlation of different sign systems' within a culture, looking especially at 'the hierarchical structures of the languages of culture, of the distribution of sphere among them, of cases in which those spheres intersect or merely border upon each other'.[9] For our purposes, different spheres would involve the traditions of text-based mainstream historiography and of antiquarianism, textual and iconic knowledges, scholarly and general-interest publications, reason and imagination. None of the oppositions are of course real in any absolute sense. Indeed, Uspenskij and Lotman's point is that internal delimitations within a culture, concerning the way it specifies discrete operations, rely on antithetical polarities for a sense of definition. Thus antiquarianism is Augustan historiography's other, without which it would lose its defining edge.

Uspenskij and Lotman distinguish between primary and secondary modelling in relation to semiotic systems. Primary modelling is defined as natural language and refers therefore to the construction of meaning from a chain of syntactically organized signs.[10] Secondary modelling refers to other systems of social communication, among which should be included works of art. Images, characteristically, are continuous, not discrete systems, and never break down into chains of syntactically organized signs although they might contain separate features whose symbolic register signifies a determinate meaning. The 'text' in such cases is an integral sign rather than a chain. Now these two modelling systems, as represented by textual (primary) and iconic (secondary) representation, are synchronic and hierarchically organized in their operation, with one or other mode dominant in different cultural circumstances. As Uspenskij further notes, a minimal requirement for culture is the existence of a pair of correlated semiotic systems, the most usual being precisely that of image and text, the visual and the verbal.[11]

Now it should, I hope, be obvious that the situation of antiquarian illustration is of especial interest in such an analytic framework by virtue of its hybridity. It uses the semiotic register of the iconic (secondary) system to make essentially discursive or informational points, a form of knowledge which is characteristically associated with the primary (textual) system. As Lotman has noted, conventional signs, because they employ syntax, are capable of telling, of creating narrative texts, while iconic signs are restricted to the function of naming.[12] Hierarchically, therefore, the illustration should support the text both because of its accustomed business in such a standardized production, but also because of wider considerations concerning the primacy of text-based knowledge in modern European culture. However, in the case of Ancient Britain, where text-based knowledge is scanty and its illumination of that past fitful and hesitant, the primacy of text is vulnerable to usurpation by the image.

This hybridized product is, semiotically speaking, active at the intersection of the differentiated spheres referred to by Uspenskij and Lotman and its position there results in an instability of meaning and purpose. The very design of Meyrick and Smith's book, as part of a genre given respect by more securely based research, allies it with the concerns for accuracy and documentation of Grose and Strutt, and it uses the same methods of presentation to offer a convincing simulacrum of the past. Yet if we try to match the detail of its plates with the letterpress on which these visual images are based we see it is only the individual elements that find anchorage in textual accounts, and in those accounts the continuous presentation of the plate is replaced by a discontinuous, discrete adumbration of detail. It is worth reminding ourselves here of Uspenskij's and Lotman's distinction between syntactic and integral texts, with the letterpress attempting to construct a linear trajectory through a fragmentary record while Havell's illustration seems to blend these elements without effort into an image that indeed shows, rather than narrates, its subject. Antiquarian illustrations thus have the power to displace the texts they are presumed to support; to show more successfully what a text attempts to describe. It is as though the reverie on fragments, the metonymic invitation to recover a lost whole has been largely effected by the artist and engraver to provide an integral and self-sufficient picture of a past which can be known in all its plenitude.

Patently a lot of this has to do with the fact that images cannot accommodate conflicting interpretations, and that a choice has to be made. Scrupulous historical research by serious antiquarian writers was marked by admission of the difficulties faced in reconstituting the ancient past, by entering into debate with other writers or recording their agreement with them, by indicating where speculation was an illegitimate inference from incomplete data and where it seemed to be justified. But in all of this activity there was no possibility of scholarly arbitration, no way of appealing to agreed standards of objective truth, as Joseph Strutt poignantly remarked:

And so it must always be, where the author is so much in the dark, as to be forced of necessity to guess at random; having besides this disagreeable circumstance attending, that, if by chance he should hit the mark, it is impossible for him to be certain that he is perfectly in the right.[13]

None of this indeterminacy can come through into illustration, whose task – to present the remote past with clarity and precision – is wholly different.

Here we might adopt one last theoretical device, Derrida's logic of the supplement. In *The Truth in Painting*, Derrida speculates on Kant's notion of the *parergon*, that non-essential addition to an entity, as, for example, drapery on a statue or the frame of a picture.[14] Derrida's point is that the relationship between *ergon* and *parergon* is highly complex, that the parergon is a supplement which is intimately bound up with its 'host', remedying its deficiencies and so making explicit the lack in what had seemed integral. The supplement is thus necessarily adjoined to the *ergon* rather than being a decorative or functional addition to it. Indeed concepts such as inside / outside, *ergon* / *parergon*, entity / supplement are unstable and cannot be maintained. Derrida has also famously been preoccupied with indeterminacy and undecidability, which he opposes to the confident logocentrism of the Western tradition. Much of his writing has been concerned with attacking that rational enterprise which is predicated on notions of the book as an authoritative discourse and of truth as something to be achieved through the operation of rigorous scrutiny of evidence and argument. I want to conclude this essay by bringing both of these insights to bear on antiquarian illustration.

Antiquarianism itself has often been accused of whimsy and credulity when compared to the protocols and procedures of a rational science and a rigorous historiography. Whiggish interpretations of the histories of archaeology or the historiography of ancient Britain routinely dismiss much of the eighteenth century's antiquarianism as a sterile period rife with fantastic theory and precious little advancement of learning.[15] As my earlier quotations from Strutt and Walker indicated, many antiquarians at the time were concerned to police their accounts, to remove the taints of fantastic invention and credulity from their publications and to secure a proper scholarly foundation as the basis for their enquiries. But given the material and textual evidence available for research into ancient Britain, all attempts to secure a foundation were vitiated by the contradictory and confusing nature of the record. Antiquarian texts concerning the remotest British history were marked by the very un-decidability and indeterminacy eschewed by rigorous scholarship, and a scrupulous antiquarian studying that period could not hope to achieve the clarity and assuredness that more recent historical eras seemed to provide. It is this lack that antiquarian illustration supplies, its very clarity and determinacy of image offering a coherent knowledge that the narrative it is presumed to supplement cannot produce. The antiquarian image thus exteriorizes the default at the heart of the antiquarian text and takes on itself aspects of the logocentricity one would normally associate with a written rather than a visual production. There is an authoritative closure about these images that effaces indeterminacy and substitutes for it a pungent and concrete reality.

Ironically it was William Borlase, whose advocacy of drawing as a form of knowledge we have already noted, who had warned against precisely this outcome in 1754: 'conjectures are no faults, but when they are either advanced as real truths, or too copiously pursued, or peremptorily insisted upon as decisive'.[16] Borlase was referring to written conjectures, but his comment may also stand as an apposite criticism of the antiquarian illustrations we have been considering. Conjecture had indeed been advanced as a truth, pursued copiously in the fullness of the image and decisively in the authority of its iconic register. Antiquarians' employment of visual illustrations of Ancient Britain had fabricated a specious authority that threatened to displace their scholarly enterprise.

Notes

1. John Law and John Whittaker, 'On the art of representation: notes on the politics of representation' in Gordon Fyfe and John Law (eds), *Picturing Power: Visual Depiction and Social Relations*, Sociological Review monograph, 35 (London, Routledge 1988), pp.178–9.

2. Joseph Strutt, *Horda Angel-Cynnan: or a compleat view of the Manners, Customs, Arms, Habits, etc. of the Inhabitants of England, from the arrival of the Saxons to the reign of Henry the Eighth, with a short account of the Britons, during the government of the Romans*, 3 vols (London, B. White, 1775), 1, p.1.

3. Quoted in G.F. Mitchell, 'Antiquities', in T.O. Raifeartaigh (ed.), *The Royal Irish Academy: A Bicentennial History 1785–1985* (Dublin, The Royal Irish Academy, 1985), p.95.

4. Letter from William Borlase to Charles Lyttleton, 6 November 1749, quoted in P.A. S. Pool, *William Borlase* (Truro, Royal Institution of Cornwall, 1986), pp.128–9.

5. Roland Barthes, 'The Reality Effect', in Roland Barthes, *The Rustle of Language*, trans. Richard Howard (Oxford, Basil Blackwell, 1986), pp.141–8.

6. For Jefferys see Aileen Ribeiro, 'The Dress Worn at Masquerades in England 1730 to 1790 and its Relation to Fancy Dress in Portraiture', PhD thesis, Courtauld Institute of Art, University of London, 1975, pp.284–302.

7. The three texts cited are Caesar's *Gallic Wars*, Edward King, *Munimenta Antiqua* (London, G. Nicol, 1799–1805), and Henry Rowlands, *Mona Antiqua Restaurata* (Dublin, Aaaron Rhames for Robert Owne, 1723).

8. B.A. Uspenskij, V.V. Ivanov, V.N. Toporov, A.M. Pjatigorskij and J.M. Lotman, 'Theses on the Semiotic Study of Cultures (as Applied to Slavic Texts)', in Jan van der Eng and Mojmir Grygar (eds), *Structure of Texts and Semiotics of Culture* (The Hague and Paris, Mouton, 1973), pp.1–28.

9. *Ibid.*, p.1.

10. *Ibid.*, pp.6–7.

11. *Ibid.*, pp.19–20.

12. Jurij Lotman, *Semiotics of Cinema*, trans. Mark E. Suino, Michigan Slavic Contributions, **5** (Michigan, Ann Arbor, 1981), p.7.

13. Strutt, *Horda Angel-Cynnan*, 1, p.1.

14. Jacques Derrida, *The Truth in Painting*, trans. Geoff Bennington and Ian MacCleod (University of Chicago Press, 1987), pp.59–71. For an analogous use of Derrida's work see Stephanie Pratt, 'From the Margins: The Native American Personage in the Cartouche and Decorative Borders of Maps', *Word and Image*, 12:4 (1996), pp.349–65. I am indebted to Stephanie Pratt for her advice.

15. See, for example, comments from David Douglas, *English Scholars 1660–1730* (London, Jonathan Cape, 1951), pp.27 and 273ff and Stuart Piggott, *Ancient Britain and the Antiquarian Imagination* (London, Thames and Hudson, 1989), p.157.

16. Preface to *Antiquities of Cornwall* (1754), quoted in Pool, *William Borlase*, pp.148–9.

3.1   R. Havell after Charles Hamilton Smith, *A Briton of the Interior* (1815), hand-coloured aquatint. Yale Center for British Art, Paul Mellon Collection

Habit of an antient Britain.

Ancien Breton.

3.2   *Habit of an antient Britain* (1772), hand-coloured etching. Yale Center for British Art, Paul Mellon Collection

4

'A small journey into the country':
William Stukeley and the formal landscapes of
Stonehenge and Avebury

David Haycock

Dr William Stukeley needs little introduction to the historian of antiquarianism in early modern Britain. Born in Lincolnshire in 1687 and educated in
medicine at Corpus Christi College, Cambridge, he moved to London in 1717,
where he became a Fellow of the Royal Society, the first Secretary of the re-
established Society of Antiquaries, and a scholarly gentleman with interests in
Newtonian natural philosophy, botany and theology.[1] However, it was
through his diligent and prolonged studies, during the summer months
between 1718 and 1724, of the prehistoric Wiltshire antiquities of Stonehenge
and Avebury (which he spelt Abury) that Stukeley made his name and
ensured his importance as an early modern archaeologist.

I intend to examine here the cultural context behind Stukeley's antiquarian
studies at these two sites, in order to show how his gentlemanly interest in
gardens and landscapes moulded the way in which he perceived, planned and
illustrated the prehistoric landscape. I shall argue that this can be detected in
the text of his two major publications *Stonehenge* (1740) and *Abury* (1743),
reflecting the express influence of contemporary, 'polite' fashions in early
eighteenth-century landscape gardening. This influence can be further
observed in the layout and design of the volumes' illustrations, and in
Stukeley's interpretation of these ancient sites in terms of 'tours' and 'pictures'. Thus it would appear that Stukeley's novel recognition of the broader
landscapes of 'Celtic' temples took its inspiration directly from contemporary
tastes in English landscaping – that is, from the vogue for gardens such as
Stowe, Stourhead and Studley Royal with their long vistas and distant views
of Classical and Gothic temples, that would have been perambulated at
leisure, and would have stimulated philosophical, political or religious
thoughts in the visitor who actively participated in their 'theatre'. It must be
emphasized however that this relationship between the 'Celtic' religious landscape and the eighteenth-century landscaped garden is never explicitly

expressed by Stukeley. Nonetheless, it is my belief that this 'way of seeing' the landscape was so sufficiently entrenched within his world view as to have existed without his having been wholly conscious of it.

The late 1710s and the 1720s was the period in which the Classical architectural style of Palladianism arrived in Britain and started to become popular. It was during these years that Sir John Vanbrugh and William Kent planned and implemented their designs for the new houses at Castle Howard, Blenheim Palace and Stowe, with their ornamental gardens incorporating temples, rotundas, pyramids, obelisks and mausolea. Though his monographs on the sites did not appear until the early 1740s, it was also during this period that Stukeley was making and writing his field notes at the 'Celtic' stone circles of Avebury and Stonehenge. 'The whole temple of *Abury*', he would suggest in 1743, 'may be consider'd as a picture, and it really is so. Therefore the authors wisely contriv'd, that a spectator should have an advantageous prospect of it, as he approach'd within view.'[2]

Stukeley was a keen gardener who travelled extensively around England, viewing and recording his comments upon the natural and man-made landscapes he encountered. He also regularly employed garden analogies and metaphors in his natural history and antiquarian writings. In his manuscript notes for a journey made to Cambridgeshire in 1754, for example, Roman Britain becomes 'a choice spot ... well-planted with citys, stations, castles, colonys, *municipia*, like delicate shrubs, & plants, & flowers of plesure ... but the Scots, & Picts ... never omitted an opportunity to ravage this garden; and serve themselves of the fruits of the labors of the Roman Britains.'[3] By assessing his interpretations of Avebury and Stonehenge in relation to this visual conceit it is possible to draw broader conclusions regarding both his theoretical interpretation of these antiquities (as historical objects rather than just as images), as well as of more current ideas of landscape design. The idea of viewing antiquities as an integral part of their landscapes has been explored in recent phenomenological interpretations of the prehistoric environment. Modern theoretical archaeologists such as Christopher Tilley have highlighted the way in which prehistoric peoples structured their monuments within the landscape, drawing upon various natural features in doing so.[4] The most recent archaeological discussion of Stonehenge also notes the 'complex web of intervisibility' of the prehistoric landscape, and suggests that 'one of the major questions about the location and siting of the monument is whether it was sited to be seen from the surrounding landscape or as a point from which to view features and sites around it'.[5] I suggest here that Stukeley was aware of such a relationship between the prehistoric archaeological site and its setting in the landscape at least as early as the 1720s.

Stukeley was familiar with and interested in the latest fashions in garden design. He recorded with some pride that his late father, who had run a law

firm at Holbeach in Lincolnshire, 'was instrumental in promoting more buildings all over the Town, & in planting Trees & quick sett hedges, so that the
Country looks all like a Garden'.[6] He enjoyed visiting stately homes such as
Chatsworth and gardens such as that of the seventeenth-century poet
Abraham Cowley, and his friend William Warburton was on close terms
with Alexander Pope, another famous poet–gardener. Additionally, Stukeley
created his own gardens and built a 'hermitage' in the garden he spent years
landscaping at his home in Stamford. In the early 1740s he also advised his
friend and patron the Duke of Montagu on the landscaping of his extensive
country park at Boughton in Northamptonshire. Stukeley suggested the
design of serpentine walks through the Duke's woods; he also produced plans
for an ornamental Gothic bridge and a mausoleum, though neither of these
were ever implemented.[7] More generally, contemporary publications such as
Stephen Switzer's *Iconographica Rustica* (1718), John Lawrence's *The Clergy-
Man's Recreation, shewing the Pleasure and Profit of the Art of Gardening* (1714)
and Joseph Addison's articles in the *Tatler* and the *Spectator* all illustrate the
growing popular interest in gardening amongst the middling, professional
classes in the first decades of the eighteenth century.

Another important developing fashion of the day was domestic tourism.
Tours of Britain were published in increasing numbers from 1700, and usually
included descriptions of stately homes and their gardens. This is a distinct
feature of Stukeley's *Itinerarium Curiosum* (1724), which included accounts of
Boughton, Blenheim and Chatsworth. Since the seventeenth century, visitors
of the right social standing had been accepted into the great houses of the local
gentry, where, if they did not actually meet the owner, they would be escorted
on a tour around the house and its garden by a senior servant. The gentry's
properties hence served as visible signs of their wealth, taste and status, and
this 'conspicuous consumption' was part of the motivation and success
behind the Dutch artists Johannes Kip's and Leonard Knyff's *Nouveau Théâtre
de la Grande Bretagne* (1707), a series of engraved views of houses set in
their gardens. As Stephen Daniels has observed, this volume also 'showed
how extensively houses had been rebuilt and grounds extended and newly
fashioned, and it acted as a pattern book for further improvements'.[8] Stukeley
was particularly impressed by the new gardens at Blenheim, and the
designer's use of a ha-ha. 'The garden is a large plot of ground taken out of the
park', he wrote,

and may still be said to be part of it. [It is] well contriv'd by sinking the outer-wall into
a foss, to give one a view quite round and take off the odious appearance of confine-
ment and limitation to the eye, and which quite spoils the pleasur and intention of a
garden. [W]ithin, it's well adorn'd with walks, greens, espaliers and visto's to divers
remarkable objects that offer themselves in the circumjacent country.[9]

Stukeley had suggested that the prints in his *Itinerarium Curiosum* 'besides their use in illustrating the discourses, are rang'd in such a manner as to become an index of enquirys for those that travel, or for a British antiquary ... The whole is to invite gentlemen and others in the country, to make researches of this nature, and to acquaint the world with them.'[10] Part of the purpose of the *Itinerarium* was to highlight the antiquities of England in an effort to encourage his countrymen to believe that they did not have to travel abroad in order to make a 'classical' Grand Tour. Stukeley never took the Grand Tour himself, observing that 'It was ever my opinion that a more intimate knowledg of *Brittan* more become us, is more useful and as worthy a part of education for our young nobility and gentry as the view of any transmarin parts.'[11] This sentiment recurred throughout his writings and both *Stonehenge* and *Abury* may be considered part of a concerted programme to encourage domestic tourism as well as the antiquarian through his fieldwork.

In both of Stukeley's monographs, his reader is treated as if they were touring the sites in person and, as I shall show below, the illustrations were tailored to support this written conceit. In the text to *Stonehenge* the reader was invited into the monument as if actually there: 'it is time to draw toward the sacred pile,' Stukeley wrote, 'and fancy ourselves walking upon this delightful plain.'[12] This description extended in its detail so that, 'Every step you take upon the smooth carpet, (literally) your nose is saluted with the most fragrant smell of *Serpillum*, and *apium*, which ... composes the softest and most verdant turf, extremely easy to walk on, and which rises as with a spring, under ones feet.'[13] In his treatment of Avebury, Stukeley pinned his description to the accompanying plates and proposed that he would 'take the reader a fine tour along with me quite round the verge of the temple'.[14] The prehistoric bank and ditch around Avebury thus became in Stukeley's words 'an agreeable terrace-walk round the town, with a pleasant view upon sometimes corn-fields, sometimes heath ... Part of this pleasant prospect I have given in plate XXIII, as seen from Abury church-steeple' (Figure 4.1).[15] Stukeley's descriptive style appealed to writers of the short guides to Stonehenge that were sold at Bath and Salisbury in the years following the publication of his book in 1740. The anonymous authors of *A Concise Account of Stonehenge, for the use of Travellers* (c.1750) and *A Description of Stonehenge, Abiry &c. in Wiltshire* (1776) may have happily plagiarized his descriptions of the monument, but also served further to disseminate Stukeley's proto-Romantic interpretation and vision of the prehistoric landscape.

Stukeley's account of Avebury also regularly pointed out the opportunities for views and prospects: he suggested, for example, that from Overton hill 'The view here is extensive and beautiful', or that from Runway hill we 'contemplate that most agreeable prospect'. He concluded with the remark that he had 'observed many of these studied opportunities in this work, of introducing the ground and prospects, to render it more picture like'.[16] John Smith, who published a work on Stonehenge in 1771, accurately remarked in passing that Stukeley's monograph on that monument 'gives many beautiful and just descriptions of the country that surrounds this temple'.[17] The many works published in the years following 1740 clearly indicate its growing popularity as a tourist spot, with short guidebooks fulfilling an explanatory function similar to those published for visitors to the houses and gardens at Stowe and Blenheim.

Catherine Levesque has recently shown how Dutch printmakers of the seventeenth century conformed to descriptive conventions whereby 'as in numerous map collections, descriptive geographies, and poetic sequences, landscape depiction is presented to the reader or spectator as part of an encompassing journey theme'.[18] To paraphrase Levesque, by presenting or inviting the reader of prints and images 'to enter into and proceed through the text or images' and by placing him in the role of traveller or spectator the objectivity and truthfulness of knowledge observed experientially was stressed, thus ensuring the 'active participation' of the observer 'in extracting information'.[19] As a work of travel literature it was appropriate for Stukeley's printed images (based on his own original sketches) to follow the same conventions in the *Itinerarium*. But this journey or tour style was used to greater success in his descriptions and illustrations to *Stonehenge* and *Abury*. In keeping with the text, the plates to both books gradually draw the reader into the landscape of the 'temples'. The first few prints depicted the roads leading to the sites and the more distant views as one gradually approached. These were followed by detailed, close prospects from various compass points and then finally again more distant views, for example of the avenues, surrounding features, and other details as one drew away. These prints, which were generally described either as 'views' or 'prospects', were clearly intended to guide the reader around the whole landscape of the site. Stukeley's engraved frontispiece to *Abury* even offered a panoramic, three-dimensional bird's-eye view of the site, as if the viewer were literally hovering a couple of hundred feet above the modern village of Avebury (Figure 4.2). This is a most dramatic and imaginative introduction to the work, and one to which Stukeley devoted considerable care and attention in the various versions and amendments he made between 1721 and 1724.[20] It provided a detailed and attractive plan for the reader unable to visit the site in person. Together with the information of their labels and the accompanying text, Stukeley's illustrated books offered a perception of the whole context of the Celtic landscape that easily outrivals even modern guidebooks.

More importantly, of all the commentators on Stonehenge, Stukeley was the first really to step away from the stones themselves in both his written and his visual descriptions. He even included views *from* Stonehenge, with the viewer's back to the monument itself – an apparently original innovation for an antiquarian image (Figure 4.3).[21] Again, this emphasized the idea that

Stonehenge was a point to look *from* as well as to be looked *at*. We may see this same idea expressed in the context of the eighteenth-century garden; for example, in Sarah Bridgeman's *View from the Brick Temple*, from her *Views of Stowe* (1739), where it is the view rather than the structure that is significant in the printed image (Figure 4.4).[22] Like Stukeley's *Stonehenge* and *Abury*, Bridgeman's collection of fifteen printed views, signed by Jacques Rigaud and 'Baron', also adopted the plan of a tour around the grounds which began with the first view of the house and the arrival and welcoming of a visitor's coach, followed by views in the garden and park becoming increasingly distant from the house.

The incorporation of spectator and landscape into the whole 'picture' of Celtic temples was therefore an important one and, as Stukeley noted, it was a relationship that had not really been recognized before, though it was frequently observed in his own writings. Thus at Stonehenge, he was the earliest observer really to draw *all* the surrounding countryside into his interpretation of the site, even beyond the barrows and ancient hill-fort that had led earlier commentators to believe that Stonehenge commemorated an ancient battle ground. In remarking upon the two-mile earth 'cursus' neighbouring Stonehenge, which he believed had been the site of ancient chariot races, Stukeley rightly commented that 'This likewise is a new unobserv'd curiosity belonging to this work, and very much enlarges the idea we ought to entertain, of the magnificence and prodigious extent of the thing'.[23] Whilst modern archaeologists consider the purpose and function of the prehistoric avenue and cursus to be enigmatic and open to speculation, Stukeley is credited as the first to recognize and remark upon them.[24] Through his discovery of this increased landscaping of the site, Stukeley remarked that:

The temple which we have hitherto been describing, considerable indeed as it really is, in itself; yet now appears as a small part of the whole. I shall therefore describe all these parts separately, to render them more intelligible: and then show their connection, and what relation they have, to one another, as well as I can. But it is not easy to enter at once, into the exceeding greatness of thought, which these people had, who founded it; bringing in all the adjacent country, the whole of nature hereabouts, to contribute its part to the work....[25]

It appears that this new perception of the landscaped site was clearly influenced by conceptions of the early eighteenth-century landscape garden, whereby any physical construction existed only as part of a broader conceptual frame. Stukeley's Stonehenge and Avebury are both clearly interpreted as man-made landscapes, modelled with the explicit intention of acting upon and being interpreted by the knowledgeable spectator who interacted with the site as well as being a simple observer of it. This point is emphasized by the staffage figures added to both Stukeley's and Bridgeman's images. For John Dixon Hunt has observed how, influenced by Italian gardens, early eighteenth-century English gardeners 'saw their designs in terms of the the-ater' and that the fabricated scenes of gardens like Stowe and Rousham 'were unthinkable except as stages for human action'.[26] As Stukeley observed in his fieldnotes at Avebury, the site was 'a fine scituation … for you descend to it from on all sides, from hills which overlook it two or three miles distant, so that it is a sort of large Theater, admirable well chose for the magnificent pur-pose'.[27] The intervening centuries had diminished the quality of this land-scape 'theatre', but Stukeley prided himself on its rediscovery, and revealed it to his contemporaries, who were accustomed to the idea of the garden prospect and tour.

His perception of his readers 'touring' the site also appears to have been related to the growing popularization in the eighteenth century of the circuit walk. As I have already indicated, in this period public and private gardens were becoming increasingly fashionable as a mode of pleasure and entertainment amongst the middle and upper classes. Public landscaped walks such as St James's Park had first been developed in London in the mid-seventeenth century, and were followed by examples at Tunbridge Wells, Exeter, and at some Oxford and Cambridge colleges. By the mid-eighteenth century many other urban centres, spas and resorts likewise boasted commer-cial pleasure gardens which followed the lead of Vauxhall and Kensington Gardens in London. It is in this context then that we can best understand Stukeley's suggestion that 'If it be not impertinent, a small journey into the country, at leisure' to visit Avebury, would be a useful diversion for the 'pleasure, health & gratification of the publick'.[28] For, as Hunt has argued, the English landscape garden 'asked to be explored, its surprises and unsuspected corners to be discovered on foot'.[29] Furthermore, Hunt also notes how 'the "action" of the garden's painting [i.e. its design] is supplied by the visitor, stimulated by the scene and its allusions; the garden visitor becomes a pro-tagonist by his act of reading these devices'. That is, 'verbal commentary was needed not only to amplify the visual but to make explicit either literary sources or a body of literary theory'.[30]

Max Schulz has also shown how the 'Practice of organizing the eighteenth-century garden as a circuit tour of a rural paradise' was already well defined by the early part of the century.[31] He suggests that such a circuit design at gardens like Stowe, Stourhead, Rousham and Chatsworth allowed the visitor to follow 'a paradigmatic action which lent itself to a secularized and (if you will) faintly frivolous parody of the soul's circuitous passage in this world from its earthly to heavenly home'.[32] Given Stukeley's interpretation of the Avebury complex as a religious symbol for the Druid conception of the deity, this analogy is interesting. In addition to the comparison with journeying or touring around the Avebury site, Stukeley developed the idea that Avebury was a 'picture' landscape that would have been 'read' by its Celtic builders and users like an 'hieroglyphic ... made in stonework'.[33] As the Druid landscape had been built to be read, so Stukeley provided the interpretative text to accompany it.

This association between the eighteenth-century man-made rural and urban landscapes and the landscape of Celtic temples may be illustrated by the poem 'The Country Seat', written in the late 1720s by Stukeley's friend Sir John Clerk of Penicuik. Clerk, a Scottish baronet who had travelled widely in Italy, has been described by John Dixon Hunt as 'among the leaders of the landscape movement' in eighteenth-century Britain.[34] In his poem he offered verse advice and instructions for most perfectly situating a country seat. He was particularly concerned with the relationship between house and garden, but his text tellingly illustrates the observations Stukeley made on the religious design of the temples at Stonehenge and Avebury:

> Come now ye rural Deities and show
> What Forms will beautify the neighb'ring Plains.
> The verdant Banks, and meads, that so they may
> With never fading Charms allure our Eyes.
> Stretch out the Lines of every Avenue
> With spreading trees in many stately Rowes. . . .[35]

To the educated eighteenth-century observer who had read John Locke and Joseph Addison, garden landscapes with their temples and hieroglyphs and inscriptions were not simply static vistas to be enjoyed solely for their beauty and design. Rather, like the gardens of Stowe with their Elysian Fields, Temples of Ancient and Modern Virtue and British Worthies, they were expected to inspire a meditative, reflective or associative response.[36] The idea that trees could be used to build sacred structures may be illustrated by Gilbert West's poem on Stowe of 1736, where he described how 'Batvian Poplars here in ranks ascend:|Like some high Temple's arching Isles extend'.[37] Michael Charlesworth has recently suggested that the eighteenth-century garden also had a clear sacred and political character and that the example of Stukeley's private gardens with their hermitages and druidic temples 'suggests that the sacred idea was a great floating signifier for the eighteenth century, in which individuals could lodge the signified of their choice'.[38] Charlesworth though does not fully expand upon the implications of this suggestion for Stukeley's writings on Celtic temples. To illustrate this point further we can return to Sir John Clerk's poem, and his perception of the private, religious purpose of the avenue in the landscape:

> That Avenue will most delight the Sight
> That on some beauteous object shapes its way.
> Such is a temple, whose high towering Spire
> Divides the hov'ring Clouds, and seems to be
> A lofty Pillar to support the Heavens.

> This lovely Prospect may your busy mind
> With useful Speculations entertain;
> Consider first, that all you do enjoy
> Is owing to the God, whose awfull Shrine
> Those sacred walks enclose, and where
> With thankful Heart you often should resort.
> And if that here your Fathers lye entombed,
> Your stately house and pleasant fields at last,
> With other charms of Life you must forgo,
> And this way travel to the shades below.[39]

Stukeley was ordained as an Anglican clergyman in 1728, and it comes as no surprise, therefore, to encounter the presence of the divine in his Celtic 'gardens'. For Stukeley, at Avebury 'fountains[,] Rivers & Mountains are introduced as scemically, to make an sepulchre'.[40] Similarly he wrote of Stonehenge that:

it must be own'd, that they who had a notion, that it was an unworthy thing, to pretend to confine the deity in room and space, could not easily invent a grander design than this, for sacred purposes: nor execute it a grander manner. Here space is mark'd out and defin'd: but with utmost freedom and openess ... Here the variety and harmony ... presents itself continually new. [E]very step we take, with opening and closing light, art and nature make a composition of their highest gusto, create a pleasing astonishment, very apposite to sacred places.[41]

Gardens have a long-standing tradition as places of thought and meditation. For many in the seventeenth and early eighteenth centuries Abraham Cowley served as a paradigm for the desire to withdraw from politics and pursue a philosophic life in their gardens. This was the case for John Aislabie, Chancellor of the Exchequer during the South Sea Bubble, who retreated to his estates near Ripon in North Yorkshire following that financial crisis and worked on remodelling his gardens at Studley Royal. Aislabie's avenue of trees, aligned with Ripon Minster, clearly evinced a patriotic, religious sentiment; it was also plainly analogous with Stukeley's image of the cursus sited on Stonehenge, and the advice given in Sir John Clerk's poem (Figure 4.5). For Stukeley, Celtic temples served, in their present form, to illustrate the temporality of man's existence, but in their original form would have served to draw the ancient viewer's thoughts up to the contemplation of the divine. Furthermore, Stukeley's Druids were not mere idolatrous pagan priests, but rather proto-Trinitarian Christians who had brought the true faith to Britain long before the Roman mission of Saint Augustine. There, according to a manuscript written some time in the 1720s:

In Bryttish Oak Groves, our old Naturalists Poets & Priests the Druids inculcated the Precepts of Religion, Studyd the Celestial Sciences, reasond of Fate, Providence, Freewill, the Immortality of the Soul, & in all History sacred or profane the Groves were places more immediately consecrate to the attention of the Supreme Being. . . .[42]

It is now apparent that in Stukeley's opinion Celtic monuments had an aesthetic aspect associated with both their religious function and their location. This fact was recognized by at least one of his contemporaries, a Charles Gray, who wrote to Stukeley from Colchester on 28 July 1749. Remarking upon several tumuli thereabouts, Gray observed how some of them were 'in such fine situations as would please your taste, *and prove the good taste of those who built them*'.[43] But as well as being apparently motivated to encourage 'good taste' in the eighteenth-century garden, Stukeley's publications in turn inspired others in their construction of physical, landscaped 'temples'. By 1728 Stukeley had already begun landscaping a circle of trees in his own garden at Grantham into 'a temple of the druids' at the centre of which, he informed his friend Samuel Gale, there was 'an ancient apple tree overgrown with sacred mistletoe; round it is another concentric circle of 50 foot diameter made of pyramidial greens ... [which] are in imitation of the inner circle at Stonehenge'.[44] The potential criticism that the Druids were known to have worshipped in groves and not stone circles posed no problem for Stukeley, for stones and trees were intricately linked in his theory of the origin of architecture. He believed that the Druid order had been established by Abraham, and that in Britain the Druids had planted groves of trees 'in regard to their great founder'.[45] As he famously observed of Gloucester Cathedral in his *Itinerarium Curiosum*, its Gothic design was 'the best manner of building, because the idea of it is taken from a walk of trees, whose branching heads are curiously imitated by the roof'.[46] Additionally, as the circular stone temples at Stonehenge and Avebury had developed out of the original circular motif of the wooded grove, so likewise the pillared 'Forums & Avenues of Athens & Rome' had been 'inspired by rows of trees, providing shade, & also the cloisters of religious houses'.[47] In a letter to Stukeley of January 1743/4, Roger Gale wrote informing him of the schemes of a 'Young Mr. Crow' who

has been much studying your Abury, & has begun a plantation of elm trees upon that plan. There will be two winding avenues to the house ... the head of the snake will be a rising tumulus, planted with several rows of trees, one above another, among which will rise an obelisk of stone for the eye.[48]

Twentieth-century archaeological excavations at Stonehenge appear to confirm that the final stone monument that we know today was preceded in earlier phases by a complicated construction made of wooden posts.[49] Then in the dedication of his *Abury* to the Earl of Pembroke, Stukeley wrote of 'the fine and costly model of Stonehenge, which Your Lordship introduces in the garden at Wilton; where, I may be bold to say, it shines amidst the splendours of *Inigo Jones*'s architecture'.[50] Again according to Stukeley, another of his patrons, the Duke of Montagu, who in the 1730s projected some seventy miles of elm avenues at his country seat of Boughton, 'honor'd all the greatest oaks in his beautiful Chases, with the names of Druids, stampt in lead, and fastened to the trees'.[51] When Stukeley discovered on top of Silbury Hill the ashes of what he believed to be the ancient king who had ordered the building of Avebury, the digging was not for speculative archaeological purposes, but 'in order to plant trees for a visto'.[52] These examples clearly illustrate the relationship between ancient temples and the eighteenth-century garden.

Finally, it has been suggested that John Wood's Grand Circus at Bath, an architectural first, is an architectural expression of Stonehenge, providing an appropriate ornament for a town that Wood considered to be the ancient metropolitan seat of the British Druids. We may note here that Stuart Piggott believed that the influence of Stonehenge on Wood's design for the Circus had, before his observation, 'not hitherto' been suggested.[53] In fact, an anonymously published tract on Stonehenge of 1776 made this connection by quoting from Lord Burlington's published collection of Inigo Jones's drawings: ' "And I believe it will scarce be doubted that Mr. [Wood], the architect of Bath, took from this, our oval [at Stonehenge], the plan of the beautiful *Circus* at the end of Gay-street, which is one great ornament of that city." '[54] As the century progressed, and as James Macpherson's fabricated ancient Scottish poems *Ossian* and *Fingal* fanned the flames of Gothic revival and the vogue for all things Druidic, the idea of constructing Celtic monuments in the landscape became more inventive.[55] The most extravagant of these must be the example of General Henry Conway, the governor of Jersey. When, in 1785, a small stone circle was discovered on the island near St Helier, the townsfolk donated it as a gift to Conway, who removed it to adorn his garden at Park Place in Berkshire. According to Conway's cousin Horace Walpole, the circle was known as 'little Master Stonehenge', and Walpole observed in a letter of 1781 that 'Dr. Stukeley will burst his crements to offer mistletoe in your Temple'.[56] It appears that we may intimately link the popular later eighteenth-century Gothic and 'Druidic' English landscape with the name of William Stukeley in a way that has not previously been considered.

Notes

*   I am grateful to Malcolm Baker, Stephen Bending, and Michael Hunter for their advice and assistance in the writing of this paper.

1. See Stuart Piggott, *William Stukeley: an Eighteenth-Century Antiquary*, 2nd edn (London, Thames and Hudson, 1985) and my revisionist interpretation, 'Dr William Stukeley (1687–1765): antiquarianism and Newtonianism in eighteenth-century England', PhD thesis, London University, 1998.

2. William Stukeley, *Abury: A Temple of the Britain Druids* (London, Printed for the Author: And sold by W. Innys, R. Manby, B. Dodd, et al, 1743), p.18.

3. William Stukeley's notes for 'Iter Cantabrigiense' (1754). MS, 494 f.i, Society of Antiquaries, London.

4. See Christopher Tilley, *A Phenomenology of Landscape: Places, Paths and Monuments* (Oxford, Berg Press, 1994).

5. Rosamund Cleal, K.E. Walker, R. Montague *et al.*, *Stonehenge in its Landscape: Twentieth-century Excavations* (London, English Heritage, 1995).

6. William Stukeley, *The Commentarys, Diary, and Common-Place Book of William Stukeley* (London, Doppler Press, 1980), p.3.

7. See Stukeley's diary 15 September 1747, at Boughton with the Duke of Montagu: 'his Grace & I rode alone round the Serpentin walks in his chase woods, wh[ich] I persuaded him to make in contrast to the strait ones.' MS. Eng. misc. e.667/5, Bodleian Library, Oxford.

8. Stephen Daniels, 'Goodly Prospects: English Estate Portraiture, 1670–1730' in Nicholas Alfrey and Stephen Daniels (eds), *Mapping the Landscape: Essays on Art and Cartography* (Nottingham University Art Gallery, 1990).

9. William Stukeley, *Itinerarium Curiosum, Or, an Account of the Antiquitys and Remarkable Curiositys in Nature or Art, Observ'd in Travels thro' Great Brittan. Illustrated with Copper Prints, Centuria 1* (London, printed for the author, 1724), p.44.

10. *Ibid.*, 'Preface' (unpaginated). Stukeley was a collector of prints, and numbered amongst his friends Samuel and Nathaniel Buck and George Vertue, the official engraver of the Society of Antiquaries. For a discussion of Vertue's work see Martin Myrone's chapter in this volume.

11. *Ibid.*, p.3.

12. William Stukeley, *Stonehenge: a Temple Restor'd to the British Druids* (London, W. Innys and R. Manby, 1740), p.9.

13. *Ibid.*

14. William Stukeley, 'Celtic Temples', MS. Eng. misc. c.323, ff.120–9, Bodleian Library, Oxford.

15. Stukeley, *Abury*, p.28.

16. *Ibid.*, pp.27–33.

17. John Smith, *Choir Gaur; The Grand Orrery of the Ancient Druids, Commonly called Stonehenge, on Salisbury Plain, Astronomically explained, and Mathematically proved to be a Temple erected in the earliest Ages, for observing the Motions of the Heavenly Bodies* (London, printed for the author and sold by E. Easton, R. Horsfield and J. White, 1771), p.29.

18. Catherine Levesque, *Journey Through Landscape in Seventeenth-Century Holland: The Haarlem Print Series and Dutch Identity* (Pennsylvania University Press, 1994), p.13.

19. *Ibid.*, pp.13–14.

20. For a reproduction, as well as an excellent discussion of these plans, see Peter Ucko, Michael Hunter, Allan Clark and Andrew David, *Avebury Reconsidered: From the 1660s to the 1990s* (London, Unwin Hyman, 1991), pp.132–56.

21. For a discussion of the developments of antiquarian aesthetics see Maria Grazia Lolla's chapter in this volume.

22. Sarah Bridgeman, *A General Plan of the Woods, Park and Gardens of Stowe* (London, S. Bridgeman, 1739).

23. Stukeley, *Stonehenge*, p.35.

24. See Cleal *et al.*, *Stonehenge in its Landscape*, pp.291–329.

25. Stukeley, *Stonehenge*, p.35.

26. John Dixon Hunt, *Gardens and the Picturesque: Studies in the History of Landscape Architecture* (Cambridge, Mass., The MIT Press, 1992), p.114.

27. Stukeley, 'Celtic Temples', f.119.

28. *Ibid.*, f.109.

29. John Dixon Hunt, *The Figure in the Landscape: Poetry, Painting, and Gardening during the Eighteenth century* (London, The MIT Press, 1976), p.143.

30. Hunt, *Gardens and the Picturesque*, pp.115–17.

31. Max F. Schulz, 'The Circuit Walk of the Eighteenth-century Landscape Garden and the Pilgrim's Circuitous Progress', *Eighteenth-Century Studies*, **15**:1 (1981), pp.1–25 and 18.

32. *Ibid.*, p.3.

33. Stukeley, *Abury*, p.50.

34. John Dixon Hunt and Peter Willis, *The Genius of the Place: The English Landscape Garden, 1620-1820* (London, The MIT Press, 1988), p.196.

35. *Ibid.*, p.198.

36. See Edward Harwood, 'Personal Identity and the Eighteenth-century English Landscape Garden', *Journal of Garden History*, 13: 1–2 (1993), pp.36–48.

37. Quoted in Michael Charlesworth, 'Sacred Landscape: Signs of Religion in the Eighteenth-century garden', *Journal of Garden History*, 13: 1–2 (1993), pp.56–68, p.59.

38. *Ibid.*, pp.58–9.

39. Quoted in Hunt and Willis, *The Genius of the Place*, pp.198–9.

40. Stukeley, 'Celtic Temples', f.175.

41. Stukeley, *Stonehenge*, p.30.

42. William Stukeley, *The Creation. Music of the Spheres. K[ing] S[olomon's] Temple. Micro- & Macrocosm Compared &c. &c.* (1718–1734), MS,1130 Stu (1), f.31 Freemason's Library, Grand Lodge, London.

43. William Stukeley, 'William Stukeley: The Family Memoirs', ed. W. C. Lukis, *Surtees Society*, 76 (1883), 2, p.159, my italics.

44. Letter from William Stukeley to Samuel Gale, October 1728, quoted in William Stukeley, 'William Stukeley: The Family Memoirs', ed. W. C. Lukis, *Surtees Society*, 73 (1882), 1, p.209.

45. William Stukeley, 'Catalogue of Druids', MS, 4720, f.2, Wellcome Institute for the History of Medicine Library, London.

46. Stukeley, *Itinerarium Curiosum*, p.64.

47. Stukeley, *The Creation*, f.32.

48. Stukeley, 'William Stukeley: The Family Memoirs', 1, pp.363–4.i

49. See Cleal *et al.*, *Stonehenge in its Landscape*, pp. 63 and 115. Recent excavations have discovered remains of a Woodhenge only a few miles from Stonehenge.

50. Stukeley, *Abury*, 'Dedication'.

51. William Stukeley, *The Medallic History of Marcus Aurelius Valerius Carausius, Emperor in Brittain*, 2 vols (London, Charles Corbet, 1759), 2, p.v.

52. Stukeley, MS Eng. misc. e.390, f.10, Bodleian Library, Oxford.

53. Stuart Piggott, *The Druids*, 2nd edn (London, Thames and Hudson, 1975), pp.143–4.

54. *A Description of Stonehenge, Abiry &c. in Wiltshire. With an Account of the Learning and Discipline of the Druids* (London, Collins and Johnson, 1776), p. 17. In this text, the anonymous author writes 'Mr. Jones' in the square bracket where I have written 'Wood'; this was clearly a transcription error.

55. For a discussion of the many representations of Druids and their monuments in this period, see Sam Smiles, *The Image of Antiquity: Ancient Britain and the Romantic Imagination* (London and New Haven, Yale University Press, 1994).

56. David R. Coffin, *The English Garden: Meditation and Memorial* (Princeton, NJ, Princeton UP, 1994), pp.121–2.

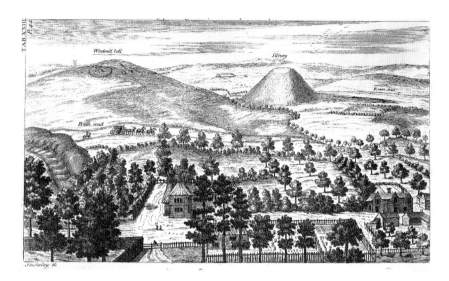

4.1   After a drawing by William Stukeley, *A Prospect from Abury Steeple* (c.1724), etching and engraving

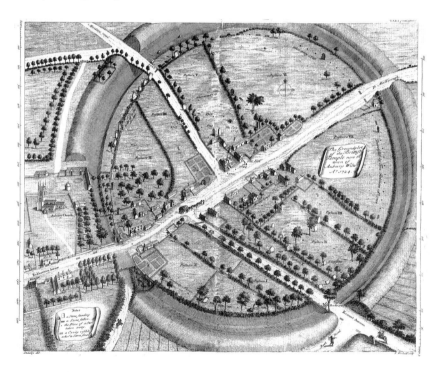

4.2   E. Kirkhall after a drawing by William Stukeley, *The Groundplot of the Brittish Temple now the town of Avbury Wilts* (1724), etching and engraving

4.3   After a drawing by William Stukeley, *Prospect from Bushbarrow* (1743), etching and engraving

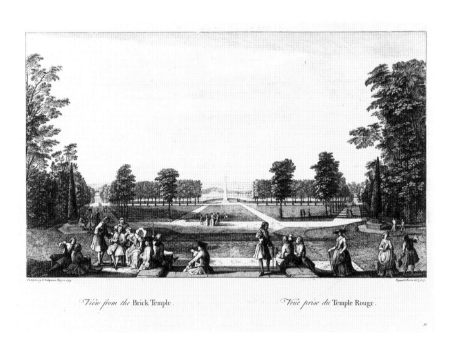

4.4   Kirkal after a design by Baron, *View from the Brick Temple* (1739), engraving

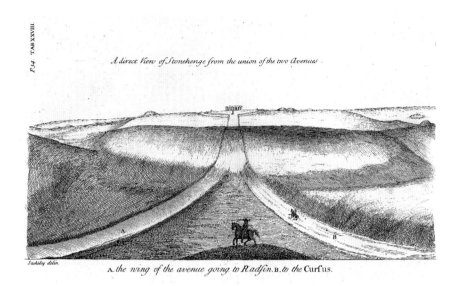

4.5   After a drawing by William Stukeley, *A direct View of Stonehenge from the union of the two Avenues* (1743), etching and engraving

5

The true rust of the Barons' Wars:
gardens, ruins, and the national landscape

Stephen Bending

An old avenue, like an old building, fills the mind with subjects of reflection. Antiquity, alone, is capable of rendering the merest trifles, things in themselves the most insignificant, interesting: as every antiquary knows.
>   William Marshall, *A Review of the Landscape; a Didactic Poem*
>   (London, G. Nicol, 1795), p.170.

And let our love to Antiquity be ever so great, a fine ruin is one thing, and a heap of rubbish another.
>   Alexander Pope, *The Prose Works of Alexander Pope*, ed. Rosemary Cowley
>   (Oxford, Basil Blackwell, 1986), 2, p.59.

One of the many values of ruins is that they incite multiple and often conflicting responses to the objects of the past, and in the following pages I will be using their appearance in eighteenth-century gardens as a way of exploring the relationship between antiquarianism and polite culture. As my two opening quotations begin to suggest, ruins can been seen in formal terms as an exemplary site for variety; they can be read as moral emblems of mutability, or of a British history of progress; they can be valued purely because they are old; or they can be no more than a heap of rubbish. It is with rubbish that I wish to begin.

Antiquarian writing in the eighteenth century is obsessed with rubbish, with the problems that rubbish represents, both physically and intellectually: it raises that perennial problem of modern culture's relationship with the objects of the past. As one reads eighteenth-century antiquarian texts, one turns up more and more rubbish. Repeatedly, there is the worry, or accusation, depending on where one stands, that the found objects of the past – precisely because they are random, because they were thrown away or left untreasured – are nothing more than rubbish, and that the study of such objects can itself only lead to the production of further rubbish. Horace Walpole, reviewing the second volume of the Society of Antiquaries' proceedings, *Archaeologia*, concluded, what 'a cartload of bricks and rubbish and Roman ruins they have piled together!'[1] Even Edward King, retiring from the presidency of the Society in 1784, felt the need to differentiate the Society's work from 'the dull, unanimated pursuits of certain Antiquaries, who are continually searching amongst rubbish, and bringing to light ... the blunders of past ages; without aiming at any one useful end'.[2]

Outside of the Society this notion of a misguided antiquarianism which must be redirected to its true purpose tends to disappear, to be replaced by more direct satires on the kind of 'Antiquarian; who cou'd tell | The Name of ev'ry Parish-Bell: | Knew to an Inch, or near the matter, | Where the last Abbot last made water'.[3] Numerous poems and one-liners continue this approach, and the persistent popular attack on antiquarianism ridicules it as misplaced enthusiasm and knowledge of no value – a knowledge which cannot be placed within a system, and which because of its lack of rigour is deemed unreliable or fanciful. That in turn points to one of the other difficulties of antiquarianism, even today: because it does not necessarily fit neatly into an academic discipline or category, it sways between the imaginative and the factual. It runs the risk of being not critical but credulous.

As many have noted, ruins become increasingly popular objects of attention in the eighteenth century and it is here that a shift has been charted from an 'antiquarian response' early in the century, to a far looser 'associative response' in terms of the picturesque by its end.[4] In contrast, however, the notion of an antiquarian response to *curiosities* remains current throughout the century. In part this is because it engages in a broader debate about value in popular aesthetics, about the possibility of subjective and objective accounts of taste; but in part also because the idea of antiquarianism itself can be so vague.[5] Certainly if one turns to popular guidebooks the needs of the antiquarian are frequently sidelined in favour of a looser response deemed more appropriate for polite society. Thus for example in the preface to *The New Oxford Guide*, of 1778, we can see how a popular guidebook attempts to negotiate between these different kinds of audiences, firstly by describing the difference between 'the antiquarian' and 'the mere spectator'.[6] Secondly, the editor offers its readers 'curiosities', but is careful to distinguish this from a compilation of antiquities suitable only for antiquarian scholars. So the projected readers become 'Parties of pleasure', neither narrow-minded antiquarians nor simply spectators, and the volume implicitly sets about flattering an audience of curious travellers, of strangers in search of 'entertainment and information'.[7] As visitors, they do not exhibit the bad-mannered enthusiasm of the antiquarian nor the vacuity of the thoughtless spectator. And while as strangers they may be uninformed, they are deemed to share a set of assumptions about cultural values, including the value of the antique.

In the 1790s, in an essay on ruins, John Aikin points to some of the problems associated with such a spectacle. Recognizing the sentimental effect of ruins, he argues quite conventionally that they work through association 'which connects animate with inanimate things, and past with present, by the relation of place'.[8] But crucially he then goes on to consider how ruins are in general confronted by fashionable day-trippers:

> I cannot but suspect, that the undistinguished passion for ruins is only a proof how little their admirers are in general sentimentally affected by them. A gay party rambling through walks of a delightful pleasure-ground, would find an unpleasant damp striking upon their spirits on approaching an awful pile of religious ruins, did they really feel the force of its associations. Were they not capable of gazing at them as mere objects of curiosity, they would be sensible of a certain incongruity of place and occasion.[9]

Evidently, Aikin wants to retain a shared public response to ruins based on their historical significance. He articulates, that is, something close to an antiquarian response to ruins, but an antiquarianism of a fairly loose sort, an antiquarianism of fancy as well as of historical accuracy. And it is this which complicates any neat distinction between antiquarianism and popular aesthetics, a complication perhaps most apparent in the popularizing work of figures like Francis Grose. In Grose's publications, antiquarianism becomes so diluted in its scholarship that it is almost indistinguishable from a text like the *New Oxford Guide*. In the preface to his *Antiquities of England* (1773–87) Grose takes care to note that he does not 'pretend to inform the veteran antiquary; but has drawn up these accounts solely for the use of such as are desirous of having, without much trouble, a general knowledge of the subjects treated of in this publication'.[10] And while Aikin might dismiss the thoughtlessness of mere parties of pleasure, Grose, for example, after the briefest account of Netley Abbey in his *Antiquarian Repertory*, remarks on the 'parties that come by water, from Southampton, to drink tea among these ruins; an expedition the Editor to this work recommends to all persons of taste'.[11] In Grose's hands, a populist interest in antiquity turns the objects of the past into the new experience of consumer aesthetics.

But Grose is strangely divided, at once defending antiquarian scholarship against its own abuses and the abuse of others, while recognizing and exploiting its commercial potential as a marketable commodity.[12] His brief satirical essay, 'Complaint of a wife at her husband's rage for antiquities', is a case in point.[13] Written in the unsophisticated voice of the wife of a wealthy citizen who has retired to live the life of a gentleman, the episode tells of how the husband is introduced to the 'Society of Antic-queer-ones' and gives up the usual haunts of polite society in favour of 'ruinous castles and abbeys, vaults and churchyards' and a collection of old glass and brass plates purloined by country sextons. Before he became an antiquarian, her husband would buy her china or plate for her mantelpiece, but now the house is full of broken pans and milk pots, and his money is spent on strange books with F.S.A. on the cover, and coffins, tombs, and ladies in winding-sheets within.

If this is a satire on the upstart citizen and his misguided form of anti-quarianism it is also surely uncomfortably close to that popular account of antiquarianism we have already encountered. What Grose demonstrates, per-haps unwittingly, is the close connection between the antiquarian past, with its drive towards collecting both objects and books, and the way in which it is conducted as another form of consumerism close to the contemporary activi-ties of polite culture. Written in the female voice, his essay plays upon the effeminacy equated with antiquarianism, on the lack of manly rationality, on a feminine inability to see the general instead of the particular, on weakness of mind, credulity and a concern with the domestic.[14] Here feminine household objects are replaced by their effeminate counterparts. Indeed, that link between the citizen, antiquarianism, and an effeminate domestic con-sumerism is frequently made, and we can see an extreme version of the replacement of one domestic collection for another in the dramatist John O'Keeffe's *Modern Antiques*, also published in the 1790s.[15] Here, the city gentleman is a Mr Cockletop who takes to antiquarian collecting and in doing so demonstrates his lack of discrimination and critical rigour. Cockletop's mis-placed pride in his antiquarian expertise leads him to agree that his nephew, Frank, may marry his niece, Belinda, only if his antiquarian knowledge can be imposed upon. Frank, taking up the challenge, duly disguises himself and offers his uncle an array of antiquarian 'rarities'. The cook's toasting fork and gridiron become 'Neptune's Trident' and a piece of 'Household Furniture from the ruins of Herculaneum'; while more strikingly, Cockletop's own hat and coat, objects of contemporary fashion, are offered as the cap of William Tell and cloth presented to Captain Cook by the queen of Tahiti.[16] Unable to distinguish between the traces of the past, the 'genuine' monuments of history, and the domestic objects of modern middle-class life, Cockletop accepts all as genuine rarities – antiquity becoming nothing more than novelty. What is played out in O'Keeffe's drama, then, is a criticism notably voiced by Walpole that the fashionable antiquarian does nothing useful and searches not for knowledge but for novelty:

they catch at the first ugly thing they see, and take it for old because it is new to them, and then usher it pompously into the world as if they had made a discovery, though they have not yet cleared up a single point that is of the least importance or that tends to settle any obscure passage in history. . .[17]

The desire for antiquities and the desires of polite middle-class consumerism become one: antiquarian curiosity merges with the same hunger for novelty which creates domestic collections and which moves the tourist around the country in search of new experiences.

What we can see, then, is the clash between a polite account of the historical past where the past is subordinated to, or consumed with, other contemporary pleasures of commercial culture – china, plate, fashionable travel, clothing, collecting – and an antiquarian past apparently distinct from that world, but which repeatedly collapses into it. The objects of consumerism may be different, but both polite culture and antiquarian culture are here driven by the desire for commodities both physical and aesthetic.[18] However, it is worth considering the particular attraction of antiquarianism and indeed what might be so threatening about it as to inspire repeated satirical attacks on the citizen collector or the polite traveller. For O'Keeffe's Mr Cockletop and Grose's city gentleman antiquarianism provides entry into a Society peopled by peers, prelates, and politicians: like the many charitable societies which emerged in the eighteenth century, it was a venue for the mixing of ranks, a chance for the middle class to claim partnership in a shared culture of polite society.[19] But buying into the objects of the past, transforming them into the aesthetic commodities of consumerism, was also the chance to buy into a shared national heritage, or at least into the beginnings of a national heritage industry. One attraction of that industry was surely that it helped allay an inherent middle-class nervousness about status based on money, or more particularly on new money. Owning, or even visiting, the material past allowed the middling sort to lay claims upon one of the means by which modern culture understood itself, even if that understanding was strictly limited. In this sense, fashionable antiquarianism lays claim to national significance through domestic acquisition and consumer aesthetics. It is perhaps this which was to prove so threatening: it offered the ability to claim one's place in the national heritage, to establish one's place in the nation without the aid of land or rank, and without the need to take action in the political arena. If we return to a figure like Grose, and his attack on the upstart citizen with his collection of cankered coins, for all that he seems to dismiss a fashionable but trivial antiquarianism, he offers his books to those who want to engage with antiquities 'without much trouble', and he recommends them most particularly because they are affordable. Back at Netley Abbey, after noting the usual attractions of ruins, he turns his attention to the different reactions appropriate to ruined castles and abbeys. Religious buildings, where we walk over the bodies of the dead, must affect us all, he concludes; but when he turns to castles and palaces he draws attention to the social class of the visitor, and writes:

> In considering a decaying Palace, or ruined Castle, we recollect, that it was the seat of some great Lord, or warlike Baron, and recur to the history of the gallant actions which have been atchieved on that spot, or are led to reflect on the uncertainty of all human grandeur, both, perhaps, from the fate of its lordly owner, and its own tottering state; but these are subjects which are like to affect the generality of beholders but very slightly; persons in the middling walk of life, happily for them, being almost excluded from those violent convulsions and sudden reverses, to which men of a more elevated rank are frequently subjected, and which is a sufficient retribution for all of their so much envied superiority.[20]

Outside that landowning élite, Grose offers us the popular aesthetics of the middling sort: an antiquarianism which rejects the dominance of a landed élite with its wealth, leisure, and ability to collect, for an antiquarianism subsumed within the vagaries of polite taste. Grose's *Antiquities* become almost indistinguishable from works like Gilpin's picturesque tours in their taste for the curiosities of the past. If populist antiquarianism seems to threaten the established culture of the landed, always nagging in Grose's work is the worry that antiquarian scholarship is properly the domain not of the city professional but of the truly leisured landed élite.

It would be tempting to suggest at this point that in the realms of landscape and garden tourism antiquarianism loses out to polite aesthetics and that scholarship is sidelined in a commercial culture. The increasing fashionability of antiquarianism in the late eighteenth century may indeed mark its decreasing claims for intellectual rigour; and conversely, rigorous antiquarian scholarship might frequently feel the need to confront its own marginal status. Arguably it is a self-marginalizing figure in the antiquarian world who was to provide one of the most influential accounts of the nation and its history. For all that antiquarianism is embroiled in commercial culture, I want now to turn to an alternative tradition of antiquarianism, and one which was to reassert the values of the landowner over the popular commercialism of Grose: Horace Walpole's 'Essay on Modern Gardening', and the numerous later eighteenth-century antiquarian works which sought to establish not only the Englishness of the English landscape garden but the centrality of a landowning élite.[21]

To approach Walpole's account of the English garden we can return to the ruin. If the spectre of rubbish, of pointless erudition on worthless objects appears throughout eighteenth-century antiquarianism, there remains the possibility that a jewel might be found in the junkyard of the past, and if not found, then perhaps recreated. William Gilpin is famous for wanting to knock down just a little bit more of Tintern Abbey, but it is also Gilpin who once wanted to create modern ruins and begged Thomas Whately, 'to use a heap of old stone & rubbish ... in something of this kind, when he had laid out the gardens at Nonsuch'. Many years later, when reflecting on his wish to turn rubbish into ruins, he concludes that the attempt must fail because it will not be authentic. Authenticity here seems less a question of age than of appearance, and it is the failure to look right, the failure to fool the viewer, which Gilpin ultimately deplores in modern ruins: 'I had not then seen', he writes, 'what I have since seen, so many awkward, ridiculous, hideous attempts'.[22] Authenticity, in true antiquarian style, is in the mind of the beholder.

Gilpin, of course, is often accused of an ahistorical formalism in his picturesque approach to the landscape, but a powerful strand of antiquarianism, albeit anecdotal, runs throughout his tours.[23] The ruins of history which Gilpin sketches on his tours are also the opportunity to affirm a history of progress from tyranny and superstition to religious freedom and political liberty: over and over again, local history and custom, anecdotes and asides, reaffirm that confidence in progress. Within such a narrative, Gothic ruins in the landscape garden stand as both reminders of a lost past, and the physical embodiment of a perfected present. The problem with sham ruins is that while they often fail visually, that visual failure is also the failure to inspire a convincing narrative of their own antiquity. Thus, at Painshill in Surrey, Gilpin is uneasy about Charles Hamilton's new ruins for their jumbling of the antique and the modern. While 'The *triumphal arch* is a most beautiful piece of modern ruin', with antique sculptures indiscriminately mixed with a modern urn, it loses all ability to inspire suitable reveries of the past,[24] when placed uncomfortably close to an unconvincing 'Gothic' summer house.

Walpole, too, found the antique arch at Painshill unconvincing, but he was far from an enemy to the modern ruin. At Hagley, he famously praised the ruins in the landscape for displaying the 'true rust of the Barons' wars', making an imaginative leap to that earlier resistance to the tyranny of monarchs. Equally famously, it is a remark he makes of ruins only recently erected; here Walpole happily accepts this modern ruin as an object of consumption for a travelling public in search of an 'antique' experience. Something of the confusion of conflicting responses to the authentically antique can be seen in Gilpin's and Walpole's reactions to the same site – Park Place, the Berkshire estate of Walpole's cousin and close friend, General Conway. On a hill looking down on the Thames Conway had placed a genuine cromlech, shipped from Jersey. According to Walpole this 'Druidic temple':

wears all the appearance of an ancient castle, whose towers are only shattered, not destroyed; and devout as I am to old castles, and small taste as I have for the ruins of ages absolutely barbarous, it is impossible not to be pleased with so very rare an antiquity so absolutely perfect, and it is difficult to prevent visionary ideas from improving a prospect.[25]

However, it was only after several reprimands from his poet friend William Mason that Gilpin could bring himself to be polite about those same antiquities. While in Gilpin's published tour Park Place hardly appears, in the various manuscript versions, it is at best 'pleasant' and at worst 'an assemblage only of primping ideas'.[26] Disagreeable chalk ruins appear in a cancellation as 'vile things', the valley is 'a mere blanket held at the 4 corners', and worst of all is the cromlech itself, described as:

half a dozen large stones brought together; (and the carriage of one of wh. cost we were told 20L) than wh. nothing can be more absurd. They neither give any idea of what they mean to represent; nor are they suited to the country, in which they are introduced. They are heterogeneous ornam[en]ts –

Additionally, in a further cancelled line he insists that they are: 'instead of being an object of the imagination, an unmeaning, affected trifle'.[27] The problem for Gilpin is that the heterogeneity of Park Place represents a discord of ideas – it becomes impossible to work up one imaginative picture of the past because competing cultural discourses draw themselves to the attention. Without a sense of locality, 'genuine' ruins lose their 'authenticity' and antiquity is replaced by an awareness only of cost and taste.

Gilpin and Walpole may react, then, in radically different ways to the same antiquarian objects, but they do so, perhaps, because of a strikingly similar notion of the antique. Both want ruins to offer some kind of direct access to the past; and to gain that access, both need to construct historical narratives in which to understand those ruins. The curiosity of Walpole's stance lies in his strange combination of attention to and lack of concern for detail in the interests of 'taste'. Indeed, despite his association with an antiquarianism of detail, of a particularity which avoids the general or the abstract, it is Walpole's antiquarianism which produces the 'Essay on Modern Gardening', an essay which is part of a far larger antiquarian project exploring gardens from Eden to the eighteenth century, and one which places the English garden as the culmination of a Whig world history.[28]

Walpole's essay sets about demonstrating the bad taste – and by extension the bad politics – of all ages before the arrival of the Hanoverians and, in true Whig fashion, he draws upon the myth of Saxon liberty to do so.[29] In this he was not alone: the second half of the century saw great effort going into producing world histories of the garden which duly found their apotheosis in the newly discovered landscape style.[30] Many of these works, like Walpole's, were overtly 'Whiggish' in their historical methods and ostentatiously patriotic in their claims: the 'English' aesthetic of variety in the garden, the rejection of geometrical form, is to be recognized as an image of the constitution and of Britons' inherent liberty. Exploring and frequently dismissing the historical record until the eighteenth century, these antiquarian works set about the double task of denying any precedent for the English garden, while at the same time using a political reading of such gardens to assert the fundamental importance of land and landowning to Britain's continued liberty at home and dominance abroad.

The success of Walpole's version of garden history lay in the fact that he was able to make an ideological polemic appear as the neutral relation of stylistic change. For Walpole, garden history is the story of great men and great gardens, one which follows the inevitable progress of these men towards the current perfection of the English landscape style. If antiquarianism is usually attacked for concerning itself with a historical and prehistoric past from which modern society can learn nothing, what happens with garden histories is in ironic agreement with this: great gardens of past ages and foreign nations are explored and consistently found to be wanting.[31] After nodding briefly at Eden, Walpole begins his narrative with Homer's description of the garden of

Alcinous and concludes that when 'divested of harmonious Greek and bewitching poetry' it was nothing more than 'a small orchard and vineyard with some beds of herbs and two fountains'.[32] The great classical garden is suddenly unworthy of its renown. Not only is it ordinary, it is small. Small, at least, when compared to the English landscape garden, a comparison Walpole consistently makes in his account of the antique. Homer's garden is demythologized before our eyes only to be re-mythologized as the landscape of Hanoverian Britain.

By the later eighteenth century a crucial element of that mythology was of a landscape garden almost miraculously 'discovered' as a wholly native art in the early years of the Hanoverian succession; and part of the power of that myth lay in political readings of English garden design as an image of English liberty. For a writer such as William Falconer in his 'Thoughts on the Style and Taste of Gardening among the Ancients' (1789), the English landscape garden is a reflection of Britain's cultural disposition, a reflection too of correct – natural – government. According to Falconer and many others, regular gardens are to be equated with despotic interests, while the 'rational' land-scape garden is a reflection of the variegated – constitutional – regime charac-teristic of Falconer's contemporary Hanoverian England.[33] In Falconer's essay, as in Walpole's, a discussion of aesthetic history becomes a discussion also of political history, and later eighteenth-century Britain (safe in the hands of a constitutional monarchy) is pronounced uniquely free from despotic claims in either sphere. Not only do these aesthetic histories provide a seemingly unproblematic account of political history and one accepted by the majority of the political nation, but, as we have seen, at the centre of such histories is the great landowner. From this perspective, the English landscape garden is to be recognized not only as a true representation of nature, but as a representation of the land – both historical and political – from which it is formed.

In such works of antiquarian history the English garden becomes a shared national achievement open to all those of polite taste, and this stands in con-trast to the cultural and political history of Britain's great rival, France, the regular gardens of which are repeatedly brought to the attention. One of the sleights of hand being practised, of course, is that the vast gardens of other ages and other cultures are equated with tyranny while English gardens – despite also being dependent on the amassing of both land and wealth at the expense of others – are characterized in terms of liberty. In this sense, anti-quarian historians of the garden act quite openly as apologists for the landed élite at a time when that élite found such apologies increasingly necessary. In the final decades of the eighteenth century the landed classes came under far heavier criticism than ever before for being both exclusive and frivolous. Histories of the landscape garden were histories of the kind of large-scale landowning open only to the aristocratic élite, but crucially they were based on the most patriotic of all things, the land itself. In the public gesture of gardening, landowners could equate themselves with the achievements of constitutional liberty and assert their dominance over aesthetic taste even as that taste was characterized as the shared property of the nation. In such histories the landed élite came to own one of the foremost expressions of national identity in the late eighteenth century, and that ownership becomes both rational and natural. Antiquarianism inevitably leads to the English garden and the English garden leads to the cultural centrality of a landowning élite.

In the popularizing work of Grose and his like, antiquarianism may seem so diluted as to disappear into the commercial world of fashion, or to be marginalized as an élitist obsession with trivia. What I am suggesting is that Walpole and other antiquarian scholars are found re-establishing its importance by providing a politicized antiquarian narrative of national success: a narrative which challenges the democratizing effects of popular aesthetics and the values of a commercial culture which together commodify the traces of the past. Equally, Walpole's insistence on taste as a necessary adjunct to antiquarianism marks once again the fragmentation of the discipline, such as it is.[34] For all that his essay appears to be the product of antiquarian research, its fundamental judgements are made at the level of taste, and a taste which is inseparable from the socio-aesthetic of landowning and from that Whig history of political progress towards constitutional liberty.

Notes

1. Letter from Horace Walpole to Rev. William Cole, 17 April 1773, reproduced in W. S. Lewis (ed.), *The Yale Edition of Horace Walpole's Correspondence*, 48 vols (New Haven, Yale University Press; Oxford University Press, 1937–83), 1, pp.304–6, p.304.

2. Quoted in Joan Evans, *A History of the Society of Antiquaries* (Oxford, The Society of Antiquaries, 1956), p.184.

3. *Veillée A La Campagne: Or The Simnel. A Tale* (London, R. Manby & H.S. Cox, 1745).

4. See, for example, John Dixon Hunt, 'Picturesque Mirrors and the Ruin of the Past', in John Dixon Hunt, *Gardens and the Picturesque: Studies in the History of Landscape Architecture* (Cambridge, Mass. and London, The MIT Press, 1992).

5. Lucy Peltz has reached a similar conclusion about the distinction of two separate concepts of antiquarian practice in her chapter in this volume.

6. *The New Oxford Guide: Or, Companion through the University. Exhibiting every Particular worthy The Observation of the Curious in each of the Public Buildings, Colleges, Halls, &c. To which is added, a Tour to Blenheim, Ditchley, Heythrop, Nuneham, and Stow … Containing an accurate Description of their Tapestry, Painting, Sculpture, Temples, Gardens, and other Curiosities. By a Gentleman of Oxford*, 6th edn (Oxford, J. Fletcher, n.d. [c.1778]), p.v.

7. *Ibid.*

8. John Aikin, *Letters From A Father To His Son, on various topics relative to Literature and the Conduct of Life. Written in the Years 1792 and 1793* (London, J. Johnson, 1793), pp.267–8.

9. *Ibid.*, pp.269–70.

10. Francis Grose, *The Antiquities of England and Wales*, 6 vols (London, S. Hooper, 1773–87), 1, p.iv.

11. Francis Grose, *The Antiquarian Repertory: A Miscellany, intended to preserve and illustrate several valuable remains. Adorned with elegant sculptures*, 4 vols (London, 1775–84), 1, pp. 244–5.

12. See, for example, his preface to *ibid.*, esp. pp. iii–vii.

13. Francis Grose, 'Complaint of a wife at her husband's rage for antiquities', in *The Grumbler: containing Sixteen Essays* (London, S. Hooper, 1791), pp.47–51.

14. For a discussion of the charge of effeminacy levelled against antiquarians in the eighteenth century see Lucy Peltz's chapter in this volume.

15. John O'Keeffe, *Modern Antiques, or the Merry Mourners, A Farce, in Two Acts* (Dublin, 'Printed by P. Byrne', 1792).

16. *Ibid.*, pp.18–19.

17. Letter from Horace Walpole to Rev. William Cole, 28 May 1774, reproduced in the *Yale Edition of the Correspondence of Horace Walpole*, 1, pp.328–31, p.330.

18. For the broader ramifications of a 'consumer culture' see Neil McKendrick, John Brewer and J. H. Plumb, *The Birth of a Consumer Society: The Commercialization of Eighteenth-Century England* (London, Hutchinson & Co., 1982).

19. Linda Colley, *Britons: Forging the Nation 1707–1837* (New Haven and London, Yale University Press, 1992), pp.66 and 91–3; Paul Langford, *A Polite and Commercial People: England 1727–1783* (Oxford University Press, 1992), Chapter 3, and esp. pp.116–21; also Paul Langford, *Public Life and Propertied Englishmen 1689–1798* (Oxford, Clarendon, 1991), esp. Chapter 1; and John Rule, *Albion's People: English Society 1714–1815* (London, Longman, 1992), Chapter 2.

20. Grose, *The Antiquarian Repertory*, pp.244–5.

21. Horace Walpole, 'On Modern Gardening', in his *Anecdotes of Painting in England . . . To which is added The History of The Modern Taste in Gardening*, 2nd edition with additions, 4 vols (London, Strawberry Hill, 1782), 4, pp.247–316; the essay was written in 1770. For a discussion of further such works, see Stephen Bending, 'Horace Walpole and Eighteenth-Century Garden History', *Journal of the Warburg and Courtauld Institutes*, 57 (1994), pp. 209–26.

22. Letter from William Gilpin to William Mason, 5 June 1783, MS Eng. Misc. d.570–1, Bodleian Library, Oxford.

23. See Carl Paul Barbier, *William Gilpin, his Drawings, Teachings, and Theory of the Picturesque* (Oxford, Clarendon Press, 1963). See also Ann Bermingham, *Landscape and Ideology. The English Rustic Tradition, 1740–1860* (London, Thames and Hudson, 1987), Chapter 2; Kim Ian Michasiw, 'Nine Revisionist Theses on the Picturesque', *Representations*, 38 (1992), pp.76–100.

24. William Gilpin, 'Miscellaneous notes', MS Eng. misc. e.522, Bodleian Library, p.26.

25. Letter from Horace Walpole to the Earl of Strafford, 12 September 1788, reproduced in the *Yale Edition of the Correspondence of Horace Walpole*, 23, pp.395–7, p.396.

26. Gilpin's description is in his *Lakes Tour*; several manuscript versions survive. I quote from the version in the *Wye Tour* manuscript in MS Eng. Misc. e.486(8), Bodleian Library, Oxford, pp.162–70, p.162.

27. *Ibid.*, pp.163, 164 and 166.

28. See Richard Quaintance, 'Walpole's Whig Interpretation of Landscaping History', *Studies in Eighteenth-Century Culture*, 9 (1979), pp.285–300.

29. See, notably, Samuel Kliger, *The Goths in England: A Study in Seventeenth- and Eighteenth-century Thought* (rpt 1952: New York, Harvard University Press, 1972).

30. See Bending, 'Horace Walpole'.

31. See Sam Smiles, *The Image of Antiquity: Ancient Britain and the Romantic Imagination* (New Haven and London, Yale University Press, 1994), Chapter 2.

32. Horace Walpole, 'On Modern Gardening', pp.250–52.

33. William Falconer, 'Thoughts on the Style and Taste of Gardening among the Ancients', in *Memoirs of the Literary and Philosophical Society of Manchester*, 2nd edn, London, Literary and Philosophical Society of Manchester, 1789), 1, pp.297–325.

34. Lawrence Lipking's discussion of the relationship between antiquarianism and taste in Walpole remains one of the most useful; Lawrence Lipking, *The Ordering of the Arts in Eighteenth-Century England* (Princeton University Press, 1970), esp. pp.140–55.

6

Caspar David Friedrich and national antiquarianism in Northern Germany

Johann J.K. Reusch

National antiquarianism became a popular field of study in Germany during the late eighteenth century and focused on recording all things local: history, natural phenomena, culture, and above all, artefacts. It was introduced into Germany from Britain in the form of illustrated antiquarian tour books that were first translated and then imitated. For more than a century, British scholars, hindered both by geographic isolation as well as by a religiously-based disdain for the Vatican had begun to shift their focus from the antiquities of Rome toward national artefacts. In Britain, nationhood, although complicated by tribal differences, was facilitated by the concise boundaries of an island, while Germany, in contrast, was composed of a kaleidoscopic array of independent states with shifting boundaries. In Britain the difference between classical archaeology and national antiquarianism had been established distinctly by the end of the eighteenth century; in Germany it had not. German scholars, for the most part, traced their national heritage to the Holy Roman Empire of German nations. Thus, they linked their common cultural and historical beginnings to ancient Rome as the origins of the civilized world and history itself. In Germany, where the scholarly lingua franca had been Latin and intellectuals had latinized their family names, antiquarianism generally had been synonymous with classical archaeology. Here, operating somewhere between the terms pre-history (*Vor-* or *Frühgeschichte*) and home-land research (*Heimatkunde*), the nomenclature of national antiquarianism clearly marginalized it at the periphery of serious academic disciplines.

The reception and pursuit of national antiquarianism in Germany can be attributed to several influences. Unlike its counterpart, classical archaeology, which had evolved from serious academic study to become the pastime of a travelling artefact-collecting élite, national antiquarianism could be practised inexpensively in one's own backyard. Germany, like Britain, began to produce a large cohort of private scholars, as study at the universities became available to a more extended social stratum who, holding appointments as clergymen, librarians or other administrative positions with aristocratic patronage, pursued antiquarian interests. Imitating illustrated British antiquarian guidebooks, German scholars provided resources to an expanding middle class for the imaginative exploration of national treasures from the armchair at home. This increasing access to a general education furthermore encouraged audiences for scholarly tourism (*Bildungsreisen*). At the turn of the century, publications describing popular antiquarian and scenic tour sites began to create a growing industry in parallel to the one that had existed in Britain for decades. At the forefront of the antiquarian movement in Germany stood the pastor Ludwig Gotthard Kosegarten (1758–1818) of Rügen. Kosegarten translated British antiquarian and scenic tour books into German and was an antiquary who collected local artefacts and recorded regional history and its sites. He owned an important collection of illustrated antiquarian guidebooks, and wrote poetry and travel accounts in the manner of the English poets of his time.

Around 1800, the painter Caspar David Friedrich (1774–1840) came into direct contact with Kosegarten and a group of German intellectuals who harboured antiquarian interests in non-classical antiquities. Among this circle were several professors from the local University of Greifswald, among them Karl Schildener (1767–1834) and Friedrich Albert Muhrbeck (1775–1827) who purchased several of Friedrich's drawings.[1] Other members included the pastors Bernhard Oliver Franck of Bobbin (1759–1833) and Adolf Friedrich Furchau (1787–1868) of Stralsund.[2] Schildener, a member of the law faculty and supervisor of the university library, was recognized as an authority on the pre- and early history of Pomerania. Furchau, the author of 'old-Nordic' epic poems such as *Arkona* (1828), was part of the bard-cult that was instigated by British antiquaries like William Stukeley (1687–1765).[3] In 1830 Furchau also wrote a definitive text on the history of Rügen for which he seems to have discussed Friedrich's participation as an illustrator.[4] Most important, however, was Kosegarten, who had a national reputation as an 'Ossianic' poet and pre-historian of the island of Rügen. Kosegarten provided lodging for visitors and led them on tours to scenic and historical sites, such as cliffs, dolmen graves, and ruins.[5] Friedrich travelled to Rügen for the first time in 1801 and visited Kosegarten who must have acted as a guide for that artist's antiquarian tour of the island.

The reasons for Friedrich's visit to Rügen must remain speculative. Rügen had already gained a reputation as a tourist site and was associated not only with Kosegarten, but with well-known public figures like Ernst Moritz Arndt and Friedrich Schleyermacher, who used to holiday there. Friedrich had already tried his hand as an illustrator of picturesque and antiquarian sites and had also worked as a tour guide in Saxony during the previous year.[6]

Contact with Kosegarten, with whom he already had many ties, would have associated him with a well-known literary personality. Kosegarten had a reputation for promoting local talent and used his influence to encourage the purchase of works by Swedish-Pomeranian writers and painters. He personally commissioned Philipp Otto Runge (1777–1810), whose artistic talent he had recognized and encouraged during that painter's childhood, to decorate his chapel in Putbus. Both Runge and Friedrich had studied drawing under Johann Gottfried Quistorp, a close friend of Kosegarten. Quistorp was the academic drawing instructor at the University of Greifswald where he taught topography, geographic survey and cartography. He had accompanied Schildener and Muhrbeck on scholarly excursions where he drafted the visual records of antiquarian subjects; and at times, during the 1790s, he seems to have taken the young Friedrich along with him.[7] It is likely that Kosegarten would have wished to further Friedrich's career, as he too was a native son of the region. Through Quistorp, or their close, regional network of acquaintances, Kosegarten would have heard of Friedrich's attempts to make a living by producing prints and drawings of popular scenic and historical sites, and no doubt they would have informed him of the success of British antiquarian guidebooks and the potential for similar studies focused on Rügen.[8]

Their first meeting was shortly after Kosegarten's publication of his pupil Karl Nernst's *Tour of Rügen* (1800), which was modelled after the British Antiquarian Tour.[9] The lack of 'newer material' forced Kosegarten to use a set of older plates by Philipp Hackert (1737–1807) as illustrations for the book.[10] This would certainly have been a topic of discussion and of great interest to Friedrich who wished to avail himself of such a commission. Kosegarten knew well the commercial potential of topographical prints through his intimate knowledge of illustrated British publications. Popular topographic prints were reprinted to be bound together with antiquarian texts and could have been found in collections owned by German antiquaries. Even in remote houses like Kosegarten's, collections of prints were so substantial that they were mentioned in the accounts of visitors to Rügen.[11]

Friedrich was thus aware of the expansion of the genre of illustrated antiquarian treatises and sensed the commercial potential of producing scenic and antiquarian views that were easily reproducible as aquatints or engravings. Most of Friedrich's drawings of Gothic ruins follow the British antiquarian model of recording such views. An important source of inspiration for Friedrich were British antiquarian guidebooks such as Francis Grose's *The Antiquarian repertory: a miscellany, intended to preserve and illustrate several valuable remains of old times* (1775–84), John Britton's *The Beauties of England and Wales; or delineation, topographical, historical, and descriptive of each county* (1801–15) as well as James Sargent Storer's *The antiquarian itinerary : comprising specimens of architecture, monastic, castellated, and domestic; with other vestiges of antiquity in Great Britain; accompanied with descriptions* (1815–18). This is evinced by comparing *Netley Abbey* (Figure 6.1), from *The Beauties of England and Wales*, with Friedrich's *Ruin of Eldena* (1825) (Figure 6.2). Indicative of his work after 1800, Friedrich abandons most trappings of the picturesque and the traditional *veduta* in favour of recording the ruinous structure in an even more clinical fashion than his British counterparts.

Most influential among the authors of antiquarian treatises was the Reverend William Gilpin (1724–1804), a theorist of the picturesque, who gained such popularity on the continent that his *Observations on the Western Parts of England* (1798) was translated into German in 1805.[12] Gilpin was seen as a kindred spirit by the circle of Protestant pastors around Kosegarten because he combined theological enquiry and aesthetic interests with national history. Many antiquarians in Britain, as in Germany, were clergymen of reformed Christian denominations who understood the transformation and employment of Christian religion in the service of late Roman colonialism. As sites of ancient antiquities and 'medieval' Gothic architecture were understood in direct opposition to pontifical colonial authority they constituted a vital effort toward ethnic self-definition. In their efforts to free their own cultural and national past from the Roman label of barbaric and uncivilized, these men traced Druid beliefs towards a nature mysticism that defied the rituals and stringent doctrines of the Roman Catholic Church. Gilpin's *The Lives of Reformers* became the standard text on the subject and had been translated into German by 1769.[13]

Gilpin's illustrations of his antiquarian and picturesque tours also reflected an increasingly popular medium, the use of brush and sepia ink drawings for mass-reproduction in aquatint etching. Due to its facility and the transportability of its materials, combined with its potential for reproduction in aquatint, sepia drawing can be considered a forerunner to modern photography. The 'snapshot' effect of this technique offered a fast and efficient way of capturing transitional half tones, volume and spatial relationships for commercial reproduction; it also provided the armchair traveller with the sensation of immediacy. Friedrich's production of a vast series of reproducible sepia drawings of German scenic and antiquarian sites seems to follow this trend, as is illustrated by a comparison of his *Ruin of Eldena* (Figure 6.2) and his *Eldena* (1837) with Gilpin's *Valley of Tweed with Melrose Abbey*, from *Observations on Cumberland and Westmoreland* (1786) (Figure 6.3).

The popularity of Friedrich's sepia drawings of Rügen grew exponentially with the antiquarian tourism in the area. Realizing the growing market for illustrated antiquarian tour guides, he was concerned that his views could be mass-reproduced by someone other than himself. Early signs of the paranoid delusions that plagued him in his later years manifested themselves during this time in a note accompanying a shipment:

Since the enclosed picture represents the essence of Rügen, and the island is being visited frequently by tourists at the moment, it could easily come to the mind of an enterprising engraver to duplicate it.[14]

Due to the lack of effective copyright laws, the plagiarist mass-reproduction of popular images was rampant in Germany; many an artist had to watch helplessly as his works were duplicated by commercial engravers who would sign the work with their own names, often omitting the original artist's *delineavit* reference. Friedrich did not trust commercial engravers, and on several occasions tried to etch his images himself.[15] He also tried to enlist his brother Christian, a cabinetmaker, in producing an edition of woodcuts and wood engravings.[16]

Despite the fact that Friedrich's drawings appear never to have been printed for any edition of an illustrated antiquarian tour, they nevertheless offer the most comprehensive and topographically exact documentation of the prehistoric graves and Gothic architecture of his time. Several of the German intellectuals who had made antiquarian and scenic tours placed Friedrich in an antiquarian context because they had themselves travelled through England, undoubtedly following the prescribed routes suggested in illustrated guidebooks.[17] A review in the *Freimüthige oder Berlinische Zeitung*, in 1803, readily interpreted Friedrich's sepia drawings as 'explaining Kosegarten's passion and the poetic fire in Nernst's tour [of Rügen].'[18] Friedrich's connection with the world of antiquarian literature and illustration was thus recognized by a contemporary audience even though his work was derided by several critics of the time as 'too architectural'. Friedrich's emphasis on architectural detail was encouraged in discussions with Kosegarten about antiquarian practices regarding the recording of architectural sites.

Kosegarten translated Thomas Gray's *Observations of Gothic Architecture* in his biographical anthology, *Etwas über Gray's Leben und Charakter* (1801).[19] No popular study of Gothic architecture existed in German, apart from Goethe's essay *On German Architecture* (1773), which in itself followed the English antiquarian effort to reclaim a national past. Kosegarten would not have missed the opportunity of discussing Gray's architectural theories with an artist like Friedrich; additionally, Goethe's essay would, no doubt, have been part of any such discussion of Gothic architecture that might have taken place during Friedrich's visit in 1801, while Kosegarten was working on the translation of Gray's *Observations*. Accuracy in identifying and recording architectural dimensions and styles was also a continuous theme in Thomas Garnett's *Observations on a Tour through the Highlands and Part of the Western Isles of Scotland* (1800), which Kosegarten translated in 1802. This was originally illustrated with 'fifty-two plates, engraved in the manner of aquatinta, from drawings taken on the spot by W.H. Watts', while the German translation was adorned with only a few vignettes. Friedrich must have seen the illustrations in Garnett's original text, such as Watts' *Dunkeld Cathedral* (Figure 6.4), which certainly served as a reference if not a model. With his focus on the Cathedral and Bishop's House at Icolmkill and Dunkeld Cathedral, Garnett's text provided exemplary methods for assessing the dimensions of architectural sites for the purpose of antiquarian cataloguing (which are echoed in Kosegarten's and Nernst's site descriptions), such as: 'The length of the cathedral from east to west, is thirty-eight yards, the breadth eight and the length of the transept about twenty-four yards.'[20] Or:

This abbey has once been a fine pile of building, though now much dilapidated; the architecture is part Gothic and partly Saxon, like most of the old abbeys. What remains of it are the tower, the two side aisles, and the nave of the church; these are in ruins, excepting the quire of the cathedral, which is converted into a parish church, and forms a sufficiently commodious place of worship. This quire was begun by Bishop Sinclair, and finished by him in the year 1350. In the middle of the eastern gable is to be seen a part of the old wall of the abbey of Culdees, which stood there before the present cathedral was built.[21]

Indeed, Friedrich's graphic œuvre after 1800 is marked by a shift from the idyllic naturalism of the traditional *vedute* towards the topographical, architecturally focused approach practised by a host of British artists who recorded antiquarian and scenic sites.

This approach reflected the imploring demands of yet another British antiquarian, Richard Gough (1735–1809). The author of a series of antiquarian guidebooks which reflect his concern with topographical accuracy, Gough pleaded before the London Society of Antiquaries during his inaugural speech as its Director to establish higher standards of topographical drawings for reproduction in antiquarian publications. He repeated these demands in his foreword to *Archaeologia* (1773–87), which became a standard antiquarian reference for years to come, and with which Kosegarten must have been familiar.

Gough placed the onus of preserving a national past equally into the hands of the antiquarian and the draftsman to whom one 'must transfer the blame from the engraver' for their poor records of architectural details.[22] Gough called for a specific 'ecclesiastic topography' by which he understood 'surveys of churches and religious houses'.[23] The antiquaries who commissioned Friedrich's work with the very intention of preserving the past through visual records shared this concern. Kosegarten would, no doubt, have sympathized with Gough's lamentation of the fate of Gothic architecture, which had lost none of its actuality, especially not for Germany where national antiquarianism was still in its infancy. As Gough had proclaimed:

One cannot enough regret the little regard hitherto paid to Gothic architecture, of which so many beautiful models are daily crumbling before our eyes ... We can go back even to the Druids, who poised immense weights almost on nothing, yet wanted the courage and contrivance to raise arches ... That fine work [Gothic architecture] which, by bringing us acquainted with the skill and magnificence of former ages, would have given immortality to our own, is laid aside. We penetrate the wilds of Europe, and the desarts of Asia and Africa, for the remains of Grecian, Roman, and earlier architecture, while no artist offers himself as a candidate for fame in preserving those of our forefathers in their own country.[24]

The effort to preserve a national past through visual records was more than an imported trend in Germany. Towards the end of the eighteenth century, the destruction of national monuments began to accelerate rapidly. Dolmen graves were dug up and their stones split and sold during an increasing demand for building materials that constituted a trade reaching from Pomerania to Holland. This practice reached such proportions in Northern Germany that towns and municipalities required 'stone passports' to trace the origins for stones shipped and transported. Fired bricks were in similar demand and were plundered from Gothic structures. During the Napoleonic campaigns, German farmers were forced by the French army to demolish historical structures in order to supply cobblestones for the building of roads.[25]

Friedrich seems not only to have relied on illustrations as a model but to have drawn inspiration from textual sources as well. Nernst's text, in fact, seems to have provided a direct model for Friedrich's production in combining scientific accuracy, mysticism, the sublime and the picturesque:

Around noon the ancient darkened castle Charenza appears after which the town is still named today. In a silent melancholy awe it still stands, a memorable relic of the past; thought inspiring and venerated as long as national history will engage someone's mind or heart. The upper enclosure of the inner plan measures about seven-hundred feet in diameter; below, a double to triple wall rises as a bastion against enemies against whose attacks the remaining sides were secured through deep swamps. Am I not mistaken, then it is the south-eastern corner of the plan which is separated by an earth wall and broken up brick construction, where most likely the large temple of idols once stood.[26]

Friedrich's professional challenge lay in translating these complex observations and experiences through his own work.

Certainly, the most frequently illustrated antiquarian monument in Friedrich's œuvre was the ruin of the monastery church of Eldena at Greifswald. British antiquarian texts had long asserted that Christian structures were usually built on the sites of ancient worship. Eldena's decayed state thus had begun to blend the forces of nature that reclaimed the site with a continuum of ancient and modern beliefs. Eldena, at least for Friedrich, constituted the Northern German counterpart to England's Tintern Abbey, one of the most reproduced subjects of any antiquarian tour guide during the early nineteenth century. This theme of Gothic architecture as spiritual and inspirational, as symbolized in the frontispiece illustration augmenting editions of Wordsworth's *A few Lines Composed Upon Tintern Abbey* (1798), may have served as a topos for Friedrich. He wrote poetry himself and must have known Wordsworth's writings, which were exceedingly popular and could have been found easily enough in Kosegarten's library. Both in Wordsworth's poem and in Goethe's *On German Architecture*, published two decades previously, Gothic structures provided a spiritual and antiquarian context that challenged Roman colonial classicist aesthetics and culture with the help of transalpine 'Germanic' architecture. That which had been dispersed by colonial acculturation could be symbolically resurrected through visionary meditation.

The force of spiritual experience, during scholarly travels to antiquarian sites, constituted an integral part of a pilgrimage into one's ethnic past. The travel correspondence of the British poet Thomas Gray, who harboured antiquarian interests which gained him an appointment as professor of history, contained passages that seem to provide the basis for Friedrich's understanding of the spirituality of landscape: 'Not a precipice, not a torrent, not a cliff, but is pregnant with religion and poetry.'[27] Kosegarten translated Gray's texts into German and wrote poetry in his style. It would have been through a discussion of his texts alone that Kosegarten would have familiarized Friedrich with the concept of the antiquarian tour. The meditative state necessary to communicate with the spiritual aspects of nature inspired not only the poetic trend of sensibility, as exemplified by Gray, but also the development of natural philosophy in Germany. It is important for this study to note that these influences predate Schelling's essay 'On the Relationship of the Creative Arts to Nature' (1807) which is widely credited as being one of the major influences upon Friedrich's work. In sum, Friedrich's whole concept of religiously imbued landscape referred back not only to the kind of nature mysticism espoused by Renaissance and Baroque mystics like Jakob Boehme and Theophrast von Hohenheim, but also to an alternative and more immediate context of 'scholarly' enquiry by eighteenth-century British antiquarians who investigated the natural religions of pre-Roman Northern Europe.

In the mind of German antiquarians the island of Rügen constituted the German counterpart to those British islands, such as the Hebrides, which were never colonized by the Romans. The remoteness of many of these sites added to their mystique and placed them in the realm of the exotic, hitherto restricted to faraway countries which, just like an ancient British past, could still be discovered and explored.[28] German guidebooks on Rügen closely followed the style of Gilpin's and Gray's coverage of the Isle of Wight, as well as the German translation of Thomas Pennant's *Voyage to the Hebrides* (1774).[29] Most prominent among these were Karl Nernst's *Wanderungen durch Rügen* (1800) and Johann Jakob Grümbke's tour through the island of Rügen, published in 1805.[30] In a reversed twist of antiquarian influences, Rügen's ancient Teutonic mystique began to intrigue an English audience and Grümbke's text was translated into English in 1807.[31] The exoticism of the island was further enhanced by its rarity and utopian potential, as the largest German-speaking island in the Baltic Sea; the island of Fehmarn, in comparison, was hardly more than a sandbank that could be reached on foot and by wagon at low tide.

British explorations into the South Sea during the second half of the eighteenth century seemed to confirm the utopian quality of island societies unspoiled by modern civilization.[32] The natives of Tahiti, for example, were thought to resemble the early pre-Roman inhabitants of the British Isles both in dress and in their carefree symbiosis with nature. This hypothesis fuelled a fascination with the islands off the coast of Britain, as places where the ancient Britons had survived the Roman conquests. Inhabitants of the Orkney Islands, where ancient monuments were known to exist, spoke an Old Norse dialect almost up to the end of the eighteenth century and were thought of as the direct descendants of an unacculturated Germanic tribe. Rügen similarly was understood as the last stronghold of Teutonic culture. Friedrich's interpretation of the chalk cliffs of Arkona as 'Germany's last crag' echoes its historic significance for antiquarian explorations. Jumping on the bandwagon of British scholarship, antiquarians identified the dolmen graves on Rügen as part of a common Celtic heritage, a belief discussed as late as the 1830s in Barthold's *Geschichte von Rügen und Pommern* (1839).[33] Kosegarten, in true antiquarian style, documented dolmen graves in his description of the Rügen fashioned as the journal of a shipwrecked traveller stranded on the island:

Several steps beyond [the hamlet of] Nobbyn, I encountered a majestic dolmen grave which is the most imposing and best preserved at the same time that I have ever seen on this island. It aligned on a north-south axis. The elliptical stone circle measures about thirty feet in length and about ten in width. The amount of stones of which it is comprised count thirty-nine. The two most monumental form the entrance and would allow an equestrian to pass below. The burial mount itself is gently curved and reaches immediately to the edge of the sea. Warmed by the sight of this noble monument and surrounded by whispers, as it seemed to me, about flash-backs from dark pre-history, I doubled my gait and moved onward.[34]

Friedrich tried to capture the experiential essence of encountering monuments of an ancient ancestral past in a series of drawings, several of which were executed as larger scale paintings. The picturesque experience of a dolmen grave set within landscape was already alluded to by Kosegarten's student Nernst, who may have referred to the same site, when he wrote, 'Exquisitely beautiful appears the outlook from that [hill] which is identified by a large dolmen grave'.[35]

In addition to his visits to dolmen graves with Kosegarten, Friedrich's drawings like *Dolmen Grave* (after 1800) (Figure 6.5), may have been inspired by British illustrated guidebooks describing megalithic architecture, such as the frontispiece to the second volume of Britton's *The Beauties of England and Wales* (Figure 6.6). Indeed, following the British antiquarian fascination with pre-Roman culture, religiosity, and antiquities, Rügen became the prime focus of German antiquarianism. Early accounts by British antiquaries about ancient temple sites inspired Kosegarten and his fellow antiquaries into expounding on the theory of a similar site on Rügen, dedicated to the goddess Hertha, the personified power of nature. This corresponded closely to the popular enthusiasm for nature mysticism, the religious concept within which many of Friedrich's works have come to be interpreted. Kosegarten dedicated several of his 'Rhapsodies' to the proposed sites of ancient worship whose perceived qualities, fuelled by the popular literary 'Ossian' cult, resulted in the inclusion of ancient Germanic sites on the new maps of Rügen during the first decades of the nineteenth century. According to accounts of the time, by the 1830s thousands of travellers descended upon Rügen to get in touch with an uncanny religious experience of ancient Germanic cult worship.[36]

Similarly, Luke Clennell's (1781–1840) *Door of Peterboro Church* (c.1808) (Figure 6.7), reproduced by William Wallis as an engraving for Storer's *Antiquarian Itinerary*, aspires to imbue antiquarian documentation with the mystical symbolism of the rites of death, the passage from the mundane to the metaphysical realm. This concept corresponded directly to Friedrich's rendering of a similar subject in the paintings *Abbey in an Oak Forest or Monk's Burial* (1810) and *Monastery Cemetery* (1819). Clennell was among the numerous artists who specialized in topographical drawings for antiquarian illustrated treatises, among them *Border Antiquities* (1814–17) by Sir Walter Scott, another antiquarian-poet of great popularity in Germany.

Friedrich also experimented with other fashionable trends which found their point of origin in British antiquarian literature. These included the use of strong chiaroscuro in order to convey a sense of mysticism through illuminating nocturnal scenes from within a central source, such as the rays of a full moon or a lantern. Having arrived in England via the Netherlandish Caravaggists, this technique was best reproduced in mezzotint, but later replaced by the aquatint. Less successfully, it was recreated through engravings which offered longer-lasting plates while sacrificing the aquatint's 'photographic' effect of immediacy. Friedrich's *The Ruin of Eldena at Night* (1803) (Figure 6.8) reflects his understanding of manipulating lighting to introduce a mystical context without compromising an architecturally accurate rendering of the subject at hand. Friedrich drawings that both reconstructed and deconstructed architectural sites, such as the illustration as ruins of Meissen Cathedral and Jacobi Church in Greifswald, ought not to be judged as deviations from topographical faithfulness but rather as an enquiry into the anatomy of a structure under the impact of time. *Jacobi Church in Greifswald as Ruin* (1815) (Figure 6.9) can be interpreted in just such an antiquarian-preservationist context as a *memento mori* to non-classical German culture, and contains a homage to the established British drive towards preserving the past.

Friedrich's interest in national antiquarianism can be understood further as a reaction to the oppressive predominantly classically-oriented curriculum at the Copenhagen Academy which he had left only recently. Several young artists of his generation, among them Philipp Otto Runge, reacted negatively to the mechanical drawing exercises of copying from plaster casts of classical sculpture under a faculty obsessed with neo-classical ideals. Of the Academy's faculty, Hans Wiedewelt had been Winckelmann's travelling companion and guide, and Berthel Thorvaldsen was later appointed Secretary of the new Archaeological Institute of the German Empire. Not only did their neo-classical theories echo the Roman view of a Barbaric northern Europe, they even denounced non-classical architecture of the Middle Ages in the words of Vasari as 'monstrous and barbarous . . . confusion and disorder'.[37]

Friedrich, as one of the first generation of academy-trained artists, saw himself as more than a mere artisan. Like Kosegarten and Quistorp, he saw himself as part of a scholarly circle with a scientific approach to recording accurately picturesque and antiquarian sites.[38] On the other hand, he wished to translate mystical and spiritual concerns of a metaphysical nature into his work, as Kosegarten did in his poetry. Many of his own statements, dating from a later period, such as that 'a painter should not merely paint what he sees in front of him', do not refer to his topographical drawings and must be understood in a poetic and metaphorical fashion.[39] Rather, the induction of mystical overtones through the manipulation of landscape and atmospheric conditions needs to be seen as referencing a performative 'bardic' tradition that aimed to convey emotional and spiritual experiences. In any case, Friedrich was best known as a draftsman by his contemporaries, and this is reflected in Goethe's attempt to commission him as an illustrator of scientific treatises. It can be safely assumed that many of Friedrich's architectural drawings were commissioned by the extended antiquarian circle with whom he was in contact and to whom records indicate sales.[40] From an economic point of view, antiquarian draftsmanship was commercially more lucrative than painting, which was more time-consuming and expensive and did not guarantee the predictable and immediate financial return of a commission. Nevertheless, many of Friedrich's topographical drawings evolved into larger-scale paintings or served as prototypical models that could be modified beyond their function as architectural records towards the more popular *vedute* for a less scholarly-minded audience.

Notes

1. Letter from Schleyermacher to Pastor Ehrenfried von Willich, 25 June 1801, reproduced in Rainer Schmitz (ed.), *Bis nächstes Jahr auf Rügen. Briefe von Friedrich Daniel Ernst Schleyermacher* (Berlin, Evangelische Verlagstanstalt, 1984) p.18. Friedrich's correspondence refers to contact with this group, as well as to sales of his works to several of its members. Muhrbeck shared a close friendship with Friedrich's admired friend Ernst Moritz Arndt. Both Furchau and Arndt tutored Kosegarten's son Johann Gottfried Ludwig. See *Caspar David Friedrich in Briefen und Bekenntnissen* (Berlin, Rogner & Bernhard, 1968) and Albert Boime, *Art in an Age of Bonapartism* (Chicago University Press, 1994), p.527.

2. Franck's antiquarian collection, including an extensive holding of minerals, was transferred to the British Museum after his death.

3. Adolf Friedrich Furchau, *Arkona: Heldengedicht in 20 Gesängen* (Berlin, Duncher u. Humblot, 1828).

4. Adolf Friedrich Furchau, *Die Insel Rügen; zwölf Gedichte* (Stralund, Struck, 1830). See also Caspar David Friedrich, *Skizzenbuch aus den Jahren 1806 und 1818*, ed. Ludwig Grote (Berlin, Mann, 1944), pp.11 and 18.

5. 'Viele Fremde, die Rügen im Sommer bereisten, nahm er gastfrei bei sich auf, da das Dorf wenig Gelegenheit zu einem anständigen Unterkommen darbot; sie verweilten mitunter mehrere Tage bei ihm und er begleitete sie nach den sehenswerten Gegenden der Insel.' Johann Gottfried Ludwig Kosegarten, *Leben Ludwig Gotthard Kosegarten* (Greifswald, Universitäts-Buchhandlung, 1827), p.171.

6. See Helmut Boersch-Supan, *Caspar David Friedrich: Gemälde, Druckgraphik und bildmässige Zeichnungen* (Munich, Prestel, 1973), p.217.

7. Gerhard Eimer, *Caspar David Friedrich und die Gothik* (Hamburg, von der Ropp, 1963), p.10.

8. For Friedrich's commercial graphic ventures until 1800, see Timothy F. Mitchell, 'From *Vedute* to Vision: The Importance of Popular Imagery in Friedrich's Development of Romantic Landscape Painting', *The Art Bulletin*, 114:2 (1982), pp.414–23.

9. Friedrich, *Skizzenbuch*, p.7.

10. *Ibid.*, p.11.

11. Johann Jakob Grümbke, *Streifzüge durch das Rügenland* (rpt, 1803: Leipzig, Edition Leipzig, 1988), p.43.

12. William Gilpin, *Observations on the Western parts of England* (London, T. Cadell, jnr and W. Davies, 1798); this was published in German as, William Gilpin, *Reise durch Westengland und durch die Insel Wight* (Leipzig, Keefeld, 1805).

13. William Gilpin, *Biographie, oder, Lebensbeschreibung der bekannten Reformatoren vor Luthero, nämlich des Johann Wikliff, und seiner berühmtesten Nachfolger des Lord Cobhams, Johann Huss, Hieronymi von Prag und Ziska* (Frankfurt and Leipzig, Mezler, 1769).

14. *Caspar David Friedrich in Briefen und Bekenntnissen*, p.39.

15. Apparently without satisfying results; Friedrich's etchings are dated between 1794–5, 1799–1800, and 1802 through to 1804.

16. *Caspar David Friedrich in Briefen und Bekenntnissen*, pp.27–30.

17. See Johanna Schopenhauer, *Journal des Luxus und der Moden* (Weimar, 1810), p.693.

18. *Die Freimüthige oder Berlinische Zeitung für Gebildete und unbefangene Leser* (Berlin, Sander, 1803), p.255.

19. Gotthard Ludwig Theobul Kosegarten, *Rhapsodièen*, 3 vols (Leipzig, Gräff, 1790–1801), pp.37–76.

20. Thomas Garnett, *Observations on a tour through the Highlands and part of the Western isles of Scotland, particularly Staffa and Icolmkill*, 2 vols (London, T. Cadell, 1800), 1, p.254.

21. *Ibid.*, 2, pp.60-61.

22. Richard Gough, *British topography. Or, An historical account of what has been done for illustrating the topographical antiquities of Great Britain and Ireland* (London, T. Payne & Son, and J. Nichols, 1780), p.xxvi.

23. *Ibid.*, p.xiv.

24. *Ibid.*, pp.xx–xxi.

25. Willi Wegewitz, *Das Abenteuer der Archäologie* (Oldenburg, Isensee, 1994), p.10.

26. Karl Nernst, *Karl Nernsts Wanderungen durch Rügen*, ed. L.T. Kosegarten (rpt, 1800: Peenemunde, Dietrich, 1994), pp.17–18.

27. Thomas Gray, *The Works of Thomas Gray*, 2 vols (London, J. Mawman, 1816), 2, p.60.

28. Even short distances on frequently travelled roads were not managed without effort, as is illustrated by the schedule of the London to Oxford coach which, by 1760, ran only three times a week and took one full day under the best of summer conditions. Stuart Piggott, *Ruins in A Landscape* (Edinburgh University Press, 1976), p.124.

29. Thomas Pennant, *Reise durch Schottland und die Hebridischen Inseln*, 2 vols, trans. J.B. Ebeling (Leipzig, Wengandsche Buchhandlung, 1779–80).

30. Johann Jakob Grümbke, *Streifzüge durch das Rügenland. In Briefen von Indigena* (Altona, n.p., 1805). Grümbke (1771–1849) was a colourful character who, after his student years at the universities of Göttingen, Erlangen and Greifswald returned to his hometown Bergen and embarked on a serious study of the history of Rügen. As an amateur artist, he also recorded the sites of the island under the Latin *nom d'artiste* 'Indigina' (the aboriginal).

31. Grümbke's tour of Rügen was published in English translation, as early as 1807, in R. Phillips, *A Collection of Modern and Contemporary Voyages and Travels*, 5 vols (London, R. Phillips, 1807), 5.

32. In 1777, the Lübeck lawyer Friedrich Overbeck even proposed to establish an intellectual colony in the unspoiled paradise of the South Sea in a letter to the playwright Anton Matthias Sprickmann. See Heinz Jansen, *Aus dem Goettinger Hainbund. Overbeck und Sprickmann. Ungedruckte Briefe* (Münster, Regensberg, 1933), p.159.

33. 'Gewagt bleibt es, die ausschliesslich sogannten Hühnengräber, die, unterscheidbar durch Form und Inhalt von den Kegelgräbern und den späteren Wenden-Begräbnissen, auf unsern Waldhöhen, unter moosigem Gestein sich noch in grosser Zahl finden, den Kelten zuzuweisen'. Friedrich Wilhelm Barthold, *Geschichte von Rügen und Pommern* (Hamburg, Perthes, 1839), p.89.

34. Gotthard Ludwig Theobul Kosegarten, *Briefe eines Schiffbrüchigen* (rpt, 1793: Bremen, Edition Temmen, 1994), pp.67–8.

35. Karl Nernst, *Karl Nernsts Wanderungen durch Rügen*, ed. L.T. Kosegarten (rpt, 1800: Düsseldorf, Dietrich, 1994), p.17.

36. Barthold, *Rügen und Pommern*, p.121.

37. Vasari, *Lives*, trans. J. C. Bondanella and P. Bondanella (Oxford University Press, 1991), p.3.

38. For Friedrich's interest in science, see Boime, *Art in an Age of Bonapartism*, pp.592–6.

39. Lorenz Eitner, *Neoclassicism and Romanticism 1750–1850*, 2 vols (Englewood Cliffs, Prentice Hall, 1970), 2, p.55.

40. See note no. 1.

6.1   W. Cooke after a drawing by F. Nicholson, *Netley Abbey (Northeast Aspect)* (1806), engraving

6.2   Caspar David Friedrich, *Ruin of Eldena* (1825), pencil and ink

6.3   William Gilpin, *Valley of Tweed with Melrose Abbey* (1786), aquatint

6.4   William H. Watts, *Dunkeld Cathedral* (1800), aquatint

6.5   Caspar David Friedrich, *Dolmen Grave* (after 1800), pen and ink

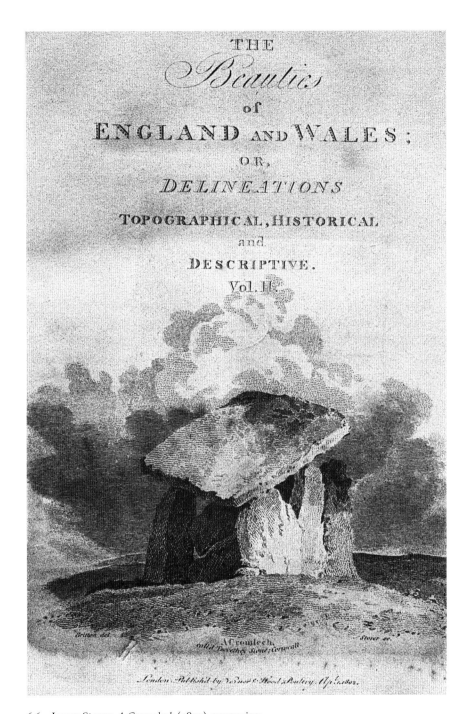

THE
Beauties
of
ENGLAND AND WALES;
OR,
DELINEATIONS
TOPOGRAPHICAL, HISTORICAL
and
DESCRIPTIVE.
Vol. II.

Britton del.

Storer sc.

A Cromlech,
called Devethy Stone, Cornwall.

London Publish'd by Vernor & Hood, Poultry, Ap.l. 1802.

6.6   James Storer, *A Cromelech* (1802), engraving

Engraved by W. Wallis, from a Drawing by L. Clennell, for the Antiquarian Itinerary.

Door of Peterbro Church.

6.7   W. Wallis after Luke Clennell, *Door of Peterbro Church* (1816), engraving

6.8   Caspar David Friedrich, *The Ruin of Eldena at Night* (1803), oil on canvas

6.9   Caspar David Friedrich, *Jacobi Church in Greifswald as a Ruin* (1815), pencil and ink

7

The extra-illustration of London:
the gendered spaces and practices of antiquarianism in the
late eighteenth century

Lucy Peltz

Extra-illustration: reading antiquarianism at the margins

Extra-illustration, often described as 'grangerization', is a process whereby published texts were customized by the cutting and pasting of thematically linked prints and watercolours. The range of titles that lent itself to this type of handling confirms one early twentieth-century commentator's opinion that 'Every book ever issued from the press is capable of some sort of extra illustration'.[1] However, research carried out in numerous libraries in Britain and the United States has proved that the greater proportion of books that underwent extra-illustration was of an antiquarian bias. Many of these books, like the Reverend James Granger's *Biographical History of England* (1769), treated biographical subjects and thus became repositories of engraved portraits of illustrious figures.[2] Antiquarian topography, which could equally encompass portraits of places, people and things, was another favourite genre for extra-illustration. As this fashionable mode of collecting and arranging diverse illustrations with antiquarian texts was carried out with considerable constancy, throughout the late eighteenth and early nineteenth centuries, it is, I think, all the more surprising that so little scholarly attention has been paid to its cultural and social implications.[3] By viewing extra-illustration as an antiquarian practice, I will here consider this novel method of enjoying texts on England's past as a symptom of both the prevailing perceptions and popularization of antiquarianism during this period.

I shall begin with an individuated artefact, which is also a paradigm. On 13 July 1811, the British Museum register of donations recorded that 'the will of Mr Crowle had transmitted ... the account of London by Pennant, in 14 Volumes, illustrated with Portraits Views Plans &c'.[4] This handsome bequest, made by John Charles Crowle and entitled *Some Account of London. By Pennant. Illustrated with Portraits,Views, Plans, &c. &c. &c* (Figure 7.1), is justly deemed one of the most celebrated and opulent examples of extra-illustration.[5] As his specially commissioned title-pages announce, Crowle's suite of volumes was based on Thomas Pennant's enormously successful antiquarian survey of London, which was first published as *Of London* in 1790.[6] Through the process of cut and paste, Crowle expanded and transformed a copy of the third edition of Pennant's single-volume, quarto publication into a lavishly bound suite of fourteen volumes, all inlaid to imperial folio size.[7] These volumes encompass thousands of supplementary engravings and watercolours garnered from a variety of sources and organized in sequence with the pages of Pennant's text. Crowle's interpolations vary from individually published prints to plates culled from the numerous illustrated antiquarian accounts of London which were issued, almost annually, after the success of John Strype's edition of Stow's *Survey* in 1720.[8] Moreover, from the inclusion of James Caulfield's etching of the Tradescant's house, we witness that Crowle was not above recourse to the many entrepreneurial publications produced specifically to exploit the growing fashion for extra-illustration (Figure 7.2).[9]

With at least thirty surviving examples, Pennant's *Some Account of London* can be said to have been the prime text to satisfy the craze for extra-illustration between the 1790s and the 1860s. The popular and anecdotal style of Pennant's antiquarian survey of the historical events and people associated with topographical locations made it eminently suitable for extra-illustration. The text, which Pennant's German translator praised for its 'sorglose Ordnung ... ei ner [*sic*] Beschreibung' (carefree order of description), readily lent itself to the incorporation of a miscellany of historical and contemporary prints of portraits, buildings, antique objects and views as visual elucidation.[10] This is demonstrated in the page spread where Crowle illustrated the narrative of the Tradescants' gardens and museum with three seventeenth-century portraits by the celebrated Wenceslaus Hollar (1607–77) alongside a modern etching of their house (Figure 7.2). This juxtaposition of rare and valuable prints with the widely circulated products of the 'Pennant Industry' suggests that the principles governing extra-illustration were less those of connoisseurial print collecting than that of an individual reading of the text. As a result, the end product of extra-illustration was a customized version of a mass-disseminated book that represented the owner's engagement and intimacy with the contents of that volume. In this regard it is helpful to observe the poet George Crabbe's comparison between the 'studious care' of 'our patient Fathers' who 'Till every note and every comment known ... mark'd the spacious margins with their own' with modern man whose 'nicer palates lighter labours seek'.[11] In sum, extra-illustration can be understood as a fashionable and perhaps playful extension of the traditional antiquarian practice of annotating texts and, arguably, as a symbolic form of conversation with Pennant's published account of London.

Given the extent and unwieldy nature of Crowle's extra-illustrated volumes and the fact that he, himself, valued them at over £5 000, they could only ever have been produced or enjoyed in the home.[12] It is this issue that leads me to consider extra-illustration in the light of Stuart Piggott's statement that, from the mid-eighteenth century, the popularization of antiquarianism saw field-work largely replaced by 'ponderous but ineffective dilettantism'.[13] During this period, in Piggott's estimation, the 'necessity of an empirical approach was forgotten' and was replaced by a 'new antiquarian public' who were 'anxious to *read* antiquarian literature'.[14] While Piggott's opinions on the evolution of new antiquarian practices and audiences help us to understand the cultural climate in which extra-illustration arose, it is important to consider the reasons for this polarization. From Horace Walpole's acerbic comment that 'The best merit of the Society lies in their prints; for their volumes, no mortal will ever touch them but an antiquary', we can infer that the popularization of antiquarianism was due, on the one hand, to developments in antiquarian publishing and, on the other, was related to the problematic reputation of the London Society of Antiquaries in the late eighteenth century.[15]

The shift in antiquarian methods from active fieldwork to passive consumption is marked by the increasingly refined, disseminated engravings of the Society, whose director, Richard Gough, acknowledged this situation in 1780, when he lamented that, with the drop in attendance at meetings and new members joining purely for the 'expensive engravings', the Society had declined from its 'Meridian Glory'.[16] While these engravings were intended as a privilege of membership, in 1756 the Society decided to make them even more widely available through the separate print shops of Boydell and Tovey.[17] Arguably, it was these publications, along with the growing industry in commercial and popular antiquarian texts by authors such as Francis Grose, James Peller Malcolm and, indeed, by Thomas Pennant, which not only encouraged an antiquarian diaspora away from the London Society of Antiquaries but also promulgated antiquarian taste to new, more diversified audiences.[18]

Evidence of the wide-scale relocation of antiquarian activities to the domestic sphere can be found in a number of sources. In 1780, George Allan wrote to Thomas Pennant complaining that 'the frequency of my being from home, has made all antiquarian matters at a stand'.[19] Pennant himself, although still publishing, declared, in 1777, that he had 'quite lost [his] spirit of rambling' and had no 'desire to leave the fire-side'.[20] That is not to suggest that antiquarianism, itself, fell out of fashion. With this antiquarian diaspora came the rise of novel pursuits, such as extra-illustration. While the wealth of antiquarian publications which could be consumed in the home may have facilitated, even accelerated, the evolution of this antiquarian diaspora, they were not the reason for its development. If we observe a selection of typical literary and visual representations of antiquarians, I believe we may discern several of the key factors that did encourage this antiquarian retreat to the domestic sphere.

The antiquarian and the fragment: gender, propriety and antiquarian satire

Thomas Pownall's *A Treatise on the Study of Antiquities* (1782) is one of many contemporary antiquarian texts which affords us some idea of the positive ideals with which antiquarians often justified their activities. In it the humanist, and specifically nationalist, qualities of antiquarianism were vaunted as a 'true and useful learning' which lead to 'the knowledge of our own country'.[21] There, following Francis Bacon's motif, he likened history to a shipwreck and proposed that the antiquarians' duty was to salvage some 'fragments of its bills of lading ... come to shore'.[22] From Pownall's unusual mercantile metaphor we can deduce that he hoped to present antiquarianism as a by-product of a modern commercial world; it also indicates the social diversity of the audience that he expected to reach. Despite his glorification of the fragment, it was evident even to Pownall that this subject should be approached with caution. Sensitive to the disjunction between the antiquarians' self-perception and more popular opinions, Pownall focused on the need for taxonomic systems in which such fragments could be organized. To illustrate this point he warned that 'to make cumbrous collections of numberless particulars, merely because they are fragments, and to admire them merely as they are antique; is not in the spirit of learning, but the mere doating of superannuation'.[23]

Such salvaged fragments were the source of some contention. It was in the light of the contrast between the liberal requirement for abstract and general knowledge and the comparative vulgarity of self-indulgent and singular interests that the antiquarians' social propriety was consistently attacked.[24] In his interpretation of the discourses of civic humanism, John Barrell has explained that the liberal and mechanic states existed in structural opposition; if narrowness and the inability to abstract material concerns typified the mechanic, then the antiquarian, who was widely scorned as without systems or conclusions, was equally held to be at risk of social transgression and 'genuine absurdity'.[25] This anxiety was directly expressed in relation to antiquarian pursuits by Samuel Paterson who, in 1772, nostalgically defined an opposition between the 'sober and judicious' antiquary of former times and the modern antiquary, whose materialism and self-gratification were typified by a love of oddities.[26] Paterson feared that the modern-day antiquarian was interested in things purely for their singularity; in short, for their detail. According to another detractor (who claimed to be a Fellow of the Society of Antiquaries), it was 'the *rust* of antiquity [that] has destroyed the *polish* of good manners'.[27] Here, the implication was that the antique fragment, which was the essence of their study, had contaminated the antiquarians' most fundamental social duties. We might therefore assume that the Society laid itself open to outright criticism when, in 1784, it made provisions for a draftsman to attend meetings and record the 'fragments of antiquity' under consideration; these were then published in *Archaeologia,* under the arbitrary heading 'Curious Communications'.[28] Consequently, the Fellows were encouraged to marvel at these fragments without the former textual anchorage of scholarly 'disserta-tion'.[29] By appearing to separate the duties of liberal abstraction from owner-ship and observation, and freeing the collector from his traditional role as expert, the Society as an urban club was no longer considered as a space for rational exchange. It became a target for charges of excess, intellectual impotence and social aberration; themes which were consistently expressed in graphic satire.

Since the early seventeenth century, graphic and literary satire had habitu-ally attacked antiquarians according to their social and sexual propriety.[30] Two typical examples sharing similar narrative structures and repeated motifs will suffice to illustrate this stock-in-trade theme.[31] The first is Francis Grose's etching, *Antiquarians, Peeping into Boadicia's Night Urn* (1770) (cover illustra-tion) and the second is *The Antiquarians* (1772) (Figure 7.3), published in the *Oxford Magazine*.[32] In these, the chamber pot did not signify some grand pro-ject of social or anthropological history. The commentary which accompanied the print in the *Oxford Magazine* made this obvious in asking 'Of what consequence is it to the public whether the chamber-utensil of Cleopatre was silver, iron … or clay?'[33] Instead, for an audience primed for satire, the chamber pot was a titillating signifier of the antiquarian's inappropriate fasci-nation with vulgar objects.[34] It spoke eloquently of the useless erudition and wasted resources associated with pedantry; a charge that was often directed at the antiquarian.

Samuel Johnson's *Dictionary* defined the pedant as 'a man vain of low know-ledge' or 'awkwardly ostentatious of his literature' and, significantly, as 'a reserve of puerility we have not shaken off from school'.[35] Pedantry thus encoded a sexual subtext that brought masculine virility into question through its associations with immaturity and impotence, both of which contradicted the premise of effective masculine leadership of family and nation.[36] In the *Oxford Magazine* engraving we see a vain, mindless fop looking through a tele-scope the wrong way to signify his narrow-minded insularity and self-interest (Figure 7.3). The phallic emblem in his wig tells us, in no uncertain terms, how to interpret him. In keeping with the tone of the accompanying text, his credu-lous companions are being duped by a charlatan, whose art seeks to invest the mundane with an aura of age and importance.[37] Equally, in the other print, the urinating dog signals the opposition between the pointless erudition of pedantry and the weighty tomes of true scholarship. Patently, the message of both these images was that the self-indulgent and introspective antiquarian, who believed his function to be national enlightenment, had completely missed his mark.

Antiquarians, Peeping into Boadicia's Night Urn and *The Antiquarians* were typical satires of antiquarian behaviour, insofar as they situated the spectacle of masculine transgression in a homosocial society setting.[38] As effective satire depends upon the immediate recognition of its theme, we can take this recurrent trope as proof of the widespread awareness of the activities of the Society of Antiquaries. While I have already mentioned that the Society became more accountable with the commercial dissemination of their publications, their growing public reputation as ineffectual, self-indulgent and divisive can have done little to help their cause. For example, in 1802, following the publicly waged battle between the draftsman James Carter and the architect James Wyatt (over the latter's restoration work at Salisbury and Durham Cathedrals), one anonymous commentator reflected with irony on 'the lessened and degraded ... title of Socius ... once so honourable and so much valued', a further indication that the reputation and work of the Society of Antiquaries was increasingly called into question.[39] So although satire, in itself, is not usually thought of as an agent of change, when intertwined with existing social tension it could act as a catalyst. Horace Walpole's reaction to Samuel Foote's theatrical satire, *The Nabob* (1772), is a case in point. In 1772, he wrote to the Reverend William Mason that 'Foote's last new piece blows us up ... as I do not love to be answerable for any fooleries but my own, I think I shall scratch my name out of their books.'[40] As Walpole was in the middle of a personal vendetta against the Society this reasoning may well have been a thin pretext; nevertheless his reluctance to be viewed as part of this collective spectacle gave him an excuse to resign from the Society and continue his antiquarianism from the retreat of his gentleman's seat.[41]

The spaces of extra-illustration: retirement, antiquarian leisure and the family

Retirement from London, 'for a person who has passed the greatest part of his life in a large and populous city', was viewed as the reward for a lifetime's industry.[42] Judging from the sentiment repeated by a number of authors, in the post-Rousseau, yet capitalist, climate of the late eighteenth century, the benefits of retirement were idealized as those of leisure, honour, refinement and an end to urban anxieties.[43] Furthermore, men retired from a public sphere gendered masculine to a domestic one gendered feminine; thus the pedantry identified with the homosocial club could be overcome in the feminized ethos of the home. James Fordyce, one of the Scottish Moralists, also advised that male manners would be refined in the company of virtuous women.[44] It is, of course, important to recognize that domestic retreat did not preclude engagement with the metropolis, nor did it limit the antiquarian's participation in the modern world. He could continue to engage with the public sphere through his freedom of movement and consumption of the many antiquarian orientated commodities which were regularly published.[45] Arguably, the antiquarian esprit was not lost in domestic retreat. It was, instead, modified to this familial setting. Extra-illustration was one novel practice that responded to the increased availability of antiquarian words and images and reflected the domestic location of their consumption.

John Charles Crowle's celebrated *Some Account of London* has already been cited as the prime example of an extra-illustrated Pennant. Unfortunately, however, there are no archives of Crowle's personal correspondence and so little is known about his life, his antiquarian interests or his collecting. In contrast, there is a wealth of surviving information which sheds light on the trend-setting activities of the MP Richard Bull (1721–1805), whose fascination with extra-illustration was originally derived from his passion for engraved historic portrait heads.[46] He is believed to have been the first person to marry published texts and images together in this way. His first venture into extra-illustration, between 1769 and 1774, produced his renowned thirty-six-volume version of James Granger's *A Biographical History of England*. Following his retirement from Parliament, in 1780, he began to focus in earnest on his favourite pastime, producing at least sixty-eight extra-illustrated suites of volumes; amongst these customized volumes are versions of nearly all of his friend Thomas Pennant's works.[47] Although there is evidence to suggest that Bull did extra-illustrate a copy of Pennant's *Some Account of London*, this project remains untraced, and so I shall now consider his two-volume, extra-illustrated presentation manuscript copy of *From London to Dover* (*c.*1789).[48] Similar to *Some Account of London*, this unpublished text expounds antiquarian topography and historical anecdotes and blends these with an account of Pennant's Thames journey, the natural history of the river-bank and patriotic descriptions of naval and commercial strength.[49] The highly ornamental extra-illustration of Bull's *From London to Dover*, like many of his other sixty-eight titles, was carried out, with his daughters Catherine (d.1795) and Elizabeth (d.1809), at Northcourt, his seat in the Isle of Wight (Figures 7.4, 7.5, 7.8 and 7.9).

In this familial context, extra-illustration not only signified Richard Bull's own retired leisure but it also represented the dynamics of his family unit.[50] While a father may rightfully have been conscious of his daughter's need to 'fill up … in a tolerably agreeable way, some of the many solitary hours you must necessarily pass at home', in keeping with his judicious concern for his daughters' reputation, Bull never actually referred to their part in his extra-illustration.[51] Instead, his passing comments were of his daughters' frailty and sickliness and, most significantly, of their improved health when returned from London to the Isle of Wight.[52] We know nothing of Catherine's extra-illustration, but Elizabeth's involvement is confirmed in a retrospective inscription on the back of the British Museum's version of a privately published mezzotint portrait of her. This proclaimed that she was 'deeply interested in her father's favourite pursuit, and in herself no less remarkable in her attachment to the same pleasurable amusement'.[53] Her participation in her father's *From London to Dover* is evident through the intricate, even expert, quality of the *découpage* decoration and pasting (Figure 7.4), all paper-based skills which were repeatedly promoted for the 'improvement of Young Ladies' in the many didactic manuals such as Hannah Robertson's *The Young Ladies School of Arts* (1757).[54] Maria Edgeworth's comment that 'a young lady ... is nobody, and nothing, without accomplishments; they are as necessary to her as fortune' reminds us that the importance of such feminine accomplishments was not simply lodged in a woman's private entertainment but also implicated her whole family and its reputation.[55] However, as women of substantial fortune, neither Catherine nor Elizabeth ever married, and it is probably as a result of their independence that they could move beyond such 'trifling', 'sedentary occupations' as japanning or scraps, to extra-illustration, which represented their engagement with texts of a topographical and antiquarian nature (Figure 7.5).[56]

As the extra-illustration of Pennant's *From London to Dover* combined this need for accomplishments with topographical knowledge it can be understood as a 'serious and instructive occupation'.[57] By embellishing a book with immediately accessible representations of illustrious people, maps and views, the extra-illustrated volume served to dramatize the antiquarian city, and to pose the print as a substitute for and souvenir of urban experience. This view is supported in the marketing device of Thomas Downes's *A Copious Index to Pennant's Account of London* (1814), which was published to encourage and guide extra-illustrators.[58] There, Downes manipulated the Horatian topos of *utile et dulci* in his assertion that 'the practice of illustrating ... is attended with so much amusement and information, by familiarizing the memory with persons and things, which would otherwise escape observation, that it is justly deemed an employment worthy of the leisure hours'.[59] Similar benefits were also articulated in Richard Bull's obituary, where extra-illustration was likened to 'Chronology, of essential service to historical literature, by contributing to render its images, clear, distinct and impressive'.[60] While the process of selecting subjects for illustration demanded a close reading of Pennant's narrative, the final, unwieldy product was, undeniably, more a spectacle than a text to be read.

The spectacle of Bull's volumes was not just enjoyed by his immediate family. They were also circulated around his social network and carried with him, on genteel visits, to entertain his hosts and share his amusements. The notoriety and celebration of his extra-illustration was, for example, noted in Lady Mary Coke's journal which remarked that Mr Walpole 'showed me a prodigious fine work ... by Mr Bull; his own *Royal and Noble Authors* ... with the prints of all the ... Personages mentioned; 'tis indeed a fine performance and must have been a very expensive one.'[61] It should also be noted that Bull exhibited his volumes beyond his immediate social group. A letter tipped into his extra-illustrated *Royal and Noble Authors*, which communicated 'how much amusement the selection of Portraits has afforded', reveals that these also found their way to Buckingham House for Queen Charlotte's entertainment.[62] Together, these two examples prove that such opportunities for display helped to identify Bull as a man of taste to a heterosocial and domestically located audience.

Despite the reiterated over-view of extra-illustration as 'the Contents of many expensive Galleries and Museums ... reduced into the narrow Compass of a few volumes', the impact of the whole was always disrupted by reference to its individual parts, especially as it was suggested that these should be 'minutely investigated'.[63] Consequently, the retired gentleman, just like the more publicly visible antiquarian who pursued such pastimes, was at risk of equivalent accusations of revelling in the detail and, more problematically, of a self-indulgent, potentially effeminate engagement with the material rather than the abstract. While the recognition that Bull's daughters had embellished these pages might have helped to preserve his masculine propriety in light of the materiality of extra-illustration, it was probably out of respect that observers rarely commented upon their work. Only Pennant, who was intimate with the Bulls, acknowledged Elizabeth's and Catherine's practice. In one letter he stated that 'I am in love with the performance in your book: & envy the fair fingers you possess which so adroitly puzzle about the inserted & non-inserted, a prodigious spectacle'.[64] In comparing the Misses Bull's dextrous handiwork (Figure 7.4) with Thomas Pennant's own, more cumbersome, extra-illustrated *Some Account of London* (Figure 7.6), we can assess the impact of a concept of skill differentiated by gender.[65] Another letter begged for Bull's daughters' recipe, for pasting prints to paper, as 'I & Moses ... bungle dreadfully', appealing again to the idea of male awkwardness with this traditionally female pursuit.[66] The 'Moses' referred to in this letter was Pennant's self-taught artist and servant, Moses Griffith. His mechanic craft and dependent status can be seen in his self-fashioning as 'PAINTER to THOMAS PENNANT, Esq', who formulated his status in opposition to Pennant's liberal persona (Figure 7.7). As this advertisement was undoubtedly published with the guidance (and permission) of his master, we can see that both Bull and Pennant sought to preserve their ideal masculine liberality through a division of labour which devolved the mechanic part of extra-illustrating to those who were considered more 'naturally' attuned to these skills; to a woman, on the one hand and to a servant, on the other.

Griffith's advertisement indicates a further assertion of masculine liberality in the project of extra-illustrating. Under Pennant's auspices, Griffith offered his services to other extra-illustrators of books. He produced heraldry and views to order and copied unobtainable prints and portraits, which allowed the extra-illustrator a greater degree of control than that afforded by the serendipity of shopping for prints. The ability to include watercolour copies after scarce prints such as the portrait of Lusty Packington (Figure 7.8), was not only a means of achieving a completeness but also served to define the cultural hegemony of the extra-illustrator as patron. Given that most extra-illustrated volumes were based on published books, the desire to reinvent a comparatively 'mass-produced' volume as a customized object, filled with rare and valuable prints, was common among extra-illustrators. However, we should not assume that Bull's pleasure at making a disseminated object unique was somehow in tension with the prevailing market economy or the ideology of social relations. He was equally willing to deal directly with artists and printmakers and to incorporate contemporary reproductive prints and modern views of sites such as Thomas Ripley's fashionable Custom House (Figure 7.9), the Adelphi or Somerset House. In fact, I conclude that the will to extra-illustrate arose from the combined impact of engraved historical por-trait-head collecting and the increased output and variety of contemporary print production. The reason that such diverse prints were deemed suitable for this sort of handling was that, within the antiquarian mentality, engravings could be principally valued as records, or didactic representations, rather than as aesthetic objects with their own intrinsic value. The implication of this excessive consumption was, I suggest, instrumental to the justification of people who were both antiquarians and extra-illustrators. As Alderman John Boydell had pointed out in promoting his Shakespeare Gallery in 1794, 'Engraving employs many persons [and] it not only brings money into, but prevents money from going out of this kingdom'.[67] Extra-illustration gained popularity in the 1790s, when the purchase of such English commodities could be justified in patriotic terms and as evidence of the antiquarian's participation in the modern world of goods. Additionally, as John Britton reflected in *Londinum Illustratum* (1819), a descriptive sale catalogue for an extra-illus-trated Pennant, such a 'vast collection … may be regarded as a library of topo-graphic and antiquarian information', which, at the same time, offered 'ocular proof' of 'the unparalleled Metropolis of England … its extent, treasures, and national fame'.[68] In sum, the extra-illustration of London was not just a brico-lage of problematic fragments 'in remembrance of the ancient state of

London', it was also tangible proof of the antiquarian's gentility, patriotism and investment in the contemporary economy.[69]

Notes

*   Much of the research for this chapter was carried out while I was George C. Cooper Fellow at the Lewis Walpole Library, Yale University. I would like to thank Janice Peltz, Anne Puetz, Marcia Pointon and Michael Willis for their support in preparing this chapter.

1. W.L. Andrews, *Of the Extra Illustration of Books* (London, Zaehnsdorf Cambridge Works, 1900), p.13.

2. The most frequent, and the most famous, biographical text to yield to extra-illustration was the Revd James Granger, *A Biographical History of England, from Egbert the Great to the Revolution: Consisting of Characters Disposed in Different Classes, and Adapted to a Methodical Catalogue of Engraved British Heads*, 5 vols (London, T. Davies, 1769). For an interesting discussion of this genre of extra-illustration see Marcia Pointon, *Hanging the Head: Portraiture and Social Formation in Eighteenth-Century England* (London and New Haven, Yale University Press, 1993), pp.53–78.

3. There are only two articles which specifically address the subject of extra-illustration. These are Bernard Adams, 'A Regency pastime: the extra-illustration of Thomas Pennant's "Of London" ', *The London Journal*, 8:2 (Winter 1982), pp.123–39 and Robert R. Wark, 'The gentle pastime of extra-illustrating books', *The Huntington Library Quarterly*, 56:2 (Spring 1993), pp.151–65. For a full discussion of the genesis, impact and implications of extra-illustration see Lucy Peltz, 'The extra-illustration of London: leisure, sociability and the antiquarian city in the late eighteenth century', PhD thesis, Manchester University, 1997.

4. *Donations* (1756–1823), 1, fol. 2502, MS, Central Archives, British Museum.

5. Thomas Pennant, *Some Account of London. By Pennant. Illustrated with Portraits, Views, Plans, &c &c &c.*, extra-illustrated by John Charles Crowle in 14 volumes folio. G 1-14, Department of Prints and Drawings, British Museum.

6. Pennant's book was originally published as *Of London* (London, Robert Faulder, 1790). Following the second edition of 1791, all subsequent versions were entitled *Some Account of London*. It went through five separate editions between 1790 and 1814.

7. Thomas Pennant, *Some Account of London*, 3rd edn (London, Robert Faulder, 1793).

8. John Strype, *A Survey of the Cities of London & Westminster & the Borough of Southwark. Containing the Origins, Antiquity, Increase, Present State and Government of those Cities. By John Stow, Citizen and Native of London, Corrected and Improved, in the year 1720, by John Strype, MA A Native of Said City*, 2 vols (London, A. Churchill, J. Knapton, R. Knaplock *et al.*, 1720). For a useful catalogue of illustrated London topography see Bernard Adams, *London Illustrated 1604–1851* (London, The Library Association, 1983).

9. Crowle's volumes drew liberally from print collections such as *Antiquities of London and its Environs; by John Thomas Smith: Dedicated to Sir James Winter Lake, Bart. F.S.A. Containing Views of Houses, Monuments, Statues, and other Curious Remains of Antiquity; Engraved from the Original Subjects and from Original Drawings, Communicated by Several Members of the Society of Antiquaries: with Remarks and References to the Historical Works of Pennant, Lysons, Stowe, Weaver, Camden, Maitland, &c.* (London, J. Sewell, R. Faulder, J. Simco, *et al.*, 1791–1800). I have discussed the 'Pennant Industry' and the commercial aspects of extra-illustration in my PhD thesis, pp.347–56.

10. Pennant, *Beschreibung Von London*, trans. Johann Heinrich Biedmann (Nuremberg, Felbeckersche Buchhandlung, 1791), p.7. My thanks to Anne Puetz for translating this preface for me.

11. George Crabbe, *The Library. A Poem* (London, J. Dodsley, 1781), p.7.

12. John Thomas Smith, *Ancient Topography of London; Embracing Specimens of Sacred, Public and Domestic Architecture, from the Earliest Period to the Time of the Great Fire 1666. Drawn and Etched by John Thomas Smith, Intended as an Accompaniment to the Celebrated Works of Stow, Pennant and Others* (London, John Thomas Smith, 1810–15), p.43.

13. Stuart Piggott, *Ruins in a Landscape: Essays in Antiquarianism* (Edinburgh University Press, 1976), p.50. For Piggott's discussion of the diminution of antiquarian methodology see also pp.1–21.

14. *Ibid.*, p.44.

15. Letter from Horace Walpole to Rev. William Cole, 1 September 1778, reproduced in W. S. Lewis (ed.), *The Yale Edition of Horace Walpole's Correspondence*, 48 vols (Oxford and New Haven, Oxford University Press and Yale University Press, 1937–83), 2, pp.115–18, p.116.

16. Richard Gough, quoted in Joan Evans, *A History of the Society of Antiquaries* (Oxford, The Society of Antiquaries, 1956), p.180.

17. 21 January and 4 February 1756, *Council Minute Books of the Society of Antiquaries of London* (11 May 1754–14 June 1774), 1, n.p.

18. See for example: Francis Grose, *The Antiquarian Repertory: A Miscellany, Intended to Preserve and Illustrate Several Valuable Remains of Old Times*, 4 vols (London, Francis Blyth, J. Sewell and T. Evans, 1775-84) or James Peller Malcolm, *Londinium Redivivum; or, an Ancient History and Modern Description of London* (London, John Nichols, 1803).

19. Letter from George Allan to Thomas Pennant, 21 April 1780, 15421 C, MS National Library of Wales.

20. Thomas Pennant, *The Literary Life of the Late Thomas Pennant, Esq. By Himself* (London, B. & J. White and Robert Faulder, 1793), p.31.

21. Thomas Pownall, *A Treatise on the Study of Antiquities as the Commentary to Historical Learning Sketching out a General Line of Research* (London, J. Dodsley, 1782), p.2.

22. *Ibid.*, p. 52. The metaphor of a shipwreck for history can be found in Francis Bacon, *The Advancement of Learning*, ed. Arthur Johnston (rpt, 1605: Oxford, Clarendon Press, 1974), book 2, ii.1, p.71.

23. *Ibid.*, pp.53–4.

24. John Barrell, *The Political Theory of Painting from Reynolds to Hazlitt* (New Haven and London, Yale University Press, 1986), pp.7–8, p.54.

25. *Ibid.*, p. 8.

26. Samuel Paterson, *Joineriana: or the Book of Scraps*, 2 vols (London, John Johnson, 1772), 'The Antiquary', 1, pp.11–29, p.11.

27. 'F.S.A.', 'Correspondence', *Gentleman's Magazine*, 73:1 (21 February 1803), pp.101–2.

28. 'Meeting of the Council, Feb. 26, 1784', *Orders and Regulations Established by the Council of the Society of Antiquaries; Concerning Forms and Proceedings to be henceforth observed in the transacting of the Business of The Society* (London, J. Nichols, 1784), pp.31–2. 'Curious Communications' first appeared as an appendix in *Archaeologia*, 6 (1785), n.p.

29. *Ibid.*, p.32.

30. It has been suggested that the first example of antiquarian satire was found in John Earle, *Micro-Cosmographie or a Piece of the World Discovered in Essays and Characters* (1628). See Joseph M. Levine, *Dr. Woodward's Shield: History, Science and Satire in Augustan England* (Berkeley, Los Angeles and London, University of California Press, 1977), p.117. One of the best known examples of antiquarian satire is Thomas Rowlandson's *The Three Tours of Dr Syntax*, 3 vols (London, R. Ackermann, 1812–21).

31. For other similar examples, see *The Antiquarians Puzzled, or the Chamber Pot Consultation*, mezzotint, P. Dawe, 1773 which recreated an identical composition to that of *The Antiquarians* (Figure 7.9) in mezzotint, Satire 7582, Department of Prints & Drawings, British Museum. Also *Antiqueerones Peeping into the P**s Pot of Heliogablus*, etching, J. Cawse, 1798, Satire 9296, Department of Prints & Drawings, British Museum.

32. *Antiquarians, Peeping into Boadicia's Night Urn*, etching, Francis Grose, 1770, was republished, posthumously, under Grose's name in Francis Grose and Thomas Astle, *The Antiquarian Repertory: A Miscellaneous Assemblage of Topography, History, Biography, Customs, and Manners*, 4 vols (rpt, 1775–84: London, E. Jeffery, 1807–9) 1, 'Rules for Drawing Caricaturas: with an Essay on Comic Painting', pp.11–21, after p.16. *The Antiquarians*, engraving, n.a., 1772, *The Oxford Magazine: or, Universal Museum*, 8 (January 1772), facing p.17.

33. 'T. B.', 'Correspondence', *The Oxford Magazine: or, Universal Museum*, 8 (January 1772), p.16.

34. Barbara M. Benedict comments on this theme in 'The curious attitude in eighteenth-century Britain: observing and owning', *Eighteenth-Century Life*, 14 (November 1990), pp.59–98, p.88.

35. Samuel Johnson, *Dictionary of the English Language*, 2 vols (London, J. & P. Knapton, T. & T. Longman, C. Hitch and L. Hawes *et al.*, 1755).

36. The significance of the 'generative' capacity in the formation of the normative masculine identity has been demonstrated by Randolph Trumbach in his discussion of the more marginalized positions of 'molly' and 'libertine'. See Randolph Trumbach, 'Erotic Fantasy and Male Libertinism in

Enlightenment England', in Lynn Hunt (ed.), *The Invention of Pornography: Obscenity and the Origins of Modernity, 1500–1800* (New York: Zone Books, 1993), pp.253–82, see esp. pp.254–9.

37. 'T. B.' concluded his letter with comments on the industry in fake antiquities and the antiquarian's inability to discern original from copy.

38. For an interesting discussion of the correlation between modes of portraiture and the growing visibility, public recognition and homosociality of the Society of Dilettanti see Shearer West, 'Libertinism and the ideology of male friendship in the portraits of the Society of Dilettanti', *Eighteenth-Century Life*, N.S., 16:2 (May 1992), pp.76–104. There West has drawn a similar conclusion on the problematic nature of sexuality and 'male solidarity' rather than with masculine individualism, p.96.

39. '*.*.', 'Correspondence', *Gentleman's Magazine*, suppl., 72:2 (20 December 1802), pp.1181–3, p. 1181. For a commentary on the Carter/Wyatt debacle, see Evans, *A History of the Society of Antiquaries*, pp.207–10 and 212–14.

40. Letter from Horace Walpole to Rev. William Mason, 21 July 1772. Reproduced in the *Yale Edition of the Correspondence of Horace Walpole*, 28, pp.38–41, p.40.

41. Walpole was offended by Robert Master's paper criticizing his *Historic Doubts on the Life and Reign of King Richard III* (1768). See Evans, *A History of the Society of Antiquaries*, p.166.

42. Edmund Bartell, *Hints for Picturesque Improvements in Ornamental Cottages* (London, J. Taylor, 1804), p.60.

43. The ideals of masculine retirement can be found, for example, in two poems by William Cowper both entitled, 'Retirement', *The Works of William Cowper, Esq.*, ed. Robert Southey, 15 vols (London, Baldwin & Cradock, 1835–7), 8, pp.93–4 and pp.283–90. See also 'On retirement', *The Freemason's Magazine: or, General and Complete Library*, 1 (July 1793), pp.127–9. One of the most famous studies of the topos of retirement in eighteenth-century poetry is, of course, Maynard Mack, *The Garden and the City: Retirement and Politics in the Later Poetry of Pope, 1731–43* (Toronto, Buffalo, New York and London, Oxford University Press, 1969), esp. pp.77–115. G. J. Barker-Benfield, *The Culture of Sensibility: Sex and Society in Eighteenth-Century Britain* (Chicago and London, Chicago University Press, 1992), also provides an interesting analysis of the representation of retirement in sentimental literature, esp. pp.222–3.

44. James Fordyce, *The Character and Conduct of the Female Sex, and the Advantages to be Derived by Young Men from the Society of Virtuous Women* (London, T. Cadell, 1776), p.8.

45. For a discussion of the commodification of antiquarianism see Stephen Bending's chapter in this volume.

46. Bull's archives are now located at Eton College Library, the National Library of Wales and Warwickshire and Northumberland County Records Offices. For a discussion of Richard Bull, see John M. Pinkerton, 'Richard Bull of Ongar, Essex', *The Book Collector*, 28:1 (1978), pp.41–59.

47. Bull's version of Granger is discussed by Pointon, *Hanging the Head*, pp.70–73 and by Wark, 'The gentle pastime of extra-illustrating books', pp. 155–8. For a full list of Bull's extra-illustrated volumes (which updates the one provided by Pinkerton in *The Book Collector*) see the appendix, 'Table of books extra-illustrated by Richard Bull (1721–1805) and his daughters, Catherine (d.1795) and Elizabeth (d.1809)', in my PhD thesis.

48. Richard Bull's extra-illustrated presentation manuscript copy of Thomas Pennant, *From London to Dover*, 2 vols (*c*.1789), is now in the Museum in Docklands, PLA Collection.

49. Thomas Pennant was as much renowned as an antiquarian as he was for the often closely associated study of natural history. The text of *From London to Dover* was published posthumously as Thomas Pennant, *A Journey from London to Isle of Wight* (London, Edward Harding, 1801).

50. For an interesting discussion of women's leisure see Ann Bermingham, 'The aesthetics of ignorance: the accomplished woman in the culture of connoisseurship', *The Oxford Art Journal*, 16:2 (1993), pp.3–20.

51. Dr. Gregory, *A Father's Legacy to his Daughters* (Edinburgh, W. Strahan, T. Cadell, J. Balfour and W. Creech, 1774), p.51.

52. See, for example, Letter from Richard Bull to Thomas Pennant, 2 December 1783, CR 2017 TP 189/1, Warwickshire C.R.O., or Letter from Richard Bull to Charles Burney, 22 November, 1784, MS, Osborn Files, drawer 46 folder 37, Beinecke Library, Yale University.

53. Thomas Dodd, MS inscription [*c*.mid-nineteenth century], on the reverse of *Miss Elizabeth Bull*, proof before letter, mezzotint, Joseph Strutt after a pastel [?] by Hugh Douglas Hamilton, n.d. [*c*.1760s–79], S. Roy 61, Cheylesmore Collection, Department of Prints & Drawings, British Museum.

54. Hannah Robertson, *The Young Ladies School of the Arts* (Edinburgh, Mrs Robertson, 1767), n.p.

55. Maria Edgeworth, *Practical Education*, 2 vols (London, John Johnson, 1798), 1, p.525.

56. They were the beneficiaries of Humphry Morice's bequest of 1786, which was valued at over £200,000. For details of this, see Pinkerton, 'Richard Bull', p. 46. *Ibid.*, 2, p.523.

57. *The Female Aegis: or, the Duties of Women from Childhood to Old Age* (London, J. Ginger, 1798), p.52.

58. Thomas Downes, *A Copious Index to Pennant's Account of London, Arranged in Strict Alphabetical order: Containing The Names of Every Person and Place Mentioned in that Popular Work, with References to Every Circumstance of Importance* (London, Taylor & Hessey, 1814), p.iii.

59. *Ibid.*

60. 'Richard Bull' [Obit.], *Gentleman's Magazine*, 76:1 (March 1806), p.289.

61. Lady Mary Coke, *MS Journals*, 22 December 1782, reproduced in *The Yale Edition of Horace Walpole's Correspondence*, 31, pp.297–8.

62. Letter from William Price to Richard Bull, n.d. [post 1792, as Price became the Queen's Vice-Chamberlain in that year], MS tipped into the front of Richard Bull's extra-illustrated copy of Horace Walpole, *Catalogue of Royal and Noble Authors*, 1, 33 3 copy 21, Lewis Walpole Library, Yale University.

63. John Simco, *A Catalogue of Books, Prints & Books of Prints for 1799* (London, John Simco, 1799), n.p.

64. Letter from Thomas Pennant to Richard Bull, 25 July 1783, 5500 C (30), MS, National Library of Wales.

65. Thomas Pennant's extra-illustrated copy of *Some Account of London* is now in the Summers Room, National Library of Wales.

66. Letter from Thomas Pennant to Richard Bull, 8 June 1781, 5500 C (13), MS, National Library of Wales.

67. John & Josiah Boydell, *A Catalogue of Historical Prints, Various Subjects, Landscapes, Sea Pieces, Views, &c. After the Most Capital Pictures in England. Engraved by the Most Celebrated Artists*, Part II (London, J. & J. Boydell, 1794), p.vi.

68. *Londinum Illustratum: A Splendid and Unique Illustration of Pennant's London* (London, C. Whittingham, 1819), pp. 5–7.

69. Ibid.

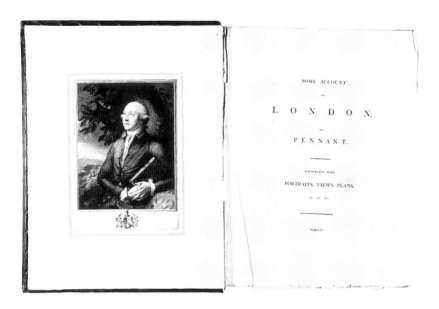

7.1 J.K. Sherwin, title page of volume one of John Charles Crowle's extra-illustrated copy of *Some Account of London* with proof before letter stage portrait of Thomas Pennant(1778), engraving

7.2 Prints of the Tradescants, in John Charles Crowle's extra-illustrated copy of *Some Account of London*

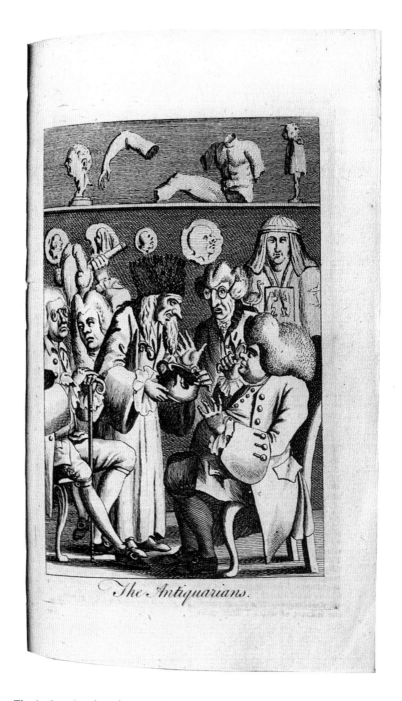

7.3 *The Antiquarians* (1772), engraving

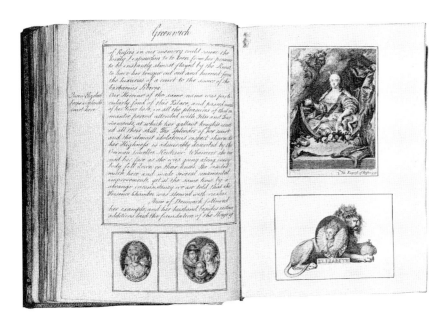

7.4 Examples of the handicraft of Catherine and Elizabeth Bull, pasted into Richard Bull's extra-illustrated presentation manuscript copy of *From London to Dover* (*c*.1789)

7.5 Prints of Admiral Trump and Michael de Ruyter, pasted into Richard Bull's extra-illustrated presentation manuscript copy of *From London to Dover* (*c*.1789)

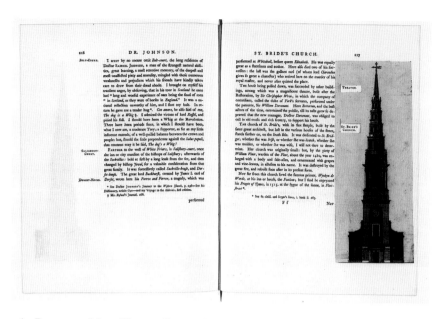

7.6 Page spread from Thomas Pennant's extra-illustrated copy of *Some Account of London*

MOSES GRIFFITH,

PAINTER to Thomas Pennant, Esq;

BY PERMISSION FROM HIS MASTER,

.Takes the Liberty of offering his Services to the
Public, at his leifure Hours,

AT THE FOLLOWING RATES.'

	£.	s.	d.
A Landfchape or Ruin, from Fifteen to Twenty Inches in Length —	1	11	6
From Ten to Fifteen Inches	1	1	—
From Eight to Ten Inches —	—	10	6
For the Margin of a Book, from Four to Five Inches — —	—	6	—
A Head, within a Margin, Five Inches by Four — — — —	—	10	6
A plain Coat of Arms — — —	—	1	3
Or with Quarters and Creft — — —	—	1	6

Wibnent, in *Whiteford* Parifh, *Flintfbire*,
.December 1ft, 1784.

7.7 *Moses Griffith, Painter to Thomas Pennant, Esq.* (1784)

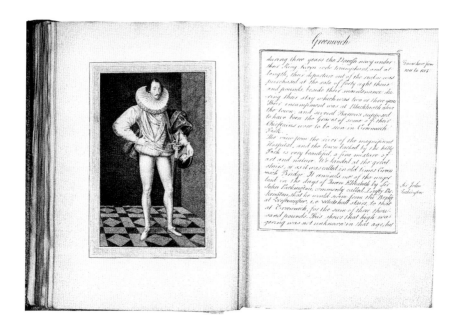

7.8   Moses Griffith, *Lusty Packington* (*c*.1791), watercolour

7.9   Map of Essex and *A View of the Custom House*, pasted into Richard Bull's extra-illustrated presentation manuscript copy of *From London to Dover* (*c*.1789)

8

The desk: excavation site and repository of memories

Annegret Pelz

Translated and revised by Anne Puetz*

> Every month I tidy my desk and it always makes me laugh; inside, it looks like heaven, all hierarchies abolished: high and low, saints, publicans and sinners, all lie in one heap.
>
> Catharina Elisabeth Goethe (1782)[1]

By the end of the eighteenth century the idea of the public museum had gained importance and, from the 1830s, this resulted in the building of museums all over Europe. This pan-European foundation of national and public museums has frequently been interpreted as an expression of the self-confidence of the educated bourgeoisie. From the viewpoint of this essay, it is significant that this era of nascent museum culture was also the period in which a number of renowned female authors, writing in German, published retrospective views of their own lives combined with a description of the desks at which they sat down to write. This chronological parallel, between the dominant museum culture and the authorial activities of a number of separate women, provides the starting point for my analysis of the relationship between the methods used in the museums process of objectifying the past and the intimate memorial techniques of these texts.

Sophie von La Roche's *Mein Schreibetisch* (1799), Caroline de la Motte Fouqué's *Der Schreibtisch oder alte und neue Zeit* (1833) and Caroline Pichler's *Zerstreute Blätter aus meinem Schreibtische* (1837) are all based on the premise that the writers' desks were both a scene of production and a starting-point for memory.[2] At the desk, these authors had spent a large part of their working lives, and writing at their desks they now attempted to capture their memories. For all three women the desk, as a piece of furniture, took on symbolic properties. It was not only, as Sophie von La Roche put it, a 'servant' of her activity, but, in its physical dimensions, it was both medium and memorial site. These authors unearthed the documents collected and deposited on the desk, picked them up, reread them and commented upon them, and thus they began to excavate their memories. In accordance with Walter Benjamin's suggestion that true memories need to locate the precise spot in which they were first experienced, these three authors not only inventoried their discoveries but also indicated the exact places in which the past was now preserved.[3] In the faithful act of listing documentary sediments and layers, these items materially re-entered their owners' lives and thereby induced 'a form of practical remembrance'.[4] As this procedure reflects the contemporary museum practices of collecting and archiving, the relationship between these 'desk' texts of personal history and the origins of the museum is apparent.[5] The focus of this essay is the examination of the volumes of La Roche, de la Motte Fouqué and Pichler, which all significantly share the reference to the 'desk' (*Schreibetisch*) in their titles.[6] La Roche's 'desk', published in 1799 (Figure 8.1), invented this physical model of literary arrangement and was, therefore, the prototype for successive texts. In contrast, de la Motte Fouqué's 'desk' follows a chronological order, which ironically emphasized the impossibility of narrative continuity, and in Pichler's text the 'desk' was now only a 'tableau' – a surface – on which a collection of texts was loosely assembled in an already established literary form.

La Roche's spatial order

Sophie von La Roche's *Mein Schreibetisch*, published in two volumes in 1799, belongs to the genre of the written description of collections. One of the oldest and most heterogeneous types of literature, this genre can be traced back to classical antiquity, and from the fifteenth century it became increasingly popular particularly as a concomitant to travel writing.[7] From 1780, Sophie von La Roche undertook several prolonged journeys to Switzerland, France, Holland and England, and produced extensive travel writings.[8] In her work, she combined the literary form of the travel report with the description of the private collection of texts and books assembled on her desk and in the adjoining study. The construction of the desk and the spatial dimensions of the room determined the structure of her text. The reader was invited to view the treasures accumulated on the desk and to follow the systematic 'course' of the pen over the desk and along its 'journey of discovery through the adjacent library and the cabinets … of the learned and the reading public'.[9] Like any other excursion, Sophie von La Roche's 'desk journey' followed a reasoning strategy within the context of the rhetorical *inventio*.[10] This sedentary journey was defined by the 'accidental' discoveries and inventions, pertaining to different places, which re-entered the writer/collector's consciousness through the viewing of her treasures.[11] The description of the material aspect of collected items, among them 'a spoilt sheet smoothed out with an iron', a portfolio with 'papers of many kinds', an edition of the English *Ladies Magazine* wrapped in 'pale-yellow paper', the letters stored in an upper drawer of the desk, all demonstrate La Roche's topical search behaviour. In this a recognition of the place of discovery triggered the release of memories, or in her own words, represented the 'markers to ease remembrance'.[12] The desk and its utensils provided the rhetoric of invention with a formalized space for the development of memories.

Seen as a collection, La Roche's 'desk' is a curious parallel to both early-modern and modern forms of the museum. The very private character of the collection of letters and souvenir fragments, the cultivation of personal whims at the desk and the emphasis on the arbitrary juxtaposition of collected items encompass characteristics of the 'peep-show principle' of curiosity cabinets and *Wunderkammern*, first developed in the sixteenth century. In these cabinets, the accumulation of curiosities had been predicated on the idea of a universal theory of combination which, as a kind of comprehensive reference system of the meanings and constellations of all signs, attempted to subject divergent interests to one general principle.[13] To the *Wunderkammer*'s cumulative principle of collection corresponds the random assemblage of quotations, comments and discursive additions in La Roche's text. However, the author's excavation does reveal a more methodical rationality in the way in which bundled up documents and 'packets' are taken up systematically. For example, the successive 'opening' of individual 'cabinets', such as Encyclopedia, novels or literature for women, suggests the influence of recent developments in classification by natural historians such as Linnaeus or Buffon, whom La Roche particularly revered.[14] While eighteenth-century natural historians supplied museums with systematically ordered specimens collected from all over the world , Sophie von La Roche placed the partly foreign-language texts within her 'desk' into new, meaningful taxonomies. Indeed, she likened her collections of books to flowers and remarked that looking at her favourites among them was as beneficial and as agreeable as looking at a leaf, a tree or a bush.[15] This application of a 'biological gaze' to her books reveals a 'botanizing' way of writing in which textual fragments, books and writing tools came to the author 'accidentally'.[16]

It is interesting that the aged author also envisaged herself within this process of fragmentation by comparing herself to a 'ruin'. In typical antiquarian terms, she repeatedly expressed her great 'pleasure in ruins' and stressed her fondness for lingering over 'fragmented thoughts'.[17] In Georg Simmel's interpretation the ruin inverts the sequence of nature and culture and commutes the work of art into an object of natural formation. It emphasizes the inherent laws of the material, destroys the aesthetic closure of form and deposes the dominance of the creative mind. The ruin also allows the human and physical aspects of the work to re-emerge and values an attitude of 'positive passivity' towards the material.[18] This correlation between destruction and tradition, embodied in the paradoxical decaying form of the ruin, corresponds to the isolated quotation of single text 'fragments' and the incorporation of these as 'relics' into the collection in La Roche's 'desk'.[19]

According to Walter Benjamin, the essential characteristic of collecting consists precisely in this removal of objects from their original functions in order to place them in the closest proximity to others of their kind within the collection.[20] By means of quotation, these text fragments of the past which had been divorced from their original contexts were given a new presence or, in La Roche's words, a 'new entrance on the stage', in a process whereby the author's contribution consisted in weaving her own 'Ariadne's thread' through a 'labyrinth of quotations'.[21]

In La Roche's concept of the recollection of memories at her 'desk' there is thus a suggestion of a system of memory that almost presages Walter Benjamin's notion of the quotation.[22] This concept corresponds to the model of aesthetic production which she promoted as her reason for writing in quotations. She made no claim to originality in the modern sense of individual authorship. Instead she propagated the open text as her ideal, when, for instance, she stated that she favoured works 'with chapters like so many entrances to a garden'.[23] In addition, La Roche designated her 'desk' as part of a series of texts whose authors, in spite of their 'own wealth', used 'the intellectual property of others' in a comparable way.[24] In this regard she mentioned Anna Laetitia Barbauld's *Das geöffnete Schreibepult* as a possible forerunner to her own text.[25] As that volume figured on her list of texts still to be read, we might thus infer that her collection not only referred back to the past, but also pointed forwards to future possibilities.

Among her predecessors from the ranks of 'great men', La Roche claimed a position alongside Cicero, Plutarch, Seneca, Bacon and Montesquieu.[26] She also made special reference to Montaigne, whom she applauded for not failing to 'borrow anything that might contribute to the embellishment of his works' from his own literary ancestors.[27] Montaigne described his writing as the 'ribbon' with which he tied 'foreign flowers' and 'borrowed jewels' into a text of his own, not in order to hide his personal contribution under these quotations but, on the contrary, in order to 'display himself' through them.[28] In her 'desk', La Roche attempted to take up his 'Ariadne's thread' and spin it forth.

De la Motte Fouqué's chronological sequence

Like Sophie von La Roche's 'desk', which was composed at the end of a long writing career at the age of nearly sixty-nine, Caroline de la Motte Fouqué's collection of texts *Der Schreibtisch oder alte und neue Zeit*, published in Cologne in 1833, is a work of old age. This posthumously published 'desk' was written when its author, as she herself said, had one foot in the grave and, feeling that she was about to depart this life, began to excavate her past.[29] As in the case of La Roche's method, the process of re-examining collected correspondences and writings helped to unearth de la Motte Fouqué's memories. In contrast to La Roche, however, de la Motte Fouqué did not sift through her desk in order to bring documents back to life; instead her intention was to organize her papers and leave them as her literary heritage. This author did not promise, as La Roche had, to 'give a *faithful* description of this desk ... *without any changes, omissions* or *addenda*'.[30] Without exception the letters and papers on de la Motte Fouqué's desk were now scrutinized (and in some cases destroyed) and finally collected into a 'desk', for the benefit of 'those left behind'. Consequently, her assemblage of texts did not conform to La Roche's principle of the desk as a system of random selection but rather to the self-representational intentions of the author.

The hint of a physical arrangement remained, however. The five chapters of the *Schreibtisch* were made to correspond to the five 'compartments' (*Fach*) of the desk. The first 'compartment' and thus the first chapter contains 'Copies of some original letters from the years 1785–1786–1790'; the second 'History of fashions of the years 1789–1829'; the third presents a 'Fragment of a stage play from the year 1819'; the fourth 'Conversations by the Fireside' and the fifth reports a 'Tournament in Potsdam'.[31] Thus, while de la Motte Fouqué exploited the possibilities of the literary desk to place unrelated material side by side, she did not pursue the 'spatial' model of text production and reading of La Roche's work. Apart from these superficial allusions to the compartments of the desk, the room and with it the framework of the 'desk journey' receded almost entirely into the background. De la Motte Fouqué's memories were not tied to the arrangement of objects in the room, but were ordered chronologically over the period of time from 1785 to 1829. As the added title 'Old and new times' and the subtitle 'History of fashions' reveal, this author considered the accumulation of texts on her desk as a contribution to contemporary history. If we compare this position with concurrent developments in museology then this heightened interest in the passage of time places de la Motte Fouqué's 'desk' in the nineteenth-century context of the progress from a natural-historical to an organic view; that is, from the physical ordering of natural history to the increased importance in the evolutionary succession of all life forms.[32] For de la Motte Fouqué, fashion was the paradigmatic expression of a person's enclosure in his or her own time. Nothing, she claimed, confirms the course of history more forcefully than the inexorable change of fashion.[33] Throughout the 'History of fashions' the 'pictorial frieze' of a variety of remembered figures formed itself into a 'historical thread through the spirit of the age', and through the mental inspection of this series of figures the writer's own past was vividly recalled.[34] Fashion and its highly memorable changes thus provided the images along which memory could travel backwards in time.

In her interpretation of Walter Benjamin, Silvia Bovenschen has explained that fashion is a measure of time which stands in close connection to the perception of biographical phases.[35] Caroline de la Motte Fouqué's perception of history was concentrated both on the French Revolution as the cause of the collapse of the entire previous apparatus of fashions, and on Romanticism as a 'transitional or transformational epoch' of fashions.[36] In her view, changes in fashion should not be imagined in terms 'of a neat succession' from one to the next, but as a confluence of 'innumerable' factors which caused the 'taste of the time to be entangled in a chaos of changing terms.'[37] The text gives examples of the changes in fashion with a collection of writings on literature, the theatre, clothing, interior decoration, language and forms of sociability.

De la Motte Fouqué's reconstruction of changing fashions presented a specifically modern image of socialization in general, and female socialization in particular, where the latter was defined by the masquerade of fashions with its multitude of successive, chrysalis-like stages.[38] Silvia Bovenschen's reading of Georg Simmel's essay *Die Mode* argues that the individual experiences the continuous changes in fashion as a crisis; as symptom of dissolving identities.[39] On the example of grimacing before a mirror, de la Motte Fouqué explained the danger that fashion presents to the development of a true, 'natural' identity. According to popular belief, a distorted face will not regain its original appearance if the grimace coincides with the striking of the clock; likewise, when the clock strikes for a new fashion, as it were, the mirror will leave the spectator unclear about her original identity: '*Mirror images* reflect themselves. We often don't know how much of them belongs to *them* and how much to *us*.'[40] Under the influence of fashion, the individual, believing itself able to act creatively upon its times, experiences itself instead as the former's 'plaything' and 'slave'.[41] In order to be able to discern any 'direction' in a time marked by the 'maelstrom' and 'chaos' of events, de la Motte Fouqué adopted the narrative stance of an author looking back from the 'shore' from a distance of 40 years.[42] Seen as a whole, the collection of texts on her 'desk' corresponded to the 'mirror image' of an identity in crisis, which may be ordered chronologically but which defies any attempt at a continuous narration. In accordance with the contemporary idea of museums, where each room, in chronological succession, was supposed to recreate the character of the century to which its exhibits belonged, but which in practice only succeeded in presenting an overall series of unrelated 'period' rooms, de la Motte Fouqué's 'text-compartments' released the memories stored in them only in fragmentary form.[43] The reader, at the same time author and collector of her texts, wandered 'through' her 'desk' as through a museum of her own authorship.

Caroline Pichler's Tableau

Like the two 'desk' texts already encountered, the text compilation *Zerstreute Blätter aus meinem Schreibtische*, written in 1835 by the Viennese author Caroline Pichler, was composed retrospectively when the author was seventy-five. Indeed, contemporary reviews praised the 'appropriately mature, happy transition from poetical creation to poetical reflection', and regarded the 'contemplative and retrospective nature of the essays' as a special quality of the collection.[44] The author herself stated that old age is the moment in which life retreats from present concerns, closes in on itself, and stimulates observations on its own past as on an 'irrefutable property, and a kind of treasure'.[45] According to Pichler, the highest priority in the act of remembrance should be the use of reason, especially in regard to the 'blind spot' towards oneself.[46] As a preface to her compilation of texts in the 'desk' she appropriated the motto 'know thyself' from a learned friend and teacher of her youth, who had fixed this adage over the door to his study, that is the place where he used 'to write and to read'.[47]

In this volume, observations and reflections (on fashion, education, painting, theatre, religion, matrimony, society, architecture, town planning, the power of ideas, as well as several obituaries), contained in texts that were up to twenty years old, were placed side by side without any fresh commentary or interpretation.[48] Although Pichler's compilation of texts did follow the already proven, cumulative principle of the literary 'desk', no specific reference to such a physical desk was actually made. Whereas de la Motte Fouqué's different 'compartments' had still indicated the boundaries between different kinds of texts, in Pichler the reference to an external system of arrangement had been replaced by the spatial metaphor of the 'church of ideas', imagined as a 'majestically tall' Gothic church with nave and aisles, 'superb carvings' and a 'daring vault carried by pillars branching out towards the top'.[49] In the case of such a complex building, she stated, 'nobody is able to fully understand the whole from a single point of view' and from every position a new 'aspect' is revealed.[50] It is this metaphor which Pichler adopted to explain both the writer's and the reader's perspective.

The medieval cathedral, as Manfred Schneider has recently described, can be interpreted as a symbolic repository of knowledge able to blend different levels of space and time into one.[51] Indeed, for Pichler it corresponded to a world whose inner complexity continuously offered new perspectives and thus endlessly referred the human being back to the limitations of his or her point of view, and in *Zerstreute Blätter*, the image of the cathedral combined with the modern image of an 'age of contrasts'. An eponymous passage communicated the author's impression of living in a time of 'antagonistic frictions', in which the requirements of people on all levels of society were subjected to conflicting conditions.[52] In the realms of literature and theatre this meant that 'the mind [formerly] in awe of and schooled in the masterpieces of the classics' was now exposed to manifold distractions, both embodied in and feeding the popularity of newspapers, journals, broadsheets and encyclopaedias.[53] The ability of these contemporary genres to point out 'knowledge in all aspects and in different directions' corresponded to the form of the 'desk' as a symbolic repository of personal memories, constructed according to a new blueprint.[54]

In the passage entitled 'The travel box' Pichler demonstrated the way in which the arbitrary coexistence of conflicting parts could be joined together to form a whole in one 'desk': at the beginning of a journey a traveller packed a small cardboard box that was to hold 'a number of small necessities, utensils and toiletries'. It took, as the writer put it, 'great skill and careful planning to fit these items into the box so that the lid could finally be closed and tied up with a piece of string.' At the end of the journey, however, when the box was opened, it emerged that the vibrations of the vehicle in transit had caused 'everything to fit together very neatly', so that each item had its proper place and the lid closed perfectly, even without the piece of string.[55] In Pichler's text the 'travel box' is thus emblematic of the 'quiet force of time and habit', by which, in the course of a lifetime, and under the influence of an external and irrefutable necessity, opposing entities were gradually brought together. It was not the chronological model of a 'path travelled' but the writing top of the desk which, both literally and metaphorically, connected contradictory fragments of texts with different time levels, people and locations as a tableau of memories, which, in contrast to La Roche's text, could no longer be ordered in physical succession.[56]

'Desk' texts – a 'kind of memoirs'

The series of 'desk' texts by renowned female authors was begun by Sophie von La Roche in 1799 and ended in 1839 with Caroline Pichler. Paralleling the contemporary history of museums – from the Louvre's opening to the public in 1793, as a repository for treasures of art amassed from all over Europe, to the historicizing monumental buildings of the 1830s – the desk had been transformed into a kind of personal museum of the author's writing.[57] Like the museum's semiophores, the desk which had been charged with the author's personal history was displayed to the viewer as a signifier to be seen in connection with and to explain the meaning of something that was, in principle, invisible.[58] In contrast to other artistic 'performances', the act of writing is invisible. For that reason, the authors 'display' the desk as an object that serves the activity of writing both materially and as a signifier. In its material capacity, the desk's writing top, its compartments and its physical dimensions refer to the entire cosmos of imaginary relations for which the desk is merely a starting point. At the same time, it is not only a signifier of the act of writing, but also an exhibition space for the author's texts. As on Catharina Elisabeth Goethe's desk, texts are placed side by side without any imposed hierarchial order and, as Sophie von La Roche has shown, they enter into independent, contingent relations with each other only through their physical proximity. Thus, the authors of 'desk' texts could be likened to curators of exhibitions comprised of written documents. They worked conceptually in that they arranged their materials and put together copies for new displays of disparate texts – some decades old, others more recent – which, at the point of their exhibition in this 'desk' format, had already existed in completed form elsewhere. The 'desk' texts are therefore primarily displays of the collected written monuments of these writers' lives, which were published, or republished, with or without extra commentaries.[59]

Caroline Pichler described this type of text collection as 'a kind of memoirs'.[60] In fact, the 'desk' texts contain, albeit in a curiously inverted form, the most important contemporary criteria of the memoir: authenticity, reliability of historical sources and memorable public action.[61] If one understands memoirs as a representation not so much of the authors themselves, but of the historical events experienced in the course of their lives, it is vital that these events were witnessed at first hand. In the words of the historian Johann Christoph Gatterer, writers of memoirs need to have been present 'quasi in the manufactory' of the historical event.[62]

The female authors' survey of their own 'text manufactory' thus turns an instrument developed for the observation of important historical events towards their own, personal histories. In view of their contemporary fame, these authors have earned the right to lay claim to memorable public action, and the criterion of authenticity has likewise been fulfilled. In order to turn their own texts into reliable sources, the authors followed the contemporary antiquarian interest in reading 'ancient documents … with searching eyes'.[63] According to Winckelmann's demand for a new, factual historiography outlined in his didactic monument *Geschichte der Kunst des Altertums*, the writing of memoirs and antiquarian practice both centred around the physical investigation of objects and on the authenticity and reliability of such fragments.[64] Johann Gottfried Herder, who dealt extensively with Winckelmann's writings, therefore proposed the distinction of the artist (writer) from the antiquary.[65] In his view, the artist needed to concentrate on the creation of beautiful or ugly forms, while the function of the antiquary was to deliver facts, to investigate and verify objects and to collect proofs for their aesthetic qualities.[66] At one and the same time, the female authors in question claimed both positions – that of the artist and of the antiquary. In the role of the former they presented texts, published them and sought proofs for the beauty of their own works. In contrast, as antiquaries, they collected, explained, ordered and investigated their works by systematically surveying and reassembling the texts deposited on their desks. In this way they erected a 'didactic monument' to their own art and created a physically rendered model of their authorial activities, based solely on the factuality of the existing texts and of the place where these activities occurred.

Notes

*   This text is a revised version of the essay, first published in German as 'Der Schreibtisch. Ausgrabungsort und Depot von Erinnerungen', in Magdalene Heuser (ed.), *Autobiographien von Frauen: Beiträge zu ihrer Geschichte* (Tübingen, Niemeyer, 1996), pp.233–46.
    Few of the German titles cited in this work exist in English translation; where English versions do exist this information has been included in the notes. In this translation, no attempt has been made to render eighteenth- and nineteenth-century German into corresponding period English; instead, the translator has provided modernized translations and these appear in quotation marks to distinguish them from the author's own words.

1. Letter from Catharina Elisabeth Goethe in a letter to Anna Amalia, reproduced in Ulrike Prokop, *Die Illusion vom Großen Paar*, 2 vols (Frankfurt a.M., Fischer, 1991), 1, p.215.

2. Sophie von La Roche, *Mein Schreibetisch an Herrn G.R.P. in D.*, 2 vols (Leipzig, Gräff, 1799); Caroline, Baroness de la Motte Fouqué, *Der Schreibtisch oder alte und neue Zeit. Ein nachgelassenes Werk* (Cologne, Bachem, 1833) and Caroline Pichler, 'Zerstreute Blätter aus meinem Schreibtische', in *Sämmtliche Werke*, 60 vols (Vienna, Pichler, 1828–45), 55. [It is worth noting that these three titles can be loosely translated as (La Roche), My desk to Mr. G.R.P. in D.; (de la Motte Fouqué), The desk or old and new times. A posthumous work, and (Pichler), Scattered leaves from my desk.]

3. Walter Benjamin, 'Ausgraben und Erinnern', ed. Tillmann Rexroth, in *Gesammelte Schriften*, ed. Rolf Tiedemann and Hermann Schweppenhäuser in co-operation with Theodor W. Adorno and Gershom Scholem, 4 vols (Frankfurt a.M., Suhrkamp, 1972–89), 4:1, pp.400–401.

4. Walter Benjamin, 'Der Sammler', in *Das Passagen-Werk*, ed. Rolf Tiedemann, 2 vols (Frankfurt a.M., Suhrkamp, 1983), 1, pp.269–80, p.271.

5. For the historiography of museums and collections see Krzysztof Pomian, *Der Ursprung des Museums. Vom Sammeln* (Berlin, Wagenbach, 1988), esp. pp.7–12 and 55–72.

6. The three famous authors, the Viennese Caroline Pichler, née Greiner (1769–1843), the Berlin writer Caroline Auguste de la Motte Fouqué, née von Briest (1773–1831), and Marie Sophie von La Roche, née Gutermann von Gutershofen (1731–1807), were associated with the great European thinkers and artists of their time: among them Madame de Staël, Dorothea and A.W. Schlegel, Grillparzer, W. von Humboldt, C.M. Wieland, E.T.A. Hoffmann, K.A. Varnhagen and J.W. Goethe. While they never met, Pichler and de la Motte Fouqué corresponded with each other and read each other's works. In the present works there are no specific cross-references to each other's texts other than the shared use of the 'desk' metaphor.

7. See Pomian, *Der Ursprung des Museums*, p. 9. For my reading of La Roche's text in the context of travel writing see Annegret Pelz, *Reisen durch die eigene Fremde. Reiseliteratur von Frauen als auto-geographische Schriften* (Cologne, Weimar, Vienna, Böhlau, 1993), pp.46–67.

8. See Wolfgang Griep and Annegret Pelz, *Frauen reisen. Ein bibliographisches Verzeichnis deutschsprachiger Frauenreisen 1700 bis 1810* (Bremen, Temmen, 1995), pp.165–73. For her journey to England see Sophie von La Roche, *Sophie in London in 1786, being the Diary of Sophie von la Roche*, trans. Clare Williams (London, Jonathan Cape, 1933).

9. La Roche, *Mein Schreibetisch*, 1, p.180.

10. *Ibid.*, 1, p.199. In rhetoric, *inventio* is the science of the discovery of subject-matter. For our authors, the desk is the treasure trove which contains the raw material for the infinite playful recombination of literary data and poetical invention.

11. 'It is delightful how chance associates ideas'. Translated from *ibid.*, 1, p.101.

12. *Ibid.*, 1, pp.78, 26, 231, 72, and 324.

13. See Hans Holländer, 'Kunst- und Wunderkammern: Konturen eines unvollendbaren Projektes', in *Wunderkammer des Abendlandes. Museum und Sammlung im Spiegel der Zeit*, ed. Hans Holländer, exhibition catalogue, Kunst und Austellungshalle der Bundesrepublik Deutschland (Bonn, Kunst und Austellungshalle der Bundesrepublik Deutschland, 1994), pp.136–45.

14. See Jens Erik Kristensen, 'Der kuriose, der klassifizierende und der biologische Blick. Die Ordnung der Natur und das moderne naturhistorische Museum', in *ibid.*, pp.127–35.

15. La Roche, *Mein Schreibetisch*, 2, p.123.

16. Although the English word 'botanizing' now conveys a sense of a systematic and structured approach to natural history, it should be noted that the German word 'botanisiren' suggests a far more accidental mode, akin to the butterfly collector, with his net, in search of chance finds.

17. *Ibid.*, 2, p.51 and 1, p.147. 'Ruins touch you particularly because you have yourself become a ruin.' *Ibid.*, 2, p.48. This remark is usually interpreted as the self-criticism of an author 'whose poetic talent . . . had already been exhausted'. See Bernd Heidenreich, *Sophie von La Roche – eine Werkbiographie* (Frankfurt a.M., Bern, New York, Lang, 1986), 5, pp.275–6.

18. Georg Simmel, 'Die Ruine' (1907), ed. Rüdiger Kramme and Otthein Rammstedt, in Georg Simmel, *Gesamtausgabe*, ed. Otthein Rammstedt, 14 vols (Frankfurt a.M., Suhrkamp, 1989–96), 14, pp.287–95.

19. 'Do letters not have the value of relics?' La Roche, *Mein Schreibetisch*, 2, p.187.

20. Benjamin, 'Der Sammler', p.217.

21. La Roche, *Mein Schreibetisch*, 1, p.183.

22. Bettine Menke, 'Das Nach-Leben im Zitat. Benjamin's Gedächtnis der Texte' in *Raum-Bild-Schrift. Studien zur Mnemotechnik*, ed. Anselm Haverkamp and Renate Lachmann (Frankfurt a.M., Suhrkamp, 1991), pp.74–110.

23. La Roche, *Mein Schreibetisch*, 1, p. 82. In secondary literature this has gained her the reproach of lacking a firm point of view. Heidenreich states that the lack of a firm position has reached its highest point, 'When in her late works (such as the Desk), passages from the works of other authors are juxtaposed without commentary or at best with a few banal words of praise.' See Heidenreich, *Sophie von La Roche*, pp.273 and 275. In Heidenreich, see also excerpts from contemporary reviews, pp.229–31.

24. *Ibid.*, 2, p.56.

25. Anna Laetitia Barbauld, *Das geöffnete Schreibepult. Zum Unterrichte und Vergnügen junger Personen. Aus dem Englischen. Ein Weihnachtsgeschenk für die Jugend* (Leipzig, Gräff, 1798–9). [This is possibly a translation of Barbauld's and Aikin's *Evenings at Home; or The Juvenile budget Opened; Consisting of a Variety of Miscellaneous Pieces for the Instruction and Amusement of Young Persons*, the 7th edition of which was published in 1807].

26. La Roche, *Mein Schreibetisch*, 2, pp.55–6.

27. 'Oh if such men with their own wealth of ideas made use of the works of others, I could well dare to do it in these pages'. *Ibid.*

28. Michel de Montaigne, 'Von der Physiognomie', in *Essays*, trans. Herbert Lüthi (Zurich, Manesse, 1985), p.835.

29. De la Motte Fouqué, *Der Schreibtisch*, 'Introduction'. Caroline de la Motte Fouqué was born in Nennhausen near Rathenow in 1773 and died there in 1831. For her literary œuvre see Dorothea Böck, 'Caroline de la Motte Fouqué. Sie hätte eine "deutsche Stael werden können . . ." ', 'Wen kümmert's, wer spricht', in Inge Stephan, Sigrid Weigel, Kerstin Wilhelms (eds), *Zur Literatur und Kulturgeschichte der Frauen aus Ost und West* (Cologne and Vienna, Böhlau, 1991), pp.139–48 and Birgit Wägenbaur, 'Caroline de la Motte Fouqué: Die lebendige Wahrheit der Kunst', in *Die Pathologie der Liebe. Literarische Weiblichkeitsentwürfe um 1800* (Berlin, Schmidt, 1996), pp.194–289.

30. La Roche, *Mein Schreibetisch*, 1, p.3.

31. De la Motte Fouqué, *Der Schreibtisch*, 'Erstes Fach. Copieen [sic] einzelner Originalbriefe aus den Jahren 1785–1786–1790', pp.1–22; 'Zweites Fach. Geschichte der Moden, vom Jahr 1789–1829'. 'Als Beitrag zur Geschichte der Zeit', pp.23–124; 'Drittes Fach. Fragmente aus dem Jahr 1819', pp.125–68; 'Viertes Fach. Unterhaltungen am Kaminfeuer im Jahre 1829', pp.169–254 and 'Fünftes Fach. Turnier in Potsdam', pp.255–80. The second compartment, 'History of fashions', was separately published several times, most recently in 1988 with added illustrations taken from the *Journal des Luxus und der Moden*, under the title *Geschichte der Moden 1785–1829*, ed. Dorothea Böck (Hanau, Dausien, 1988). The various editions show differences in text.

32. Kristensen, *Wunderkammer des Abendlandes*, p.134.

33. De la Motte Fouqué, *Der Schreibtisch*, p.26.

34. *Ibid.*, p.27.

35. Silvia Bovenschen, 'Über die Listen der Mode', in *Die Listen der Mode*, ed. Silvia Bovenschen (Frankfurt a.M., Suhrkamp, 1986), pp.19–20. This volume, edited by Bovenschen, compiles the most important contributions to the discourse on fashion of the last century, including: F.Th. Vischer, W. Sombart, T. Veblen, E. Fuchs, G. Simmel, R. Barthes, R. Sennett.

36. De la Motte Fouqué, *Der Schreibtisch* , pp.68 and 117.

37. *Ibid.*, p.2.

38. *Ibid.*, p.45.

39. Georg Simmel, 'Die Mode', in *Philosophische Kultur. Gesammelte Essays* (Leipzig, W. Klinkhardt, 1921), pp.29–64. See also Bovenschen, *Die Listen der Mode*, pp.13–14 and 179–207.

40. De la Motte Fouqué, *Der Schreibtisch*, p. 26. The emphasis is de la Motte Fouqué's.

41. *Ibid.*, p.26.

42. *Ibid.*, pp.50–51.

43. Jørgen Jensen, 'Das goldene Zeitalter der Museen', in *Wunderkammer des Abendlandes*, pp.160–9, p.162.

44. See the review by Andreas Schumacher in *Der Telegraph*, 1 (Vienna, 1836), pp.508–9, quoted in Emil Karl Blümml (ed.), *Caroline Pichler, Denkwürdigkeiten aus meinem Leben*, ed. Emil Karl Blümml, 2 vols (Munich, Müller, 1914), 2, n. 563 p.602. On Pichler see Barbara Becker-Cantarino, 'Caroline Pichler und die "Frauendichtung" ', in *Modern Austrian Literature. Journal of the International Arthur Schnitzler Research Association*, 12:3/4 (Riverside, Ca., University of California, 1979), pp.1–24.

45. Pichler, *Zerstreute Blätter*, p.8.

46. *Ibid.*, p.10.

47. *Ibid.*, p.7.

48. In one notable instance two obituaries of the poet and narrative writer Louise Brachmann (1777–1822) and the poet Maria Therese von Arntner (1772–1829) refuted the critiques put forward by Carl Wilhelm Otto August von Schindel. See Carl Wilhelm Otto August von Schindel, *Die Schriftstellerinnen des neunzehnten Jahrhunderts. Drei Teile in einem Band* (rpt, 1823–4, Hildesheim and New York, Olms, 1978), 1, pp.13–30, 39–57 and 3, pp.22–53. See also Susanne Kord, ' "Und drinnen waltet die züchtige Hausfrau?" Caroline Pichler's Fictional Auto/Biographies', in Jeanette Clausen and Sara Friedrichsmeyer (eds), *Women in German Yearbook. Feminist Studies in German Literature and Culture*, 8 (1993), pp.141–58. A revised, two-volume edition of *Zerstreute Blätter*, originally published in 1839 under the title *Zeitbilder*, is reprinted in Caroline Pichler, *Sämmtliche Werke* (Vienna, Pichler, 1845), pp.59–60.

49. Pichler, *Zerstreute Blätter*, pp.12–13.

50. *Ibid.*

51. Manfred Schneider, 'Das Kino und die Architekturen des Wissens', in Georg Christoph Tholen and Michael O. Scholl (eds), *Zeit-Zeichen. Aufschübe und Interferenzen zwischen Endzeit und Echtzeit* (Weinheim, Bundesrepublik Deutschland, 1990), pp.281–95.

52. Pichler, *Zerstreute Blätter*, p.83.

53. *Ibid.*, pp.160 and 83.

54. *Ibid.*, p.83.

55. *Ibid.*, pp.146–7.

56. In this way, aged fifty, Caroline Pichler describes her life as a 'path travelled' in her autobiographical 'Überblick meines Lebens aus dem Jahr 1819'; see Pichler, *Denkwürdigkeiten*, 2, p.395, see also 1, p.3.

57. The British Museum opened to the public in 1759; the Fridericianum was built in Cassel in 1769: the Louvre was opened to the public in 1793 and a year later the French National Archives were founded as the first, and for a time the only institution of its kind; the foundations of the new British Museum were laid in 1824, and its equivalents, the Altes Museum in Berlin and the Munich Glyptothek, were completed in 1830. See Pomian, *Der Ursprung des Museums*, p.67 and Jensen, *Wunderkammer des Abendlandes*, p.160.

58. Pomian, pp.84 and 95.

59. Walter Benjamin, 'Ich packe meine Bibliothek aus. Eine Rede über das Sammeln' in *Gesammelte Schriften*, p.388. This work exists in English as, 'Unpacking my Library. A Talk About Book Collecting', in *Illuminations*, ed. Hannah Arendt, trans. Harry Zohn (London, Fontana, 1992), pp.61–9.

60. Pichler, *Denkwürdigkeiten*, 2, p.379.

61. Johann Christoph Gatterer, 'Vom historischen Plan, und der darauf sich gründenden Zusammenfügung von Erzählung', in *Allgemeine historische Bibliothek von Mitgliedern des königlichen Instituts der historischen Wissenschaften zu Göttingen*, ed. Johann Christoph Gatterer (rpt, 1767–71, Hildesheim, Olms, 1994); the quote is taken from the full microfiche editions. See also Günter Niggl, *Geschichte der deutschen Autobiographie. Theoretische Grundlegung und literarische Entfaltung* (Stuttgart, Metzler, 1977), p.56.

62. *Ibid.*

63. Albrecht von Haller thus characterizes Gotthold Ephraim Lessing's working method in his antiquarian writings, *Laokoon* (1766) and *Antiquarische Briefe* (1769). See Albrecht von Haller, 'Rezension des "Laokoon"', in *Göttingische Anzeigen von Gelehrten Sachen*, 12 and 18 September 1766, quoted in *Gotthold Ephraim Lessing. Werke und Briefe in zwölf Bänden*, ed. Wilfried Barner *et. al.*, 12 vols (Frankfurt a.M., Deutsche Klassiker Verlag, 1990), 5:2., pp.674–734, p.681.

64. Johann Winckelmann, *Geschichte der Kunst des Altertums* (rpt, 1764, Vienna, Phaidon, 1934), preface, pp.9–22, p. 10. This work exists in English translation as J.J. Winckelmann, *The History of Ancient Art*, trans. G.H. Lodge (Boston, J. Rosgoode & Co., 1880).

65. Johann Gottfried Herder, 'Die Kritischen Wälder zur Ästhetik', in Johann Gottfried Herder, *Werke in 10 Bänden*, eds. Günter Arnold, Martin Bollacher, Jürgen Brummack *et. al.*, 10 vols (Frankfurt a.M, Deutsche Klassiker Verlag, 1985–97), 2, pp.9–422.

66. See Johann Gottfried Herder, 'Denkmal Johann Winckelmanns', in Winckelmann, *Geschichte*, p.431.

8.1   N.a., *Sophie von La Roche, Mein Schreibetisch*, frontispiece (1799)

9

Antiquarianism, connoisseurship and the Northern Renaissance print: new collecting cultures in the early nineteenth century

Heather MacLennan

The antiquarian print collector was a significant figure in Britain in the late eighteenth and early nineteenth centuries, existing as both a cultural historian and connoisseur and contributing to a rich museum heritage through the legacy of some extraordinary print collections.[1] Previous research has concentrated on print collections rather than their context and circumstances. Yet investigation of the activity of middle-class print collectors in the late eighteenth and early nineteenth centuries reveals much about the new collecting culture.[2] A few pioneers admired categories of art otherwise neglected by higher art criticism. An instance of this is the enthusiasm shown by antiquarian print collectors for the Northern Renaissance print. Styles of linear engraving and fifteenth- and sixteenth-century iconography seemed so outmoded that they appeared redundant to many early nineteenth-century viewers, who were more interested in Classical aesthetics. Among the few artist observers who expressed admiration, the figure of William Blake stands out.[3] Variable impressions and prints made from reworked plates added to the confusing late eighteenth-century picture of the early art of engraving. Many prints that were bought and sold cannot be identified exactly; indeed, prints of the fifteenth century were not fully catalogued until the early twentieth century, notwithstanding the pioneering work of earlier cataloguers.[4] Many unidentified masters and their workshops were only known by their monograms.

Given these circumstances as well as the climate of opinion, the commitment of some early nineteenth-century print collectors to the category of Northern Renaissance art seems all the more remarkable.[5] The topic raises questions about connoisseurial and antiquarian attitudes to print collecting. Since interest in early Northern printmaking was largely antiquarian, reasonable assumptions might be made concerning levels of interest. However, within print collecting culture there was evidently a free exchange of ideas about aesthetics and cultural history. This study demonstrates some of the rich range of responses that Northern Renaissance prints evoked, raising questions about the definition of the antiquarian particularly as far as certain categories of prints are concerned.

The flourishing of print culture during the Renaissance was recognized as an important historical phenomenon by early nineteenth-century antiquarians who appreciated the distinctive role of early engravers in the rise and expansion of print design and technology, as culture progressed. Original engravings were fully recognized in the advertising of print sellers from the 1770s onwards.[6] In the 1790s, the collecting of early Northern prints predates the development of interest in Northern Renaissance painting, with one or two exceptions. A few important sales indicate the relative significance of these prints.[7] Among these were the sales of the collections of Sir Joshua Reynolds (1798) and Charles Rogers (1799). Reynolds's collection served to illustrate the history of art and the techniques of the masters. He owned several paintings and very many engravings by Northern Renaissance artists.[8] The Northern Renaissance prints owned by Rogers were thought to be remarkable.[9] In some circles, at least, early Northern Renaissance artists were well known, but this was not a category of art normally sought out by collectors notwithstanding the reputation of artists such as Dürer and Van Leyden, who in any case were thought to have transcended their Gothic origins in their embrace of more graceful Italian styles of representation. The most sought-after prints and those that fetched the highest prices tended to be associated with artists such as Van Dyck or Rubens, and the seventeenth-century Italians.

Collectors such as Douce, Roscoe, Ottley, Kerrich and Fitzwilliam represent a new cultural development. Informed, independent and motivated by a serious regard for the art of engraving and its history, their collecting ambitions coincided with a buoyant period in the art market, a time when inexpensive and good impressions could be obtained. Histories and dictionaries of engraving encouraged a more sophisticated approach to the collecting of old master prints, and especially of Northern Renaissance engravings.

The prices of rare and early prints increased in the period. In January 1817, Douce observed that old prints were costing more than some paintings, and that prices were once again on the increase. In the Seratti sale (1816) two early Italian prints fetched nearly £50 each. In January 1821, Douce commented to Kerrich on the occasion of the second Lloyd sale, on two 'lions', a supposed Finiguerra, sold for £53 and 'a little print of a Madonna under a Gothic canopy, presenting an apple to her infant' with the undoubted date of 1460, he said, very early for a copper plate.[10] It sold moderately; Douce had not bid, as he knew that Dimsdale (a dealer) had intended to bid high to obtain it.[11] The Lloyd sale was a good one from the point of view of Northern Renaissance engravings. 'The Martin Schoen's at this sale have not diminished the present value of yours,' Douce told Kerrich.[12] The status of Northern Renaissance prints within this collecting culture was changing.

The art of the connoisseur

The antiquarian print connoisseur's cabinet was constructed neither to demonstrate fashionable taste nor to serve the higher cause of classical aesthetics. The aim was to represent past printmaking achievement in its diversity, inspired by the intrinsic qualities of the print impression. The autograph print had high status in such collections. Ideas about the appraisal of master prints were influenced by specialist publications on engraving, which gave full consideration to the history, technique and merits of the print.[13] Growing appreciation of the originality of early engravers was understood in relation to ideas about the *peintre-graveur* particularly emanating from Bartsch.[14] Indeed, the impact of Bartsch's volumes did much to redress the imbalance of viewpoints affecting the low status of early examples of the autograph print during an age in which the reproductive image seemed to dominate.

Huber's *Manuel des Amateurs* encouraged the observer to use his eyes, develop expertise, and apply newly acquired knowledge when making judgements about the quality or state of an impression. This is the art of the connoisseur.[15] Robinson describes the connoisseur as motivated by the beauty of the impression and the uniqueness of the proof. Such a collector is discerning, seeking after fine quality impressions by outstanding practitioners in the field, valuing clear early impressions on well preserved paper. Many connoisseurs tried to collect the whole of an artist's œuvre, and each known state of a particular print image.[16]

Huber's distinction between an antiquarian approach – in search of rarity rather than artistic merit – and that of the true print connoisseur – moved by a sense of history and aesthetics – sets up an interesting opposition, which is too stark to be helpful, particularly when trying to understand the range of reasons why print images of the Northern Renaissance were admired in Britain.[17] Prints had a literature largely independent of fine art hagiographies and aesthetic prejudices. Writers on engraving sought to present the production, study and collecting of engraving as a liberal art, which led to better consideration of all print styles. While criticism was still directed at the Gothic aesthetic, recognition was given to the significant role of early engravings in the history of art. Furthermore, German writers promoted the cause of great Northern engravers and their talented precursors.[18]

For Douce and Kerrich, issues of authorship and circumstances of production were key concerns. They both realized the significance and difference of

the early autograph print, and showed insight into the genesis of the repro-
graphic image. Kerrich's experiences as an artist and printmaker gave an in-
depth understanding of the processes and techniques of engraving. Douce
applied his interest in social history and iconography.

In 1807, Douce started to collect old master engravers seriously, particularly those of the Northern schools. Aldegrever, Van Leyden, Dürer, Beham,
and Schongauer are all mentioned in his record of purchases; for instance in
November 1807, among unidentified prints he notes the acquisition of an
impression from Van Leyden's *Passion of the Crown of Thorns (of Palser)*, and
Dürer's *Woman and Satyr*. In June 1808, he bought Dürer's *Jacob and Thamar*, M.
Schoen's *Virgil* and 'lots of old masters at Allen's sale in July (Dodd)'.[19] Also in
1808 he obtained a 1460 Annunciation, work by Aldegrever, Van Leyden's
designs of the *Wise Men and the Resurrection*, Van Meckenem's *Death of the
Virgin*, Beham's *Adam and Eve*, M. Schoen's *Assumption of the Virgin, Christ
before Pilate*, Dürer's *Virgin and Child* (1511) and other versions and copies,
many of which came from the Richardson sale in October. By 1809 he was
buying 100 or 200 prints at a time. He did buy more mainstream Italian prints,
particularly Mantegna and Marc Antonio, but he mostly acquired early
Northern engravings. This period coincides with an increase in his intellectual
awareness of the old master engravers and the history of engraving, which can
be traced in his record of 'Books Read' and in his correspondence with Kerrich,
where, in 1808 and 1809, there is a lively debate over the authorship, identity
and production of early Northern prints.[20]

During this period, Douce was working at the British Museum as Keeper of
Manuscripts. He had access to the print collection and was very interested in
its contents, although, as with much else at the British Museum, he despaired
of its organization. In 1809, Douce began an unofficial record of the early
Northern prints held by the British Museum, which may have been solely for
his own interest, although this date coincides with Philipe's contract with the
Museum to sort and catalogue the collection.[21] Douce's notebook is entitled
'An account of the very early engravings on copper formerly in the collection
of Dr Monro and now in the British Museum, 1809'. Working through an
album of recently sorted prints, Douce attempts to identify each impression,
referring to Bartsch, Heinecken, Strutt, and Ottley.[22] He commented on similar
impressions in private collections, including his own, and noted whether they
changed hands. Many British Museum prints were finer than others he had
seen. Exasperated at the incompetence of the British Museum sorters and the
wisdom of the curator's identifications, he noted that Italian prints were
mixed in with Northern examples, and Schongauer's prints were either inter-
spersed with prints by Van Meckenem or wrongly attributed. At the back of
his notebook he listed printmakers' names and monograms and early prints
dating between 1461 and 1499.

Douce identified prints by the Master ES (known as the Master of 1466), Schongauer, Israel Van Meckenem, Wenzel von Olmütz, Mair von Landshut, Dürer, and monogram artists, among whom are the Master WH, the Master AG and the Master BM, to name but a few. Douce's connoisseurial instinct led him to make accurate visual connections between styles and identities, in order to establish the date and œuvre of unattributed prints; Bartsch references were added. Detailed descriptions and narratives helped in the identification of impressions, but in several instances an antiquarian purpose is revealed where he noted costume fragments and annotated his text with sketches of shields or head-dresses as an *aide-mémoire*. An amazing head-dress attracted his attention in Dürer's *Young Couple Threatened by Death, or, The Promenade* (1498) (Figure 9.1) and thus he provided a sketch (Figure 9.2).[23] In the case of Item 15 in the notebook, Douce's description and sketch detail were accurate enough to identify a print by the Master ES, *Virgin Praying in a Gothic Chamber* (1467) (Figure 9.3). Douce noted, 'Behind her a vessel of holy water & a basin', in red in the margin he added the date, 1467, and commented, 'I have this print'.[24] The sketched motifs of shields and the monogram and date are copied (Figure 9.4); the print is still in the Museum collection and like many of the images Douce itemized came from the collection of Dr John Monro.[25]

Known for his researches into medieval customs, Douce was captivated by unusual subjects and costume details; for instance, regarding one engraving by the monogrammist WH, *The Garden of Love* (Figure 9.5), he wrote:

A large & very curious print ... representing a number of young men & women, recreating themselves in a garden. At a table, spread with fruit, are two young men, one playing on a guitar; another offers a cup of wine to a lady who rejects it; by her side sits a young female with her hands crossed. Near the table is a beau of the time, a feather in his cap & pointed shoes, who presents a cup to the last mentioned damsel. In another part of the garden are two other pairs of lovers, two standing, the others sitting. At the gate of the garden a female has seized a fool by one of the apes ears of his cap, & with the other hand picks his purse or pocket.[26]

Additionally, he sketched the fool and added, 'W is on the stomacher of a lady sitting on the ground'; and, 'This print is very interesting for the dresses which resemble those in V. Meckeheim's prints. Some of the women have an odd sort of cap or bonnet. All the men have pointed toes.' He speculated that it might be a copy of a similar subject by Master ES.

What was Douce thinking when he contemplated these prints? He was drawn to the Gothic period and its characteristic design styles, and his lively descriptions focus on people, their role, character and costume detail. His response is thus not primarily aesthetic, it is antiquarian.[27] He has unhesitating praise for the skill and artistry of master engravers such as Schongauer, for their qualities of observation, of drawing and of mark making; indeed, he is struck by the quality of the impression, especially *The Flight into Egypt*, of which he wrote, 'A fine Impression of a beautiful print'.[28] He mentioned a large version of 'Christ bearing the cross', by Schongauer, about which he noted, 'The head of Christ is beautiful beyond description'.[29] Also,

A very beautiful print by M Schoen with his usual mark of an ecce homo, attended by the Virgin and St John; she is weeping … the head of Christ is extremely fine & marks the great superiority of Schoen over all his contemporaries. Indeed A Dürer himself has not equalled the heads of christ in this print.[30]

Douce, the print connoisseur, attends to authorship and establishing an artist's œuvre. He is observant of excellent impressions, seeking to identify originals and thus prototypes and to distinguish these from copies. He notes relationships between drawings and print compositions, as in the case of a Dürer study; his comment on a large drawing of Christ delivering John from Purgatory, dated 1510, was that 'It seems the original sketch for the print of this subject in the large wooden Passion (see my comparison of it with the print in my Albert Dürer Book 6)'.[31]

A simplified idea of late eighteenth-century antiquarianism does not necessarily apply to print collectors in the period; circumstances suggest a far more complex set of criteria than the caricature constructed by contemporary observers of an enthusiast, obsessed with minutiae and the barely significant. Wainwright refutes such an image of the antiquarian.[32] Serious antiquarians were interested in tracing the origins of ideas and technologies and recognized the social importance of artefacts. They were pioneer cultural historians, but this does not mean they were unreceptive to aesthetic approaches. What constituted an antiquarian was a topic for much satire in the period, and self-parody in the case of Douce and Kerrich. Kerrich had little time for valuing artefacts *per se*, and would only consider them worth recording if they had artistic value. The cultural value of the print to the antiquarian was immense, but to say that all antiquarians displayed an attitude that was external to the field of art is to assume that distinct discourses operated in isolation from one another.

An interesting question is raised in respect of Northern Renaissance prints. Because they did not readily submit themselves to classical criteria of appraisal – seeming outmoded in a period in which styles of engraving served reproductive purposes – it was more likely that these prints should be fulsomely appreciated by antiquarians and print connoisseurs for whom, as I have said, the unique qualities of the print and its imagery were paramount. These viewers did not necessarily require that the print should display the softly modulated tonal effects needed to imitate a painting or drawing. Robinson hints at this difference between the connoisseur and the critic when he discusses the appraisal of sixteenth- and seventeenth-century Northern prints in the age of Rembrandt: 'Seventeenth-century collectors applied the criteria of print connoisseurship in evaluating an individual impression. Critics, however, invoked a different set of principles in their appraisals of a printmaker's style.'[33] There were different discourses at work. Robinson continues, 'Although critics enjoyed the neatness and finish typical of engravings by Dürer and Lucas, they reserved their warmest praise for printmakers who created effects of light and tone that simulated the fluidity and coloristic richness of a painting or wash drawing.'[34]

This useful distinction may be applied to analysis of early nineteenth-century criticism, suggesting that within the dialogue of print collectors, viewpoints were not constrained by academic criteria. This was neither an artist's nor a critic's discourse. Antiquarian print collectors inspired by the print artefact approached Northern Renaissance images afresh, without aesthetic prejudice. Lipking has observed the growing awareness of the importance of history as well as the new approaches to learning that encouraged attributes of wisdom and usefulness rather than amusement and curiosity.[35] Indeed, Lipking charts the passage from curiosity about the past to serious interest and connoisseurship.[36] This new direction can be observed in the approaches of serious print connoisseurs in their researches into the genesis and history of printmaking forms.

Artists, artisans and copy engravers

Douce and Kerrich shared knowledge about prints and printmaking in their correspondence, between 1803 and 1827. They met in each other's homes, or kept a rendezvous in a Lincoln's Inn Fields coffeehouse, and talked about the content of their respective print cabinets with their reference books before them. Over the years, their opinions were gradually transformed, inspired by new encounters with print impressions, or engraving texts.

Except for the posthumous catalogue on Heemskerck, Kerrich's extensive views on print collecting and early Northern categories of artists and printmakers were never published, although he did consider the possibility.[37] Ideas about the early Northern printmakers evolved from the on-going dialogue conducted between himself and close friends, particularly Douce and his circle of acquaintances, which included Fuseli, Balme and Cotman. When Kerrich was confined to duties in Cambridge as University Librarian, or if he was on holiday at the Norfolk coast, he corresponded with Douce, exchanging views on print collecting. It was in the private world of collecting and talking that his ideas developed.

While Douce did publish his research into cultural history, this was not directly related to his study of the single-leaf print. There is a manuscript on early print processes and images, titled 'Origin of Printing',[38] which was prepared for a lecture at the Society of Antiquaries, but was never published. Douce's views on prints and printmaking are otherwise to be found in his private correspondence, where the status of the print and the artist–engraver were frequently debated. Early in 1805, a lecturer on the art of engraving at the Royal Institution (probably Landseer), had approached Douce to look at old prints in his collection. Douce wrote to Kerrich:

My long lethargy … as to old prints was lately interrupted by an application from the lecturer on the art of engraving at the royal institute to look at what I had in this way. I was a good deal surprised to find that he was an entire stranger to prints of the 15th and 16th centuries as well as to every book that has mentioned them. Most of these I pointed out to him, & being really a man of quick apprehension & real genius, he has contrived to write a lecture of much interest & far too good for the motley & lounging auditory at the above place. He unfortunately read this lecture at my house in the presence of Barry the painter which he had solicited & who contrary to all expectation gave it the toughest reception you can imagine, as it seemed to tread over some of the same ground he had taken in his own academy lectures; & you must know besides that he regards engravers just as a physician of the first eminence would a journeyman apothecary.[39]

Kerrich responded:

Perhaps I have as little respect for mere Engravers who only copy other peoples works as Mr Barry: they can be considered only as transcribers, or if they ever reach to the merit of Translators, it is the utmost that can be allowed them; & that is no very great matter. The old masters who engraved, or etch'd their own designs, are creatures of a quite different species. But, if I understand you right the merit of Engravers, or the rank they ought to hold amongst men, seems to have been entirely out of the question: the subject of your lecturer's Discourses was the Art of Engraving itself: concerning the Importance of that, there can, I should suppose, be no doubt. Without the assistance of Engraving Mr Barry & all the other painters would in a few centuries fall into oblivion … However I do not know that it was the Lecturer's business to set forth all this; We must take it for granted that the People at the Royal Institute, consider'd the Art of Engraving as a thing of some consequence, & wish'd to be informed & instructed in it, or why did they set him to talk about it: and if he gave them the information & introduction they wanted, clearly, & intellegibly [sic]; he did what he had undertaken, & deserves great praise.[40]

That there was a public airing of the topic of engraving and a debate about its status is apparent. Kerrich had pragmatic respect for the necessity of copy engraving, since the reproductive print served a useful purpose to artists, communicating an idea of their work in their own time and for future generations. Kerrich alluded to Barry's stance vis-à-vis the reproductive print and its engraver–producer, whom Barry apparently considered to be a mere transcriber, which was a conventional viewpoint. How did Barry regard his own printmaking output? As reproductive engraving and etching, or as art? Barry should have been in an ideal position to make a distinction between the utilitarian purpose of the engraver's craft and the expressive power of the artist working freely in this medium, as he was a printmaker of some experience. He is known to have worked on engravings and etchings from his own designs at home. Inventories of the contents of his house include etching equipment, and there is a fragment of a note on the etching process that suggests an experimental approach.[41]

The Kerrich letter clearly demonstrates its author's feeling for the Renaissance original print. He states quite clearly, 'The old masters who engraved, or etch'd their own designs, are creatures of a quite different species'.[42] In other words, he does not see them in the same light as modern copy engravers. In his sensitivity on this issue, he is not too far distant from twentieth-century attitudes to such artists. Kerrich had a profound understanding of the circumstances in which the artist's print was produced within the Renaissance engraver's workshop, and he was evidently aware of the change of circumstances between the old engravers of the fifteenth century and the high Renaissance exemplified by Dürer. Bartsch's coining of the phrase 'Le Peintre Graveur' would have had some significance for Kerrich, although he did not obtain a copy of Bartsch before 1812. Barry's views are those of a practising artist taking a modern stance on the art of engraving; Kerrich occupies a connoisseurial position in this debate, and shows appreciation for the special circumstances of the early engraving and its artist–producer.

Identifying authorship, genesis and production

A marked feature of the correspondence between Douce and Kerrich is the discussion of authorship and the methods by which print images were produced, and the effect this had on their consequent artistic status. The central issue was the artisanal element of print production. The subject of identification was important in evaluating the master print, and was a topic debated by Kerrich with reference to the very old engravers known only through their monograms. The discussion about authorship partly focused on technical procedures in as much as these could be reconstructed in the early nineteenth century.

In 1804, Kerrich had apparently been puzzling over the significance of engravers' marks and the extent to which these might be successfully interpreted when determining authorship. He wrote the following letter to Douce (for Kerrich, who revered the designer, it is the identification of the artist as author that was uppermost in his mind, though he did retain some respect for the inspired engraver):

But in order to form any satisfactory opinion concerning the meaning of these marks upon old prints, & determine to whom they refer, we must make the enquiry upon as

large a basis (if I may so speak) as we can, & consider who they are that can be said to
have a property to the work – that can have any right to call it theirs. The very old
engravers seem to have had the matter entirely to themselves. They appear to have
been the Designers Engravers etc etc & nobody else had anything to do with it. But it
was not so with their successors – Albert Dürer himself is a very puzzling fellow, & if
we consider his works, with any attention, we must conclude, that the mark has very
different meanings upon different prints. In some of them I *must* believe whatever may
be said (I mean without proof) he was both the Inventor & Designer, & engraver or
cutter, in others he might be the Inventor or the Designer & even draw the whole upon
the block ... in which case not only the Invention & outline, but the shading & very
lines & Hatchings would be his also – in others he might only be author of the picture,
or wash'd Drawing, & the Engraver work from it, in which case the lines and
Hatchings would not be his, but yet he might fairly claim it as his Design, & put his
mark to it.[43]

Douce preferred to think that Dürer cut all his own prints himself. He
regarded the master engraver as someone who saw the process through to the
end. He eventually came round to Kerrich's way of thinking about the woodcuts. Kerrich doubted that in all cases Dürer was both designer and executor
(*formscheider*). He regarded the mechanical execution of the drawn lines, however excellent, as a craft activity, of less importance than the skill and imagination required to design and draw out the image, which was the part of the
process he most admired. This extract highlights how one might interpret the
authorship of each part of the process of print production and shows Kerrich's
appreciation of the realities of the output of a Renaissance workshop. Douce
and Kerrich shared an intense interest in Dürer's achievements and in understanding the process of engraving or woodcut. They appreciated the
Renaissance artist's skill and valued the original print. Ultimately, for Kerrich,
it was Dürer's authorship of the design that determined the principal merit of
the engraving or woodcut. But as the point demonstrates, identifying the
authorship of prints was a complex matter. The value thus placed on the
generation of artist–engravers that preceded Dürer is fascinating. Here, the
very distinction made later by Landau and Parshall about early engraving and
the original print can be seen to be fully acknowledged by Thomas Kerrich.[44]

The application of criteria normally discussed in the presence of paintings,
as recommended to British readers by Gilpin, inevitably excluded early
Northern examples, which were in a stylistically difficult category of their
own. Whereas in accounts of painting there was an effort to transcend the
mechanical in order to promote the idea of painting as a liberal art, this was far
more difficult in the case of the early engraving, which lent itself, in appraisal,
to those aspects of the vocabulary of criticism devoted to the technical.
Evidence of mastery over the medium of engraving and of skill in rendering
detail appealed to the antiquarian and the connoisseur. While admiration of
technical skill was a well established aspect of all art criticism, as a particular
quality it was insufficient to admire technique alone; style was far more

important, and this worked against the wider acceptance of Northern Renaissance prints as art.

Antiquarian approaches to artefacts certainly did not conform to the perspective of artists, critics or academics, and, it could be argued, represented a separate discourse. Yet within the definition 'antiquarian interest' there were diverse approaches to the print artefact. Douce and Kerrich evidently had an enlightened understanding of early engraving, a well-debated topic, informed by contemporary attitudes to the reproductive print process. The question of how to appraise and determine the authorship and status of early prints was of importance, and a distinction was made between the modern copy engraver and the old artist–engraver. This difference and thus recognition of the value and character of the Northern Renaissance print was very significant. German scholarship helped provide the necessary encouragement for Northern Renaissance printmaking to be fully appraised. The connoisseurial approach to the print as an art form was influenced by European attitudes. But it was principally close attention to the print image and an independence of outlook that enabled Douce and Kerrich to approach early prints positively.

Evaluating prints as art, even by some antiquarian writers, tended to be determined by an overriding Classical taste that marginalized the Northern Renaissance engraving style. This accounts for the neglect of such artistic achievement within higher art criticism of the early nineteenth century. However, for some collectors, the study of Northern Renaissance engraving was indeed born out of recognition of the special qualities of these prints and of their significance as valuable repositories of cultural history. In theory, an identifiable connoisseurial discourse existed in the period, at least in tomes such as Huber's, but in practice the range of ideas that prints evoked was complex. A study of the correspondence of Douce and Kerrich reveals a rich set of attitudes to early Northern prints well before works by these artists became sought after as collectors' items and Dürer or Van Leyden or indeed Schongauer were fully accepted in the pantheon of art.

Notes

1. For instance, Francis Douce (1757–1834), who bequeathed his collection in 1834 to the University of Oxford; and Reverend Thomas Kerrich (1748–1828), part of whose print collection is in the Fitzwilliam Museum, Cambridge. Other neglected figures include Lord Fitzwilliam (1745–1816), the founder of the Fitzwilliam Museum, all of whose prints were retained by the Museum, and Dr John Monro (1715–91) whose early Northern engravings were bought by the British Museum in 1806.

2. See Antony Griffiths, *Landmarks in Print Collecting, Connoisseurs and Donors at the British Museum since 1753* (London, British Museum Press, 1996).

3. Blake reveals his respect for Dürer, Schongauer, Leyden, and Beham in his discussions about engraving style. See William Blake, 'The Descriptive Catalogue' (printed to be distributed at Blake's exhibition of August–September, 1809), in G. Keynes, *The Complete Writings of Blake* (London, Nonesuch Press, 1957). See also Blake's 'Prospectus for the Chaucer Engraving' (1809) (*ibid.*) and the manuscript for the unpublished 'Public Address' (1810). Blake kept a copy of Dürer's *Melancolia* above his

engraving table. The situation and status of the printed image and its executor in the eighteenth century certainly concerned Blake. In a discussion about Blake's 'Public Address', Bindman comments, 'To proclaim a taste for Albrecht Dürer and early Northern engravers in 1810 was rare although by no means unique, but their appeal to Blake was due as much to the fact that they engraved their own designs as to the character of their work'. David Bindman, *The Complete Graphic Works of William Blake* (London, Thames and Hudson, 1986) p.19.

4. For later authoritative catalogues see, Max Lehrs, *Geschichte und kritischer Katalog des deutschen, niederländischen und französichen Kupferstichs im XV Jahrhundert*, 9 vols (Vienna, Gesellschaft für vervielfältigende Kunst, 1908–34); Max Geisberg, *The German Single-Leaf Woodcut, 1500–1550*, rev. and ed. Walter Strauss, 4 vols (New York, Hacker Art Books, 1974); F.W.H. Hollstein, *Dutch and Flemish Etchings, Engravings and Woodcuts, c.1450–1700* (Amsterdam, M. Hertzberger, 1949); M. Hertzberger, *German Engravings, Etchings and Woodcuts, c.1400–1700* (Amsterdam, M. Hertzberger, 1954) and Campbell Dodgson, *The Masters of Engraving and Etching: Albrecht Dürer* (London and Boston, The Medici Society, 1926). According to common practice, all specific impressions of prints cited in this chapter are referenced according to Lehrs or Dodgson.

5. The heyday of print scholarship of the Northern Renaissance masters lasted between the 1890s and the 1930s, with notable contributions by Lehrs, Geisberg, and Dodgson. In recent years there has been a spate of excellent exhibitions dedicated to the subject and a revival in debate about the topic following on from new research. For a summary of recent exhibitions and catalogues see G. Bartrum, *German Renaissance Prints 1490–1550* (London, British Museum Press, 1995). See also the exhibition catalogues *Fifteenth-century German Line-engravings and Dotted Prints* (Oxford, The University of Oxford, Ashmolean Museum, 1991) and Ursula Meyr-Harting, *Early Netherlandish Engraving c.1440–1540* (Oxford, The University of Oxford, Ashmolean Museum, 1997) which include many Douce prints.

6. See Walter Shropshire's Sale Catalogues of 1770 and 1771, British Museum Print Room Library [hereafter BMPL].

7. See the McFarquer Sale Catalogue (May 1796), BMPL (Thane's copy).

8. Reynolds's Prints and Drawings sale was in March and May 1798 at Philips. Included are prints by Dürer, Van Leyden, Aldegrever, and also Schoengauer. See Thane's catalogue, BMPL.

9. See BMPL catalogue which belonged to Thane, pp. 78–98. Also Griffiths, *Landmarks in Print Collecting*, pp. 19–36. Rogers was one of the first British collectors fully to appreciate the significance of Northern Renaissance engravings.

10. 6 January 1821, MS Kerrich 606, f.174, Corpus Christi, Cambridge.

11. It might have been *The Smallest Madonna of Einsiedeln with St Meinrad*, by the Master ES; see M. Lehrs, *Late Gothic Engravings of Germany and the Netherlands* (New York, Dover, 1969), pl.218. The composition that Douce describes is similar to two larger prints of the Madonna, both of which are dated 1466. The Master ES *Madonna* (Lehrs 68) is seated underneath an elaborate architectural Gothic canopy, on either side an angel and a saint. She is offering either a pear or an apple to the child.

12. 6 January 1821, MS Kerrich 606, f.174. Douce had a good deal of respect for Lloyd's collection.

13. Among these: Michael Huber, *Notices générales des graveurs divisés par nations, et des peintres rangés par écoles précédées de l'histoire de la gravure et de la peinture, et suivies d'un catalogue raisonné d'une collection choisie d'estampes* (Dresden, J.G.I. Breitkopf, 1787) and M. Huber and C.C.H. Rost, *Manuel des Curieux et des Amateurs de l'art contenant une notice des principaux graveurs, et un catalogue raisonné de leurs meilleurs ouvrages*, 9 vols ([1 and 2] London, H. Escher [3–9] Zurich, Orell, Fuessli & Co., 1797–1808).

14. Adam von Bartsch, *Le Peintre-Graveur*, 21 vols (Vienna, J.V. Degen, 1803–21); see also Bartsch, *Catalogue des Œuvres de L. Van Leyden* (Vienna, J.V. Degen, 1798). While Bartsch's approach to the classification of the original print was systematic and ground breaking, some of the ideas about the appraisal of the printmaking image had been anticipated, for instance in William Gilpin, *An Essay Upon Prints*, 2nd edn (London, G. Scott, 1768) and in Huber, *Notices générales des graveurs*, who was influenced by Gilpin.

15. The Dutch dealer in prints and collector, J.P. Zomer, as described by W.W. Robinson, also fits Huber's definition of the connoisseur; see William W. Robinson, 'This Passion for prints, collecting and connoisseurship in Northern Europe during the seventeenth century', in Clifford S. Ackley (ed.), *Printmaking in the Age of Rembrandt* (Boston, Massachusetts, Museum of Fine Arts, 1981), pp.xl–xli. See also Huber and Rost, *Manuel des Curieux et des Amateurs*, 1, pp.58–77. Zomer is described by Robinson as a sophisticated collector of prints, among the first of those amateurs 'whose entire approach to collecting was based upon the values of print connoisseurship. Concentrating on the quality and rarity of the individual impression, he strove to establish a choice collection, not a universal one.' (p.xli).

16. *Ibid.*, pp. xlii–xliii. Robinson is sure that the characteristics of the modern print connoisseur were in evidence as early as 1700.

17. Huber and Rost, *Manuel des Curieux et des Amateurs*. Huber's account of the art of the connoisseur draws on Gilpin. Huber constructs the print as art and its appraisal as aesthetic. He is dismissive of the pursuit of rarity for its own sake.

18. See C.H. von Heinecken, *Idée Générale d'une Collection Complette d'Estampes, avec une dissertation sur l'origine de la Gravure et sur les premiers Livres d'Images* (Leipzig and Vienna, Jean Paul Kraus, 1771); and Heinecken's *Dictionaire des artistes dont nous avons des estampes*, 4 vols (Leipzig, J.G.I. Breitkopf, 1778–90). See also Huber, *Notices générales des graveurs*, and Bartsch, *Catalogue des Œuvres de L. Van Leyden* and *Le Peintre-Graveur*.

19. Douce's *Collecta* (1805–34), 1808, MS Douce e.66–68, Bodleian Library, Oxford.

20. See Douce notebooks, MS Douce, ff.14–17, Bodleian Library, Oxford. See also his letters to Kerrich at this time, MS Kerrich 606.

21. MS Douce e.61. This notebook consists of 38 leaves, mostly written recto and verso, in Douce's own handwriting. Thomas Philipe had been commissioned by the British Museum to mount and sort the print collection, and worked on this task between 1808 and 1810.

22. Many of these references were probably added later. Douce read the manuscript for William Young Ottley's *An Inquiry into the Origin and Early History of Engraving Upon Copper and in Wood with an account of engravers to the time of M.A. Raimondi*, 2 vols (London, J. McCreery for J. and A. Arch, 1816).

23. MS. Douce, e.61, f.13 r.

24. *Ibid.*, f.6 v.

25. British Museum, E 1–24. All 'E' numbers on mounts refer to the earliest acquisitions in the Museum. Monro's prints are mentioned in Joseph Strutt, *Biographical Dictionary of Engravers*, 2 vols (London, R. Faulder, 1785–6). See Volume 2, p. 21 for a list of prints by the Master ES, among which is Lehrs 2.61. The identification of Monro's prints, which has been a problem since Philipe masked the collector's marks with new mounts, is now more feasible thanks to Douce's notebook.

26. MS Douce e.61.f.7 r. (Figure 9.4).

27. See S. G. Gillam (ed.), *The Douce Legacy* (Oxford, Oxford University, Bodleian Library, 1984). Douce's authorship focused on what is best defined as cultural history, on subjects such as the Dance of Death, and the Illustrations of Shakespeare. See his publication, *Illustrations of Shakespeare, and of ancient manners: with dissertations on the clowns and fools of Shakespeare; on the collection of popular tales entitled Gesta Romanorum; and on the English morris dance*, 2 vols (London, Longman, 1807), also *The Dance of Death; painted by H.Holbein, and engraved by W.Hollar. The daunce of Machabree, made by J. Lydgate* (London, Edwards, c.1794). A later edition was entitled *The Dance of Death exhibited in elegant engravings on wood, with a dissertation on the several representations of that subject, but more particularly on those ascribed to Macaber and Hans Holbein* (London, William Pickering, 1833). See Gillam, *The Douce Legacy*, pp.71, and 102, for a discussion.

28. Schongauer, Lehrs 5.7.

29. Schongauer, Lehrs 5.9.

30. Schongauer, Lehrs 5.34 (i). Douce owned the second state.

31. MS Douce e.65, f.45.

32. Clive Wainwright, *The Romantic Interior* (New Haven, Yale University Press, 1989).

33. Robinson, 'This Passion for Prints', pp.xliv.

34. *Ibid.*

35. Lawrence Lipking, *The Ordering of the Arts in Eighteenth-Century England* (Princeton University Press, 1970), p.8.

36. *Ibid.*, pp.144–5.

37. Thomas Kerrich, *Catalogue of the Prints after Heemskerck* (Cambridge, J. Rodwell, 1829).

38. MS Douce b.7. In a different (red) ink at the top of the MS, and probably in Douce's hand, 'Written long before W O's work appeared.' He refers to Ottley's *Inquiry* of 1816. This account was written around 1812–14, that is before Dibdin's *Bibliographia Spenceriana* of 1814, which he refers to in connection with Earl Spencer's wood-cut of St Christopher, which Douce dates to 1423. The account focuses on the origins of print processes from early block books to 'pious' images printed alongside blocks carved with text. He considered whether Schongauer and Gutenberg were once engravers on

wood, deciding they were not. He attributed to Wolgemuth, the master of Dürer, the beginnings of the art of the woodcut.

39.   25 January, 1805, MS Kerrich 606, f.9.

40.   Letter dated 12 February 1805, MS Douce d.36, Bodleian Library, Oxford. Landseer was preparing a series of talks to be given at the Royal Institution in 1806.

41.   This fragment is now held in the Lewis Walpole Library, Connecticut. Whether Barry retained a more elevated view of the artist's print because of his own experience is not, alas, apparent from the quoted letter; other information indicates that Barry's was an ambivalent position. See Gillam, *The Douce Legacy*, p.4, on Douce's relationship with Barry, which very possibly began around 1800.

42.   12 February 1805, MS Douce d.36.

43.   29 September 1804, MS Douce d.36, f.5.

44.   See D. Landau and P. Parshall, *The Renaissance Print, 1470–1550* (New Haven and London, Yale University Press, 1994). These authors explore the theme of the artist–engraver from the early developments of the 1470s, which they describe as 'the critical stage in the maturation of early printmaking as an art form', p.v.

9.1   Albrecht Dürer, *Young Couple Threatened by Death, or, The Promenade* (1498), engraving

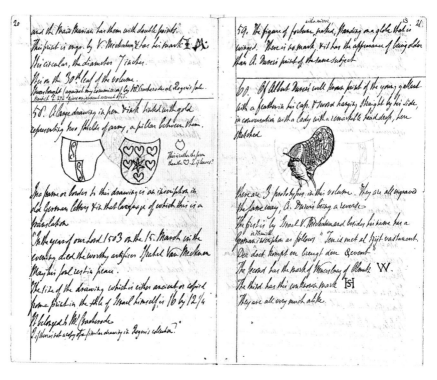

9.2   Francis Douce, *Early Prints in the British Museum* (1809)

9.3   Master ES, *Virgin Praying in a Gothic Chamber* (1467), engraving

9.4   Francis Douce, *Early Prints in the British Museum* (1809)

9.5   Master WH, *The Garden of Love* (n.d.), engraving

10

Science and sensibility:
architectural antiquarianism in the early nineteenth century

Alexandrina Buchanan

It is a truth universally acknowledged that at some point in the nineteenth century, antiquarianism lost its significance as a field of intellectual endeavour. As Momigliano put it, 'The question to ask about the antiquarian studies in the nineteenth century is not why they were discredited, but why they survived so long'.[1] The aim of this essay is to question what happened to antiquarianism during this period by examining certain aspects of a single topic: the study of medieval architecture.

Antiquarianism was an amateur interest which flourished in a period before the construction of disciplinary boundaries. It is thus very difficult to define, especially given the pejorative overtones the term has carried for some commentators since the eighteenth century, if not earlier. For the purposes of this essay, I shall consider as antiquarian any relationship with the past which seeks rather to describe and categorize its physical remains than to draw from them any wider message or moral. The study of medieval architecture was usually included within antiquarian literature, though it could also be classed as aesthetics, and the influential remarks on the subject by Sir Christopher Wren were drawn from his son's *Parentalia* (1750), a work hard to classify but certainly not antiquarian in intention. Medieval buildings were first studied as one element within wider topographical studies, which could occasionally provide surprisingly detailed descriptions of individual structures and sometimes accurate chronologies of their construction, though they had little to say on architecture in the abstract.

During the second half of the eighteenth century, changing aesthetic sensibilities combined with political factors to engender new interest in national antiquities, and medieval architecture started to attract notice in its own right. From around 1800, texts devoted to the subject began to appear with increasing frequency, aimed at every level of the market. Through the publishing boom, antiquarianism, which had formerly been the hobby of a small coterie with well-understood aims, became a mass pursuit and one from which there was money to be made. Personal and intellectual disputes had commercial implications and books on architecture written in the early years of the nineteenth century reveal the concerns of their authors regarding the explosion of antiquarian activity. The promise of accuracy of fact and validity of methodology were becoming selling points, even above beauty of production or fineness of illustration.

Although association aesthetics and patriotism had made Gothic popular, they had not made it rational, and in 1800 it was not yet confirmed as a subject appropriate for intellectual enquiry. It had to be released from the emotionalism engendered by its eighteenth-century admirers; the style itself had to be seen as being as regular as Classicism and the methods for its study needed to be rational and objective.

This was the intellectual context for the study of Gothic in the years around 1800. The works of Sir James Hall exemplify the attempts to give rationality to the subject. As he put it, his object was to restore Gothic to its due share of public esteem:

chiefly by shewing, that all its forms may be traced to the imitation of one very simple original; and, consequently, that they are connected together by a regular system: thus proving, that its authors have been guided by principle, and not, as many have alleged, by mere fancy and caprice.[2]

The original to which Hall traced the origin of Gothic was a rustic hut of woven wickerwork. Having noted the visual correspondence between the curving lines of willow branches and Gothic tracery, he endeavoured to prove his theory by the experiment of growing his own willow church, of which he published an illustration as part of his study (Figure 10.1). His aim was twofold: to provide the Gothic style with an origin and to show that its practitioners followed rules in its usage. Both ambitions follow closely the pattern of scholarship regarding Classical architecture, with the arboreal origin echoing the theory of the primitive hut as expounded by Laugier.[3]

As well as being a keen antiquary, Hall was also active in what we should now term scientific pursuits. As a member and later President of the Royal Society of Edinburgh, he was a close associate of James Hutton, described as the founder of modern geology, who championed the so-called 'Vulcanist' position that the Earth had a core of molten rock, which welled up to form mountain ranges, which were then worn away to create the sedimentary rocks, in an endless cycle.[4] After Hutton's death, Hall tried to provide proof of his friend's theories by heating stones under pressure, in an attempt to simulate conditions at the centre of the earth.[5] To a modern scholar, this approach seems very close to his attempts to demonstrate his theories about Gothic. In both investigations he was attempting to provide proof by an appeal to the new scientific technique of experimentation, though in neither case could his evidence be conclusive: showing that events *could* take place under similar conditions was no guarantee that reality replicated the experiment.[6] Hall himself, however, made no attempt to draw parallels between his two fields of interest. He did not liken his antiquarian work to science but to another branch of intellectual enquiry, namely 'theoretical history' as defined by Dugald Stewart and practised by Voltaire.[7] By this he meant that his version of antiquarianism was not simply descriptive but aimed at a wider relevance by providing causal explanations.

The writings of Sir James Hall have a dual significance. They reveal a desire to legitimize antiquarian arguments by appealing to a discourse already high in public esteem. Nevertheless, they suggest that in 1797 science had yet to achieve sufficient status for Hall to present his antiquarian methodology in a scientific light. This situation was soon to change.

Historians seeking to understand what happened to antiquarianism in the nineteenth century have frequently appealed to science as a key to the problem. The scientific model has operated at three levels. The work of the earlier historians of science (including those of the nineteenth century) saw the period as a march of progress, a 'scientific revolution', which, whether true or not, has served to make the nineteenth century seem an age of science, whose 'progressive' tendencies would inevitably be scientific. This *Zeitgeist* interpretation is to be found, for example, in Paul Frankl's *The Gothic* (1960), in which he wrote of 'The Scientific Trend'. Revisionist historians of science have disputed this picture and have supplied the student of antiquarianism with exemplary models for analysing the emergence of disciplines and the functioning of scholarly communities.[8] When speaking of science, I am following their lead in referring merely to a historical discourse rather than to a metaphysical absolute. For my purposes it is unhelpful to equate scientificity with logicality and objectivity or to use the adjective 'scientific' as a value-judgement on the methodology of antiquarian authors. Finally, evidence from the nineteenth century itself seems to point to scientific influence. In comparison with eighteenth-century treatment of medieval architecture, the literature of nineteenth-century architectural antiquarianism is presented logically and detachedly; it makes appeal to evidence rather than theory and is filled with scientific imagery.

In re-evaluating the relationship between antiquarianism and science, my aim is not to deny the importance of the latter but to question our interpretation of the scientific model. Historians of science themselves have shown that during the period under discussion, science itself was very far from stable as a concept and the individual branches of science, such as geology or chemistry, were not fully formulated. In England, science remained a largely amateur pursuit and, like antiquarianism, represented a field of knowledge with which a gentleman of culture was expected to be familiar. Even in the nineteenth century, it was not uncommon for individuals to be active in both scientific and antiquarian spheres. Spencer Joshua Alwyne Compton (1780–1851), the second Marquis of Northampton, was President of both the Royal Society and the Archaeological Institute in the 1840s, and Cambridge scientists such as William Whewell and Robert Willis wrote major works on medieval architecture.

Seen from a scientific perspective, antiquarianism might even have seemed to have achieved a cultural status worthy of envy and emulation. Whewell, for example, cited the prevailing system of architectural nomenclature as the exemplification of his dictum about the invalidity of numerical terminologies.[9] Still more telling is a passage from Cuvier's *Recherches sur les ossemens fossiles de quadrupèdes* (1812), in which he chose to describe himself not as a biologist, nor as a scientist (for the word had yet to be invented), but as a historian, or even an antiquary, examining skeletons as though they were buildings.[10]

The traditional application of the word science to systematized knowledge in general, allowed antiquarianism to be categorized as a science, in accordance with a discourse dating from the seventeenth century at the latest. Antiquities had been included within the inductive programme of Francis Bacon as a subject suitable for research, and the Royal Society which tried to put the Baconian programme into practice had included antiquarians as well as those interested in science in its more restricted sense.[11] The main outlet and focus for seventeenth- and eighteenth-century antiquarianism, the County Histories, often treated the flora and fauna as well as the historical aspects of the region, and this link carried on into many of the local field clubs and archaeological societies established during the nineteenth century, as well as the earlier volumes of the Victoria County History.[12] The use of the word 'science' in architectural antiquarianism of the early nineteenth century therefore has to be treated with caution, as it may represent merely a belated usage in its traditional sense, rather than a metaphor. In researching this essay, I have considered as relevant only those instances when it is clear that the word is used in its restricted sense, either because a particular branch of science is quoted or because specific characteristics are identified.[13]

The citation of science seems to occur most frequently in reviews of books on architectural history or similar analyses of scholarship, and should perhaps be seen as an attempt to explain or contextualize antiquarianism for the non-practitioner. For most authors, the use of scientific imagery represents primarily a series of metaphors, rather than a considered statement of methodological intent. By employing such analogies, writers were endeavouring to link antiquarianism with the associations brought to mind by science. As we have said, certain affinities already existed, but the intention was also polemical; using the metaphor to create a similarity which would thereby reform the associations of antiquarianism. For many of the antiquarian authors who drew the analogies, these represent the only statement of their views on science, and thus it is difficult to be certain what associations were intended. Generalizations, however, can be made about popular conceptions of science in the early nineteenth century, which may be relevant to the antiquarian viewpoint.

1. Science was believed in itself to be systematic and to provide proof of the underlying order of the Universe.
2. Knowledge was believed to be progressing more quickly in science than in other fields and at a rate faster than at any previous period.
3. Scientific method was inductive.

Instead of using the term 'antiquarianism', nineteenth-century practitioners often preferred to describe their scholarly relationship with the past as 'archaeology'. This term encompassed the study of buildings, which also received the epithet 'architectural history'.[14] As one contemporary later put it:

they called it now Archaeology, because they wished to denote the fact that it was no longer a mere enquiry, no longer a mere indulgence of curiosity, but that it had become a science with certain rules and definite objects.[15]

A similar sentiment lay behind the coining of the later term 'ecclesiology', which was likewise claimed as an inductive science.[16] When describing their field of study as archaeology (from *archaios*, ancient and *logos*, discourse – the Greek equivalent of the Latin-derived antiquarianism), scholars were attempting to give it intellectual distinction, just as contemporaries had redefined natural philosophy as biology, geology and so forth. There was also a desire to dissociate their subject from the moribundity of the 'chartered body of imbecile old women called the Antiquarian Society'.[17]

The use of the word 'archaeology' became common during the second decade of the nineteenth century and is therefore too early for us to be certain that the intention of its original users was to recall science in its restricted sense. Metaphors which were undeniably scientific, only began to be used regularly in the 1830s.

The most common of the scientific metaphors likened antiquarianism to palaeontology, the study of fossilized skeletons, which was of vital importance to the nineteenth-century development of biology and geology, and of great popular interest. As far as the general reader was concerned, the most significant achievement of palaeontologists such as Georges Cuvier (1769–1832), in France, or Richard Owen (1804–92), in Britain, was their reputed ability to reconstruct on paper an entire skeleton from the remains of a single part (Figure 10.2), based on a belief that each element was functionally related to the whole. Their achievement was broadly similar to claims put forward by architectural antiquaries and also restoration architects, who used surviving fragments to produce reconstructions, either on paper or in stone, of the building at a single point in its history (Figure 10.3). *The Ecclesiologist* provides a typical example of the comparison:

A vaulted church is thus a kind of organic whole; and it is scarcely fanciful to say that a Willis – the Owen of the comparative anatomy of architecture – could reconstruct such a design from a few of its bones.[18]

The citation of palaeontology for polemical purposes does not, however, require it to have been an influence on the original methodology of the architectural antiquary. It provided a powerful metaphor because it fed into the existing obsession of scholars with the rationalism of Gothic. Their desire to prove that the style had a structural rationality, with each part functionally related, and that Gothic architects had followed fixed rules in their designs, made the simile apposite. Nevertheless, the reconstruction of whole buildings from their parts has at least as long a history as the corresponding practice in science. Paper reconstructions of Classical buildings had been attempted since the Renaissance, governed by the Vitruvian precept that Classical architects had followed fixed rules in their designs.[19] Although the Middle Ages had produced no treatise comparable to Vitruvius, the recognition that Gothic architecture could be systematized and rules abstracted from comparison of its specimens, meant that medieval buildings could also be reconstructed, using the paradigms of the stylistic table to supply missing elements.

The modern term 'stylistic table' refers to the chronological division of medieval architecture into a number of discrete groupings, or styles, identified by abstracting from the comparison of a large number of buildings certain significant elements such as the shape of the arches, forms of tracery or the profiles of the mouldings (Figure 10.4). The use of the word 'style' to describe these groupings did not, for the great majority of English antiquarians, carry with it the connotations it today bears of formalism and Germanic philosophy.[20] It provided a systematization of what was known about medieval buildings and hence rendered the information 'scientific' in the traditional sense of the word.

The stylistic table is primarily associated with Thomas Rickman, whose stylistic terminology has become the common currency of medievalists. However, his work, first published in 1812, has a historical context, of which he was well aware. He had read widely in antiquarian literature, as is proved by the fact that each element of the stylistic table he popularized, from the dating of the stylistic phases to their terminology, can be traced in earlier works.[21]

The first recorded scholar to group medieval architecture by isolating a diagnostic feature was John Aubrey, writing in the late seventeenth century, who concentrated his analysis on window tracery.[22] Aubrey was a Baconian and a member of the Royal Society, and undertook many field trips on which he examined geological formations as well as monuments of archaeology and architecture, using his knowledge of one to inform his studies of the other.[23] His work remained largely in manuscript, but it was nevertheless well known to eighteenth-century antiquaries, such as Charles Lyttleton and Andrew Ducarel.[24] The aim of the group of scholars of which Lyttleton was a member was to discover an alternative to chronicles as a means of dating medieval buildings, for to put it crudely, chronicles were written by monks, monks believed in miracles and therefore chronicles were not always to be trusted.[25] In Aubrey's groupings of similar buildings, coupled with their own observations, Lyttleton and his fellow antiquaries suggested style as an alternative means of dating. A number of stylistic sequences were proposed, the first being by Warton in his *Observations on the Faerie Queen* of 1762.[26]

It is obvious that the creation of the stylistic table must ultimately be attributed to the methods of seventeenth-century research, servicing eighteenth-century demands. It soon proved its worth, partly because it enabled antiquaries to give dates to undocumented buildings, particularly parish churches, and, a consequence which is less frequently acknowledged, because it provided an alternative source which permitted them to reject documented dates which did not fit in with their chosen theory.[27] Indeed, the suspicion antiquaries felt towards their textual sources made recourse to non-textual evidence easier than was the case, say, in geology, where the primary text was the Bible.[28] The place of the stylistic table in the developing methodology of architectural antiquarianism was assured when Rickman and Britton both employed and further developed the system and it was seen to fit in with the ideals of nineteenth-century scholarship.

Although not a nineteenth-century innovation, it was only during this period that the chronological series of styles began to be illustrated in tabular form (Figure 10.4). This manner of presentation may be likened to the geological columns of strata which were then becoming a common way of embodying a similar set of data (Figure 10.5); similarly, the schematization of the architectural history of an individual building by the division of its plan into a series of areas represented by different shading corresponds to the communication of geological information on coloured maps (Figure 10.6).[29]

To the modern observer, the practice of geology presents many similarities to architectural antiquarianism, in particular the study of 'building stratigraphy', that is to say the analysis of the successive phases of construction as identified by changes in style and breaks in the masonry.[30] Surprisingly, however, geological metaphors were not widely used at the time – a rare (and belated) example is E.A. Freeman's comment that 'the antiquary works with his buildings in exactly the same way in which the geologist works with his strata'.[31] There is no evidence that the recognition of such phenomena can be closely associated with advances in geology. The study of masonry jointing was first developed by the Cambridge architect James Essex in his Report on Lincoln Cathedral, produced for restoration purposes in 1761, in which he included a considerable amount of research into the history of the building in order to explain which of the cracks were due to structural failure and which were merely the signs of a temporal break in the work.[32] His innovatory comparison of literary and structural evidence was motivated by a supremely practical purpose – a desire to avoid repairing fissures that were no threat to the building. Works of the 1760s and 1770s which used a similar methodology may all be shown to have had some connection with Cambridge antiquarian scholarship, but there is no perceivable link with those who were concurrently discovering the stratification of rocks.[33]

Early nineteenth-century discussions of the stylistic table and architectural antiquarianism in general are overwhelmingly obsessed with the issues of terminology and nomenclature. This is something new; and whilst the interest in Gothic naturally led to a need for a more detailed vocabulary, it nonetheless seems probable that the importance accorded to the issue owes much to public perceptions of scientific advances. The second half of the eighteenth century had seen the fields of botany and chemistry transformed by the adoption of the systems of binomial nomenclature, and early nineteenth-century antiquaries were quick to draw comparisons.[34] For example, a review of Robert Willis's work on architectural nomenclature argued that:

Nothing conduces more to the diffusion and popularity of any science than its being provided with a sufficient complement of names for every part and subdivision of the subject to which it belongs. This appears to be the true secret of the almost universal taste for botany, and the other minutely classified sciences, which immediately followed upon the publication of the Linnaean system.[35]

It may not be reading too much into the system proposed by Rickman to see in its division of Gothic architecture into Early English, Decorated English and Perpendicular English an attempt at an antiquarian binomial nomenclature.[36] Many of the early architectural antiquaries, such as Dawson Turner of Norfolk and Arcisse De Caumont of Normandy, were important members of Linnaean societies, and De Caumont's Société des Antiquaires de Normandie was consciously modelled on such bodies. It was also De Caumont who popularized the notion of the stylistic table in France. The need for a universally accepted system of stylistic terms was keenly felt by antiquaries, who all conceded the usefulness of the theory of stylistic dating. However, the slippery nature of style, combined with the rewards of being seen as the originator of the definitive system, meant that the issue was still unresolved in the 1850s.[37]

As well as developments in systematic terminology, the early nineteenth century saw a rapid advance in the complexity of architectural nomenclature, that is to say the words used to describe the individual elements of buildings. Terms such as 'plate tracery', 'dogtooth mouldings' and 'nook-shafts' are all creations of the period. This too is analogous to developments taking place in the sciences and was a self-conscious development, aiming at the advancement of architectural antiquarianism by an increased precision of language. The construction of a specialist language resulted in the creation of a scholarly community, even before the foundation of the various archaeological societies, and the recognition of the rights of certain writers to create or reform architectural terminology was an assertion of their position within the scholarly hierarchy.[38]

Despite its obvious value to architectural antiquarians, the scientific metaphor did not go unopposed. What we might identify as a Romantic appreciation of Gothic could coexist with an analytical examination of its features – I have found little evidence that attempting to understand medieval architecture was considered to detract from the aesthetic appeal which, according to eighteenth-century theories, had lain in its mystery and appeal to the senses rather than the intellect. What was considered problematic about the new approach was that by concentrating on external forms, it paid little attention to the functions of the buildings, in particular their religious and historical significance.[39] From the point of view of its practitioners, this was on the one hand an attempt to avoid the charge that medieval architecture was inherently ritualistic (and it may be of significance that Rickman was himself a Quaker) and on the other hand a belief (which was rarely articulated) that style and ritual had no inevitable connection.[40] For the ecclesiologists in particular, however, the perceived linkage between a scientific approach and an irreligious attitude was a problem which their reviews of offending books took pains to expose and their own works endeavoured to avoid.[41]

Returning to the problem posed by Momigliano, we are now perhaps in a position to suggest that antiquarianism was not so much discredited as transformed. In today's terms, there was a successful 'public relations campaign' which employed fashionable concepts to redefine the subject. Many of the aims and methods of antiquarianism remained the same, but they came to be viewed differently, and the repackaging of the subject was so convincing that we too can be led to believe that it had entirely changed. By looking at the products of this operation, my analysis cannot address the underlying problem of why the transformation occurred, but I hope it suggests that the relationship with science was more complicated that it at first appears. The so-called 'scientific revolution' cannot alone provide sufficient explanation for any changes.

Acknowledgements

An early version of this essay was presented at a symposium at the History of Art Department of the University of Manchester in April 1994. I should like to

acknowledge the assistance of Dr Christopher Wilson and Professor Richard
Marks.

Notes

1.   A. Momigliano, *Studies in Historiography* (London, Weidenfeld & Nicolson, 1966), p.25. See also P.
        Levine, *The Amateur and the Professional. Antiquarians, Historians and Archaeologists in Victorian
        England, 1838–1886* (Cambridge University Press, 1986), p.38.

2.   Sir James Hall, 'Essay on the Origin and Principles of Gothic Architecture', *Transactions of the Royal
        Society of Edinburgh*, 4 (1798),papers of the literary class, pp. 1–27.

3.   The theory that Gothic originated in the emulation of the groves of trees in which the Goths wor-
        shipped was current in eighteenth-century England, but in its concentration on the human manip-
        ulation of natural materials, Hall's argument is closer to that of Laugier.

4.   V.A. Eyles, 'Sir James Hall, Bt., 1761–1832', *Endeavour*, 20 (1961), pp.210–16. This makes no mention
        of Hall's architectural studies, for which see J. Rykwert, *On Adam's House in Paradise. The Idea of the
        Primitive Hut in Architectural Theory*, 2nd edn (Cambridge, Massachussetts and London, MIT Press,
        1981), pp. 82–7. D.R. Dean, *James Hutton and the History of Geology* (Ithaca and London, Cornell
        University Press, 1992).

5.   Dean, *James Hutton*, pp.88–92.

6.   Hall's arguments did not prove convincing to his successors, though he has achieved lasting
        significance as the first scholar to identify and label the tracery cusp. Such observations were
        applauded and, more importantly, there was also praise for the manner of their presentation: R.
        Willis, *Remarks on the Architecture of the Middle Ages, especially of Italy* (Cambridge, J. & J.J. Deighton,
        1835), p.57, n, and F.A. Paley, *A Manual of Gothic Architecture* (London, Van Voorst, 1846), p.160, n.

7.   Hall, 'Essay on the Origin and Principles of Gothic Architecture', p.13.

8.   The literature of the history of science is vast and I shall make no attempt to summarize it here. The
        scientific model has been employed in particular by Levine, *The Amateur and the Professional*. This
        article and the paper on which it was based were written before the publication of the article by C.
        Yanni, 'On Nature and Nomenclature: William Whewell and the Production of Architectural
        Knowledge in Early Victorian Britain', *Architectural History*, 40 (1997), pp.204–21.

9.   W. Whewell, *The Philosophy of the Inductive Sciences*, 2 vols (London, J.W. Parker and Son, 1847), 2,
        p.531, n.

10.   'I am attempting to travel along a road where no one has chanced more than a few steps, and to
        make known a genre of monuments which are almost always neglected despite being indispens-
        able for the history of the Earth. As a new type of Antiquary, I have to learn how to decipher and to
        restore these monuments, to recognise and to reassemble in their original order the scattered and
        mutilated fragments from which they were composed.' G. Cuvier, *Recherches sur les ossemens
        fossiles de quadrupèdes*, 4 vols (Paris, Deterville, 1812), 1, pp.1–2 [my translation]. For comments on
        the sources and significance of Cuvier's metaphor, see M.J.S. Rudwick, *Georges Cuvier, Fossil Bones,
        and Geological Catastrophes* (Chicago and London, University of Chicago Press, 1997), p.35, n.2,
        and p.174.

11.   F. Bacon, *The Works of Francis Bacon*, ed. J. Spedding, R.L. Ellis and D.D. Heath, 7 vols (London,
        Longman & Co., Simpkin & Co., Hamilton & Co. et al., 1858–9), 4, pp.303–4. For the Baconian
        movement, see S.A.E. Mendyk, *'Speculum Britanniae': Regional Study, Antiquarianism, and Science in
        Britain to 1700* (Toronto, University of Toronto Press, 1989), in particular Chapter 6.

12.   For example, the Warwickshire Natural History and Archaeological Society (founded 1836).

13.   I have endeavoured to read every British text dealing with medieval architecture published
        1750–1850, and their reviews in the more obvious periodical literature, though out of consideration
        for the reader I shall limit my quotations. Except where stated otherwise, each quotation could be
        paralleled by many similar examples.

14.   The term was apparently coined by William Whewell and first used to describe a particular work
        of scholarship by Robert Willis, *The Architectural History of Canterbury Cathedral* (Oxford and
        London, J.H. Parker, 1845). It is possible that Willis employed the term 'architectural history' to
        suggest that his method was more closely based on textual than structural evidence: A.C.
        Buchanan, 'Robert Willis (1800–1875) and the Rise of Architectural History', PhD thesis, University
        of London, 1994, Chapter 3.

15. *Associated Architectural Societies Reports and Papers*, **8** (1865–6), p.lvii.

16. *The Ecclesiologist*, 1 (1841), p.56. See J.F. White, *The Cambridge Movement: The Ecclesiologists and the Gothic Revival* (Cambridge University Press, 1962), Chapter 3.

17. *The Athenaeum* (1844), p.175.

18. *The Ecclesiologist*, **16** (1855), p.45. This comment on Robert Willis is prefigured by a similar analogy (but with Cuvier as the archetypal palaeontologist) by R. Billings, *The Power of Form Applied to Geometric Tracery* (Edinburgh, W. Blackwood & Sons, 1851), pp. 21–2. It seems to have become naturalized within the discipline and was echoed, for example, in a comment on Rickman by the Bishop of Peterborough: *Associated Architectural Societies Reports and Papers*, 8 (1865–6), p.lviii. The metaphor was still current in 1913: F. Bond, *An Introduction to English Church Architecture. From the eleventh to the sixteenth century*, 2 vols (Oxford University Press, 1913), 1, p.235; and Gothic structures continue to be described in terms of skeletons, e.g., J. Bony, *French Gothic Architecture of the Twelfth and Thirteenth Centuries* (Berkeley, L.A., University of California Press, 1983), p.7.

19. Early reconstructions 'restored' the ruined monuments of Classical antiquity to their supposed original state, as for example Francesco di Giorgio Martini's drawings of the Colosseum: C. Maltese (ed.), *Francesco di Giorgio, Trattati di architettura ingegneria e arte militare*, 2 vols (Milan, Edizione Il Polifico, 1967), **1**, p.275 (and corresponding plates) or the drawings of Roman temples in the *Libro d'Antonio Labacco appartenente a l'architettura nel qual si figurano alcune notabili antiquita di Roma* (Rome, ascribed to V. & L. Dorichi, 1557). The earliest skeletal restoration is said to be that of a unicorn, constructed from bones now known to have belonged to a mammoth, by Otto von Guericke in 1663: W.E. Swinton, 'Early History of Comparative Anatomy' *Endeavour*, 19 (1960), pp.209–14.

20. The work of William Whewell is the notable exception to this generalization. For the use of the word 'style' in English discussion of architecture, see E.S. de Beer, 'Gothic: Origin and Diffusion of the Term; the idea of style in Architecture', *Journal of the Warburg and Courtauld Institutes*, 11 (1948), pp.143–62 and G. Germann, *Gothic Revival in Europe and Britain. Sources, Influences and Ideas* (London, Lund Humphries for the Architectural Association, 1972), pp.24–7.

21. J. Baily, 'Thomas Rickman, Architect and Quaker, the Early Years to 1818', PhD thesis, University of Leeds, 1977, p.313.

22. H.M. Colvin, Aubrey's *Chronologia Architectonica*, in J. Summerson (ed.), *Concerning Architecture. Essays on Architectural Writers and Writing presented to Nikolaus Pevsner* (London, Allen Lane, The Penguin Press, 1968), pp.1–12.

23. Mendyk, *Speculum Britanniae*, pp.170–84.

24. C. Lyttleton, 'Dissertation on the Antiquity of Brick Buildings in England', *Archaeologia*, 1 (1770), pp.140–48. That he was aware of these ideas from the 1750s is suggested by his remarks in 'Some Remarks on the Original Foundation and Construction of the Present Fabric of Exeter Cathedral', in *Exeter Cathedral*, Society of Antiquaries Cathedral Series, 1 (London, 1754), pp.1–12.

25. For example, W. Warburton, *A Critical and Philosophical Enquiry into the Causes of Prodigies and Miracles as related by Historians* (London, T. Corbett, 1727).

26. Reprinted in J. Taylor (ed.), *Essays on Gothic Architecture* (London, J. Taylor, 1800).

27. The evidence of style was favoured in particular by those who favoured Saxon dates for Romanesque buildings, especially John Carter (a list of whose works may be found in J.M. Crook, 'John Carter and the Mind of the Gothic Revival', *Society of Antiquaries Occasional Publications*, 17 (London, 1995), pp. 80–90) and Edward King, *Monumenta Antiqua; or, Antient Castles*, 4 vols (London, G. Nicol, 1799–1805).

28. For the relationship between scripture and geology, see R. Porter, *The Making of Geology: Earth Science in Britain, 1660–1815* (Cambridge University Press, 1977), pp.65–70 and 107–10. Porter argues that geology freed itself from textual evidence before other disciplines, a statement with which I would have to disagree. For the importance of non-textual evidence in antiquarianism, see Momigliano, *Studies in Historiography*, Chapter 1.

29. Whewell may have been the first to present the styles in tabular form in 1823: J.M. Stair Douglas, *The Life and Selections from the Correspondence of William Whewell* (London, C. Kegan Paul, 1881), p.38. The first coloured plans belong to the lectures given by Willis to the British Archaeological Association and the Archaeological Institute, printed in monochrome, e.g., in Willis, *Canterbury Cathedral*. The earliest coloured geological map of any part of Britain was that published by William Smith in 1815.

30. The term is used and described by W. Rodwell, *English Heritage Book of Church Archaeology*, revised

edn (London, Batsford, 1989) and T. Tatton-Brown, *Great Cathedrals of Britain* (London, BBC Books, 1989).

31.   E.A. Freeman, *The Methods of Historical Study. Eight Lectures read in the University of Oxford* (London, Macmillan & Co., 1886), p.232.

32.   J. Essex, 'Report to the Dean and Chapter of Lincoln' (1761), 'The Ark', folder 22, Lincolnshire Archives.

33.   H. Malden [actually by T. James], *An Account of King's College-Chapel, in Cambridge* (Cambridge, Fletcher & Hodgson, 1769) and W. Gostling, *A Walk in and about the City of Canterbury* (Canterbury, Simmons & Kirkby, W. Flackton, 1774). Gostling had corresponded with Essex about such structural evidence: see letters copied by William Cole, Add. MS. 5842, ff.173v–174, British Library.

34.   For the relevant scientific advances, see M.P. Crosland, *Historical Studies in the Language of Chemistry* (London, Heinemann, 1962) and W.C. Anderson, *Between the Library and the Laboratory. The Language of Chemistry in Eighteenth-Century France* (Baltimore, Johns Hopkins University Press, 1984).

35.   *The Ecclesiologist*, 3 (1843), p.146. One author, Bell, had not been so enthusiastic about linguistic revolution, contrasting the longevity of antiquarianism and the widespread acceptance of its existing terminology with the newness of chemistry at the time of its terminological shift: T. Bell, *An Essay on the Origin and Progress of Gothic Architecture, with reference to the ancient history and present state of the remains of such architecture in Ireland* (Dublin, W.F. Wakeman, 1829), pp.27–8. Hence he was using the scientific metaphor in a negative manner, cavilling at the substitution of the term 'Gothic architecture' by the term 'English architecture'.

36.   T. Rickman, *An Attempt to Discriminate the Styles of English Architecture, from the Conquest to the Reformation* (London, Longman, Hurst, Rees, Orme & Brown, 1817).

37.   See for example E. Sharpe, *Seven Periods of Architecture* (London, George Bell, 1851).

38.   Whewell was very interested in the role of specialized language in scientific advance and was himself a notable linguistic innovator: W. Whewell, *The Philosophy of the Inductive Sciences*, 2 vols (London, J.W. Parker, 1840), 1, p.xlviii and 'On the Influence of the History of Science upon Intellectual Education', in *Lectures on Education Delivered at the Royal Institution of Great Britain* (London, J.W. Parker & Son, 1855), pp.32–3. Whewell's philosophy of language is discussed by S. Schaffer, 'The History and Geography of the Intellectual World: Whewell's Politics of Language', in M. Fisch and S. Schaffer (eds), *William Whewell. A Composite Portrait* (Oxford, Clarendon Press, 1991), pp.201–31. The role of language in antiquarian group identity is discussed in my PhD thesis, *op. cit.* at note 14, pp.199–200.

39.   Paley, *A Manual of Gothic Architecture*, pp.ix–x. Similar sentiments were expressed by Freeman, *A History of Architecture* (London, Joseph Masters, 1849), p.xiii.

40.   See, for example, the unpublished comment by Willis: 'It is necessary that this distinction between the aesthetic character, mechanical arrangement & the symbolism of a building should be very clearly understood for the want of this classification has been the source of an error unhappily too prevalent in the present day and which leads to the most fatal consequences … In short I believe it is our duty as Antiquarians and Architects to study the architecture of past ages so as to develope [*sic*] the cause and principles by which they reached so high & perfect a power over the aesthetic character which I have endeavoured to show is wholly independent of the ritual itself.' Add. MS. 5135, ff. 46–8, Cambridge University Library.

41.   For example, a review of Willis, *Canterbury Cathedral*, in *The Ecclesiologist*, 4 (1845), pp.220–22.

10.1   W. & D. Lizars, *The 'Willow Cathedral' built under the direction of Sir James Hall*, etching

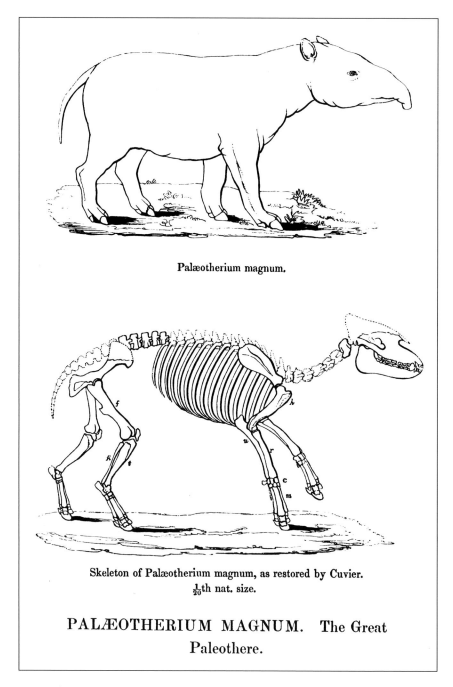

Palæotherium magnum.

Skeleton of Palæotherium magnum, as restored by Cuvier.
$\frac{1}{20}$th nat. size.

PALÆOTHERIUM MAGNUM.   The Great
Paleothere.

10.2   After an illustration by C. Laurillard, reconstructions of the Great Paleothere
from its fossilized skeleton, wood engraving

10.3   G.B.S., Edmund Sharpe's reconstruction of the east window of Tintern Abbey, wood engraving

10.4   Robert Willis's tabulation of the stylistic sequences proposed by earlier scholars

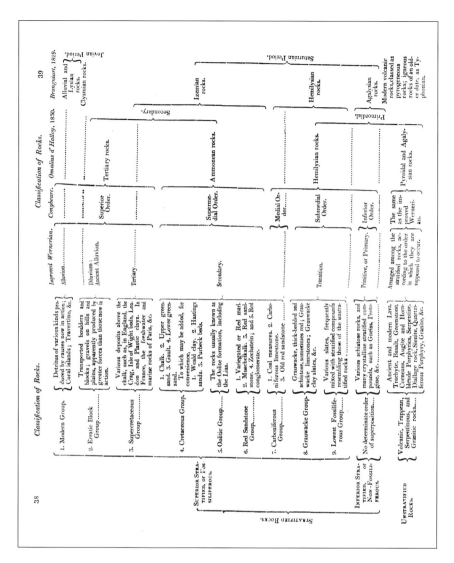

10.5   Henry de la Beche's tabulation of the geological systems proposed by earlier scholars

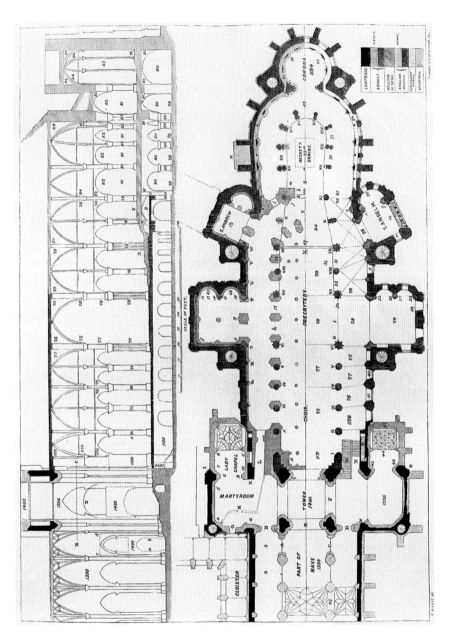

10.6   Drawn by R. Willis, engraved by Delamotte and Heaviside, Robert Willis's historical plan of Canterbury Cathedral, 1843, wood engraving

11

Story, history and the passionate collector

Susan A. Crane

Late eighteenth-century antiquarianism is marked by the presence and absence of particular desires. The desire to possess the past in the form of arte-facts and to own relics which had metonymic relationships to stories about the past or about myth, were key characteristics of collectors who sought, as Krzysztof Pomian puts it, to hold in their hands the physical ties between 'the visible and the invisible worlds'.[1] At the same time, antiquarianism displayed a general lack of desire to preserve the past *in toto*; antiquarians remained con-cerned with fragments and specialized collections based on objects of personal interest, rather than coherent, inclusive, instructive collections which would be accessible to the broadest possible public. A remarkable shift in the desires and activities of collectors occurred around the turn of the century: some for-mer antiquarians and other, newer types of historical collectors began to take a passionate interest in historical preservation and the production of public museums which removed the desired objects from the personal provenance of the collector, and placed them in the public view as collective, indeed national, property.

The antiquarians became figures of ridicule and contempt from the nine-teenth century onward, their status reduced to that of 'dilettante'. Writers such as Sir Walter Scott and the poet Annette von Droste-Hülshoff caricatured the older type of historical collector as one hopelessly behind the times, in an era when the passions of historical collecting had shifted from personal, idiosyn-cratic, and élite networks to nationalist, collective and representative ones. The transition from one form of passionate historical collecting to another can be described as a shift from stories to histories, from fragments to totalities, from cabinets to museums. The displacement of the antiquarian, the devalua-tion of one form of passionate interest in artefacts, and the subsequent burial of a personalized expression of historical consciousness, then came to characterize the museums, historical profession, and historiography of the nineteenth century, particularly in Germany. The antiquarian thus represents a pivotal figure, both actor and artefact, in the story of the shifting desires for history in modern Europe.

Writing in 1822, Professor Friedrich Kruse, one of the founders of the Thuringen-Saxon historical association for the study of national antiquity, quoted a fellow co-founder approvingly: 'antiquity does not give us history, collecting does: collection of what is left to us from antiquity, what is preserved by old reports and by accident'.[2] The general public was so unconcerned with the past that it was merely accidental that the past remained present at all, but for the activities of collectors; and yet they had diverse motives. Only recently had scholars such as Kruse joined in collecting efforts. Karl Preusker, an advocate of preservation, noted in 1829 that a new consolidation of collectors and collective interests was transpiring. Reviewing the inaugural issue of another historical association's journal, he noted that:

> the editor shows how in recent times the welcome efforts of so many friends of history and antiquity in almost all provinces of Germany have become noticeable, and how through many newly-founded associations ... not only was more attention than before dedicated to all monuments (*Denkmäler*) and remains of the past, but also fundamental interest and sharpened criticism sought results for science ... otherwise one very often had piled them up as curiosities full of show or pomp and not considered them as means to a higher purpose, in connection with all the sources of history. Everywhere now the trend is towards a worthy display of the treasures of antiquity. One seeks meaning and connection therein, and strives after instruction.[3]

Preusker clearly notes the change in attitude characteristic of his time: co-operation among like-minded, 'scientific' collectors is necessary for a true understanding of the desired artefacts, which otherwise would suffer under the (implied) misuse of the antiquarian, the collector of mere curiosities. The value of 'curiosity' both as an attitude and as a type of object was changing; the collections housed in curiosity cabinets were being revisited and revalued, their contents subject to a new scrutiny.

The word 'curiosity' indicates a human passion or desire to know, and the cabinet was intended to open the mind to the wonders of the world just as much as it was intended to invigorate further study. However, it was already generally assumed, in the early modern period, that most people would not be able to appreciate both facets, and that the knowledge achieved by the curious was not as substantial as that gained by scholarship. Zedler's *Universal-Lexikon* of 1732 separated the general quality of curiosity from what he called 'intellectual curiosity':

> In common curiosity, one delights oneself in those things which concern the external senses, memory and ingenuity, as when one always enjoys seeing something, listening to pleasant anecdotes (*Histörchen*), or wanting to read clever and funny writings ... intellectual curiosity is when one takes a delight in clever inventions ... But not to

ignore the curiosity which belongs in cabinets: here again it is the intellectual curiosity
… which awakens reflection; reflection in turn produces discerned truths and these
show a previously unknown and diverse usefulness of the things.[4]

This definition stresses the pleasure derived from the satisfaction of curiosity,
but common curiosity is limited to responsiveness, whereas intellectual
curiosity involves study. Therein lies the implicit relation to antiquarians and
natural historians. 'The curiosity which belongs in cabinets' could mean either
the attitude of the individual to the cabinet, or the object itself; either way, this
curiosity 'proper' to its cabinet domain is a characteristic of the intellectual
who has brought it – the object or the emotion – with him.

  Krzysztof Pomian has traced the early modern meanings of the French
words *curieux* and *curiosité* and shown that they could define a particular individual. The French Academy, in its 1694 dictionary, gave the following definition of *curieux*: 'someone who takes pleasure in collecting rare and curious
objects or who is very knowledgeable about them; an enthusiast's cabinet; he
[who] mixes daily with those who have an inquiring mind'. *Curiosité* similarly
means the objects of the *curieux*'s interest: 'It also signifies a rare and curious
thing; "his museum was full of curiosities" '.[5] The object and the collector were
defined in terms of each other. The value judgement placed on this identity,
however, was laden with moral strictures against the common aspects of
curiosity: indecent curiosity, wanting to know too much, and its potentially
sacrilegious effects were all to be avoided.[6] To this negative potential we
might add another: that of dilettantism. Pomian cites an antiquarian's text
from 1739:

This word '*Curieux*' is very ambiguous indeed and its meaning should be determined
once and for all. In effect, if this term applies to any man who builds up a collection of
Medals, the man of Letters becomes confused with that ordinary mortal, the simple
man of taste, who only seeks and values in Medals the beauties of ancient engraving.
The true scholar is no longer differentiated in any way from him who merely seeks to
appear to be and whose wealth permits him to satisfy his vanity, since both collect
Medals, even though to very different ends. Their Collections are therefore entirely
dissimilar, and the studious man who toils uniquely for his proper instruction will
assemble objects with care, objects which will be neglected by him who seeks to flatter
his self-esteem or his taste, rather than to form his mind and perfect his knowledge.[7]

During the course of the eighteenth century, the 'merely curious' collector
began to be disparaged in opposition to the 'connoisseur'. The distinction
rested primarily on the amount of skill brought to the study as well as the
depth of the desire to learn, which was opposed to the desire of having one's
own glory reflected through possession of curiosities. The stigma attached to
'dilettante' derives from this early-modern association of 'curiosity' with
acquisitiveness, lack of seriousness, idiosyncrasy and a desire to improve
social status.[8]

The term 'curiosity' refers to both the desire to know and the object of interest; not surprisingly, therefore, the desire and the object come together in the form of the story that the object represents. Curious collectors were attracted to objects either because they represented a world-view consonant with plenitude, or because the particular object had a significant connection to some kind of information, whether a myth or a scientific endeavour. The object represented a part or the whole of a story. 'Curiosity' was a broad category, including natural-historical as well as man-made objects, antique as well as contemporary objects, art as well as objects lacking any aesthetic value – and rarities whose authenticity lay as much in their very existence, as in their purported origin. There is considerable evidence of these storied relationships between objects and collectors which the historiography of collecting and museums faithfully replicate.[9]

Though labels or signs did not always indicate it, many of the objects in a curiosity cabinet were essentially accompanied by stories. A guide would relate the story. Random access to a cabinet's contents was unheard of; cabinet visits took place in the presence of the owner or a designated guide, until late eighteenth-century experiments with the first public museum days.[10] In essence, modern histories of these cabinets reproduce the guided visit, by listing the stories along with the object. The following stories are culled from a recent example of this historiography, Arthur MacGregor's excellent collection, *Tradescant's Rarities*. In the collection of Duke Albrecht V of Bavaria (1528–79):

> another personal obsession manifested itself in a series of plaster casts of deformed limbs and paintings of dwarfs, human deformities, bearded women and convicted criminals, the latter complimented by an inventory enumerating their crimes – one such person was said to have been wholly or partially responsible for the murder of 745 people.[11]

In the famous cabinet founded in 1590 at the University of Leiden, known for its medical specimens, 'In addition to various animals, ranging from a ferret to a horse, the rearticulated skeletons of a number of notorious criminals could be seen. These included the remains of a sheep-stealer from Haarlem and of a woman strangled for theft; more impressively, one could see "The Sceleton of an Asse upon which sit's [sic] a Woman that Killed her Daughter" and also "The Sceleton of a man, sitting upon an ox executed for Stealing of Cattle." '[12] In the collection of Bernard Palissy (1510–90), Huguenot potter and philosopher, 'His large shell-collection contained foreign as well as local varieties, and fossils were also richly represented. One of Palissy's particular interests was petrification, the basis of which he discussed [in his philosophy]: no doubt his interest was fuelled by the tales he records of whole companies of men and animals and even entire villages turned to stone.'[13] In the Bodleian Library at Oxford, the following highlights were recorded by visitors: ' "a piece of the

salt pillar" (which may have been intended for Lot's wife), and a coat attributed to Joseph "which he wore when he was sold to the Egyptians." '[14] In the
Tradescant natural historical collection in London, *c.*1683: 'More widely
appreciated (and collected) were the "Barnacles", of which the Tradescants
had four sorts. Barnacle geese attracted the curiosity of collectors on account of
the tradition, enshrined in their name, that they sprang from barnacle shells
adhering to driftwood and trees rather than from eggs.'[15] Finally, the
Tradescant collection included 'the remora, a sucking fish (*Echeneis remora*)
anciently believed to have the power to bring ships to a halt by attaching itself
to the keel'.[16]

   These stories amply illustrate two important, and distinct, points. First, the
desirability of the curious object lay in its relation to a known or acceptable
story; why otherwise would it have mattered which human skeleton or
deformity one was viewing? And why else that fish, or that oxbone, unless it
had a tale to tell? And even where the objects did not refer to a particular tale –
say, the samples of geological materials or a butterfly collection – they could
be said to refer to another narrative, the one constructed taxonomically
around their distinction into species and categories by type. This was a narrative of scientific knowledge, and a story that would be just as well known (to
the scientists) as the fantastic tales were to the larger cabinet-visiting public.
Secondly, historiography of the cabinets, and therefore of museums, repeats
the story for the very same reason, even though we supposedly no longer
believe in the mythic or fantastic origins of the objects: because the desire for
the story remains, even if the desire for the object has subsided.[17]

   The desire for stories persisted through the transition from curiosity cabinets to modern museums and was reflected in the historiography of museums,
which reproduced the earlier stories even in an attempt to displace or recast
them. The first modern German history of museums, to my knowledge, was
written by Gustav Klemm, librarian to the king of Saxony and director of the
royal porcelain collection. Klemm's *Towards a History of Scientific and Art
Collections in Germany* (1837) rehabilitates earlier libraries, cabinets, museums
and archives as precursors of the modern historical museum. Two of the most
famous early modern collections, those of Ole Worm and C.F. Nieckels, are
discussed at length as examples of collections in which 'the historical viewpoint dominated'.[18] Klemm then provided a detailed listing of significant contemporary collections of all types, with a separate category for 'collections of
history and ethnography'. Klemm reinterpreted the perpetually-present
desire to collect as a progressive history of collecting for the representation of
history – sometimes misguided, sometimes misrepresented, but always
recognizable as a trend toward the current era's historical interests.[19] This
interpretation prevails even though, as Klemm also notes:

Certainly collections were formed whose beginnings clearly reflected the character of their times, when one laid particular value on the unusual, rare and remarkable, and where it was enough to bring the materials together in order to judge first of all according to their scope, to be able to sort and order according to their differences.[20]

Such collections – Klemm cites that of August I, forerunner of the royal Dresden collection of art and antiquities – are characterized as 'jumbles', well-intentioned but limited by the sixteenth-century scientific world-view. Klemm contrasts early eighteenth-century cabinets – 'conglomerates of the fruits of bad taste, which offer food for conversation but at best only rarely can provide instruction' – with the museums of his time, in which the attempt was being made 'to create organic wholes, to vouchsafe as complete as possible an overview of the subject ... before it takes into consideration the superfluous or the mere curiosity'.[21] This overview, the organic form, was History. In crediting selected earlier collections with 'an historical viewpoint', he subtly and successfully translated any earlier evidence of interest in narrative organization into a prehistory of the modern historical museums. Natural history continues to benefit from collection of specimens, Klemm argued, but historical museums need to be developed so that their collections offer instruction to the viewer, through a visible historical narrative.

What happens to the 'curiosity' under this new collecting rubric? Curiosity is no longer sufficient grounds, nor a satisfactory object, for museum collecting; plenitude is no longer representative of a world-view but of disorder; and persistent interest in curiosities now relegates the collector to the status of dilettante. Desire for stories is replaced by a desire for a particular kind of story, history.

'No mere attribute of age or empty curiosity value' would give an object a place in the Berlin royal antiquities collection under the direction of E.H. Toelken in 1835.[22] The new museums wanted to represent history through selected historical objects, whose historical value was not determined by sheer age or uniqueness. If curiosities are 'empty', lacking historical value or unable to fit into the story to be told, they do not qualify as monuments (*Denkmäler*) of German history. The German word for memory, *Erinnerung*, literally means filling-in (*erinnern*), and a *Denkmal*, as opposed to a curiosity, is an object of memorial which best effects this memory-process. The difference between a curiosity and a *Denkmal* is crucial to understanding the changes in historical collecting which began at the end of the eighteenth century.

To understand Toelken's position, we can look to earlier descriptions of antiquarian collections and see how historical value was attributed. One of the best-known collections of the later eighteenth century in Cologne belonged to the Baron Johann von Hüpsch (1730–1805), who collected antiquities as well as natural-historical objects and what would now be considered ethnographical objects (costumes, weapons, handcrafts). The antiquities came from all over the world and were not intended to represent local history. The personal nature of the collector's enterprise becomes clear when we look at Hüpsch's attempts to sell the collection as a single unit. As was often the case, potential buyers desired only certain objects from the collection – which also supports the argument that collector idiosyncrasy was still a determining factor in collecting during this period. Another hindrance was the lack of a catalogue or inventory. Hüpsch did not catalogue his own collection because, as Gudrun Calov explained, 'one could not understand the overall sensibility of his cabinet from a ''systematic'' presentation, because for him from the very beginning it was a matter of an overall conceptualization, not of the individual curious objects'.[23] French authorities interested in the collection (during the Napoleonic occupation of the Rhineland) offered to buy it intact if the disorder of the collection could be remedied by a catalogue. Hüpsch, despite financial straits and a desire to preserve his collection intact, refused.

The collector was able to maintain whatever sense of order he desired so long as the collection remained in his cabinet, but once the collector tried to market it, the collection had to offer something besides the fascination it held for its creator; the multitude of stories associated with individual objects needed to be contained within a transmittable master narrative. What for Hüpsch was representative of plenitude became to observers a sign of disorder. Later visitors to the cabinets who had an interest in purchase, including the illustrious Johann Wolfgang von Goethe (himself a passionate collector), complained of the disorder that characterized some of the best collections of antiquities. After 1813, Goethe undertook to visit and describe the major collections of art and antiquities in the Rhine and Main regions, and was also asked by the Prussian government to make recommendations regarding the purchase of some of these collections for Berlin. Goethe's reaction to the collection of Ferdinand Franz Wallraf, professor of botany and rector of the university at Bonn, is typical of this new criticism:

He [Wallraf] belongs to that sort of people who from a boundless desire to possess things, are born without any methodical sensibility or love of order ... The chaotic condition in which the priceless objects of nature, art and antiquity lie is unthinkable: they lie, stand and hang all over and under each other. He protects these treasures like a dragon but without at all sensing that day by day something exquisite and worthy is losing its value through dust and dry-rot, and through being shoved and rubbed and stuffed together.[24]

A contemporary drawing depicts Wallraf amidst his objects, very much like Goethe's dragon in his lair: his foot resting royally upon a book, objects piled about him, the knights in their armour almost alive to his interests (note that he has his hand resting possessively on what appears to be a medieval relief) (Figure 11.1). The critique of disorder can be seen as a development from the descriptions of early modern cabinets in which the proximity of different

kinds of objects made for an impression of plenitude. Goethe was impressed
by the sheer amount of interesting objects, but did not see in Wallraf's protec-
tiveness the kind of protection – preservation – which historical collectors
desired.

In contrast, Goethe visited another famous Rhineland collection in 1815,
that of Franz Pick (1750–1819), which impressed him more favourably. Early
in his career, Pick had served as house chaplain and secretary to Graf Franz-
Wilhelm von Oettingen-Baldern, who possessed an art and curiosity cabinet
'in the style of the 16th century'.[25] Pick's interest in collecting was developed
along with this collection, and he became friends with Wallraf. By the time of
his death, Pick's own collection included 'about 250 paintings, 7500 engravings, 200 wood carvings (including 35 by Dürer), hundreds of manuscripts,
valuable books including those printed before 1500 (incunabula), medieval
stained glass, Roman stone monuments, antique coins, ivories and antiquities
from several centuries' – most of them local artefacts.[26] Clearly this was no
curiosity cabinet, nor yet was it a '*Schatzkammer*' of royalty; it was a collection
in which the historically sensitive observer could find much food for the soul.
Goethe found that Pick's collection stimulated the historical sensation:

This bright and clever man has conscientiously collected each and every antique thing
which came into his hands, which would be enough of a service, but he has served an
even greater purpose in that he has earnestly and wittily, sensitively and cleverly
ordered a chaos of ruins, enlivened them and made them useful and enjoyable . . . one
looks through the collection with ever changing interests, which each time necessarily
take a historical direction.[27]

The collection might still appear a 'chaos of ruins' to modern observers, since
period or type did not necessarily order the objects. The effect the collection
had on Goethe seems to have been intensified by its situation in Pick's own
house: his house *was* the collection. Goethe wrote in a recommendation to
Berlin that 'to move Pick's collection from its place would be to destroy it;
while in contrast one must move Wallraf's collection if one is to make anything
of it'.[28]

The curious collector and the eccentric antiquarian were beginning to be
socially and intellectually isolated in the nineteenth century. They became
objects of derision in contemporary literature. Dickens and Flaubert each
poked fun at the figure of the eclectic collector in the novels *The Old Curiosity
Shop* and *Bouvard and Pecuchet*, respectively; Flaubert's pair were a distinct
parody of the collector who wished to recreate the macrocosm of the world in
the microcosm of a private cabinet.[29] Walter Scott's title character in his 1817
novel *The Antiquary*, Jonathan Oldbuck, was a curmudgeon whose refuge
from 'female foolery' and the general irritations of the world was his 'sanctum
sanctorum', the chaotic jumble of his private study-cabinet. A similar characterization appears in a letter from Annette von Droste-Hülshoff, whose sister

Jenny married the antiquarian and philologist Joseph von Lassberg. Describing one of her visits to them at the castle of Meersburg on Lake Constance in the 1840s, Droste-Hülshoff wrote:

Aside from the ladies of Thurn [herself and Jenny], not one wench entered the house, only men all of one type, antiquarians who wished to grub around in my brother-in-law's musty manuscripts; very learned, very famous people in their own rights – but oh so boring, like unto death, mildewed, corroded, prosaic, rough as a horsebrush, hardened despisers of all new art and literature.[30]

Lassberg himself was not above joking at the expense of antiquarians. He recalled seeing an English poem around the turn of the century which related the story of an antiquarian visiting Shakespeare's birthplace, 'who found a broken pisspot in the garden and donated this priceless treasure to the British Museum'.[31]

The antiquarian today is himself something of a historical relic. The late historian Arnaldo Momigliano described the antiquarian as the type of man 'so near to my profession, so transparently sincere in his vocation, so understandable in his enthusiasms, and yet so deeply mysterious in his ultimate aims: the type of man who is interested in historical facts without being interested in history ... Nowadays the pure antiquarian is rarely met with'.[32] The pure antiquarians are those who remained behind after the majority went on to collective collecting, or as Momigliano writes, 'As soon as the antiquarian leaves his shabby palace which preserves something of the eighteenth-century and enters modern life, he becomes the great collector, he is bound to specialize, and he may well end up as the founder of an institute of fine arts or of comparative anthropology'.[33] The isolations of Lassberg's castle or Oldbuck's 'sanctum sanctorum' were deserted in favour of public spheres of collecting.

So popular was the trend toward group organization that this period of German history was even at the time called 'the era of the association' (*Verein*).[34] The production of collections was undertaken in common cause, and the results were intended to be publicized and displayed to a widening public. Associations of historical preservationists flourished in Germany after 1820. Each association sought to build a collection of historical objects and to publish a journal that reported on their collection and preservation efforts. When they could afford to, they purchased extant collections; in addition, they urged members to contribute (donate) objects and their own collections to the association museums. These museums were then housed in such small, rented rooms as were available, and made accessible to association members on a regular basis. The stated purpose of these associations was to preserve and display objects of historical interest, rather than to produce written histories. Nevertheless, these museums were to be organized according to historical narratives, so that the visitor to the museum would be instructed in the historical sensation (as opposed to history). What Goethe described as the historical feeling in Pick's house was to be reproduced in local museums in each province of Germany. The members of the historical associations took it upon themselves to be guardians and custodians of the historical object: they alone were qualified to identify, collect, preserve and organize the objects of historical perception.

The persuasive force of these collectors was formidable. They discouraged the individual collector from dabbling in historical objects, arguing that although the historical sensation could be experienced alone, efforts to preserve that sensation would be lost even if the objects were saved, unless the historical perception was shared. Personal passions and the right ideas were insufficient means for achieving the goal of preservation; alone, the collector was an object as incomplete and dispersed in effect as were any of the artefacts and objects the collectors wished to find and save:

No one can say with certainty that it might not be possible for an individual to succeed in saving important antiquities, and to bequeath them to the association for use in scientific study. When individuals collect, these collections are important to them and are in good hands – as long as they live. After their death, it is all lost again. But if a well-grounded association collects – then this loss is not to be feared, and future generations are assured the advantages of the earlier work and collection; they at least enjoy the fruits of our labor![35]

Individuals, acting alone, are as mortal as the uncollected object: their work will become a ruin, in danger of perishing unless united in the collective effort, whose ongoing continuity ensures its posterity. The association was more than the sum of its individual parts, and would survive them.

This lesson in historical consciousness was tested and tragically revised in the case of the founder of the Germanisches Nationalmuseum, Hans von Aufsess (1801–72). An amateur collector and historical preservationist, Aufsess liked to 'live in' and amidst his collection of historical objects (Figure 11.2). His collecting career, begun in the 1820s, was characterized by his interest in two fields: his family history, which entailed the history of German nobility dating from the Middle Ages to the present; and, following from this, German medieval art and artefacts. Aufsess was part of the Romantic nationalist groundswell of interest in reclaiming Gothic art as German, and recovering its relics from neglect and ruin. He retained another, characteristically Romantic, subjective interest in these objects, in that he genuinely believed that these objects had a personal connection to him, through the legacy of his nobility. The personal connection was established not by provenance but by ownership; not by family heritage but by class prerogative turned into personal possession. Members of the nobility, Aufsess argued, had a special relationship to the artefacts of the past. Insofar as these artefacts had survived into the present due to their monetary or religious value, it could be argued that valuable artefacts necessarily owed their origin to the class that had been

able to afford them. But Aufsess also collected domestic objects, kitchen imple-
ments as well as icons and armour. For Aufsess, the entire material cultures of
the past belonged to him, his class, and the future – in that order, and in his
own home.[36]

Aufsess founded the 'Society for the Preservation of the Monuments of
older German History, Literature and Art' and edited its publication, the
Anzeiger für Kunde des deutschen Mittelalters, begun in 1831. With the foundation of the society, Aufsess began to contemplate creating a museum for the
display of his collection and that of the Association (also largely comprising
his own objects). The Association was very much a provincial one, dedicated
to collecting local historical objects and promoting their national significance.
At the same time, the professionalization of history was proceeding apace,
with chairs being created for history professors at the universities, and
historicism becoming the dominant scholarly-theoretical persuasion. Aufsess
and his fellow collectors, passionate dilettantes all, found themselves in conflict with the professional historians who, although they benefited from the
diligent collecting of society members, distrusted the collectors' scholarly
abilities. Aufsess for one consistently denied that he had any interest in
writing history; he saw his historical mission as that of the collector and pre-
server of artefacts which might otherwise fall into ruin, disappear, and be lost
to historical memory. But he learned that the historians were unwilling to trust
him with the very objects he found, collected and preserved.

The tensions between Aufsess and the scholarly community are clearly
illustrated in a remarkable drawing that appears in the guestbook of Schloss
Aufsess. The artist Wilhelm von Kaulbach, a friend of Aufsess's, drew the
image: he depicts Aufsess as a knight astride a white horse, skewering with his
lance the representatives of 'scholarly conceit' (*gelehrten Dünkel*) and the
'moralizers' (*Moralprediger*) (Figure 11.3). Aufsess as the hero of historical
preservation is protecting not only his autonomy as a collector, but also his
claim to interpret his collection as he chooses. The selection of objects in the
collection reflected Aufsess's intention to portray local-noble heritage as a
national identity. After over twenty years of struggling to create a suitable
display space – which he believed must necessitate removal of the objects from
his house to a public building – Aufsess received the endorsement of the Duke
of Saxony and the first assemblage of a national, rather than provincial,
German historical association in 1852. The motto he chose for the new
museum was 'Property of the German People' (*Eigenthum des deutschen
Volkes*). He deliberately chose to remove the collection from his own home to a
public museum, and publicly announced this self-alienation of property, from
private to public, from provincial to national.

The German nation, for Aufsess, was the concept which best expressed his
personal, familial and provincial sense of identity. He chose it in defiance of

the scholars of the day, and eventually suffered the repercussions: Aufsess, initially the director of the Germanisches Nationalmuseum, lost his position ten years later after a review by representatives of the scholarly community indicated that they considered him unfit to direct a museum of national importance. The museum in Nuremberg, brought under Prussian jurisdiction, had succeeded where Aufsess had failed: the collection itself was valued for its contents, but its collector was not to be trusted with the interpretation of the collection. Even though Aufsess understood his collection to represent the nation, others who would 'speak for' the nation wanted to tell a different story with the same objects.

Ironically, Aufsess lost the war by winning the battle: in establishing a museum whose contents were to represent the nation, he succeeded in creating a national museum, but the personal- and class-based story of the nation was displaced by the discourse of nationalism. As the *großdeutsch* and *kleindeutsch* factions fought out the destiny of German unification, Aufsess sank into despondency and isolation, alienated from his all-too-national collection, his own right to 'speak for' the nation, its people, its nobility, and its history.

The narrative of nation created by Aufsess rested on an idiosyncratic notion of personal history and class heritage; for Aufsess, the nation was an intimate and meaningful concept precisely because he provided his own understanding of it. He began to lose his personal possession of the past the moment he decided to create a museum, both because he gave away his possessions and because his personal vision clashed with that of rapidly professionalizing and nationalizing historians. If the academics and nationalists can be said to have caused Aufsess's downfall, there is only one further ironic, perhaps tragic note to add to the story: Aufsess attended a parade to celebrate the anniversary of German unification, and was mistakenly overheard to criticize the new nation, whereupon he was attacked by patriots, beaten, and died a few days later of his wounds.

Storied objects continued to be processed into national historical narratives throughout the nineteenth century. The antiquarian did not so much disappear as fade away, while the new custodians of historical narrative sought to collect objects which inspired a historical sensation and which, rather than invoking the notion of plenitude or rarity, could participate in the story of an essential recognition of 'the past'. Passionate collectors of artefacts, no longer guides and tellers of the stories they longed to relate, joined like-minded fellows in association to pursue the common goal of historical representation.

Notes

1. Krzysztof Pomian, *Collectors and Curiosities: Paris and Venice, 1500–1800*, trans. Elizabeth Wiles-Portier (London, Polity Press, 1990), p.7.

2. Friedrich Kruse, 'Introduction', in *Deutsche Alterthümer*, 1 (1824–26), p.33.

3. Karl Preusker, 'Alterthumsforschung', *Westfälische Archiv*, 4 (1829), p.233.

4. Johann Heinrich Zedler, *Grosses vollständiges Universal-Lexikon aller Wissenschaften und Kunste* (rpt, 1732; Halle and Leipzig, Graz, Akademische Druck, 1961), p.173.

5. Pomian, *Collectors and Curiosities*, p.56.

6. *Ibid.*, p.59.

7. *Ibid.*, p.125.

8. Pomian's thesis is that 'it is the social hierarchy which necessarily leads to the birth of collections, those sets of objects kept out of the economic circuit, afforded special protection and put on display', *ibid.*, p.32. In the case of Diderot and the Encyclopedists, he argues that they attacked *curiosité* as 'a "desire to acquire" not only the sort of object with which the enthusiast filled his rooms but also, if not above all, a social position enabling one to exert a decisive influence on the lives of artists and on their art itself', *ibid.*, p.137.

9. O.R. Impey and A. MacGregor, *The Origins of Museums: The Cabinet of Curiosities in 16th–17th Century Europe* (London, Oxford University Press, 1985); Barbara Jean Balsinger, 'The Kunst- und Wunderkammern: A Catalogue Raisonné of Collecting in Germany, France and England 1565–1750', PhD thesis, University of Pittsburgh, 1970; Eileen Hooper-Greenhill, *Museums and the Shaping of Knowledge* (London, Routledge, 1992); Paula Findlen, *Possessing Nature: Museums, Collecting and Scientific Culture* (Berkeley, L.A., University of California Press, 1994).

10. An earlier history by David Murray cites the exasperation of a French visitor to the British Museum in 1810, who reported that 'We had not time allowed to examine anything; our conductor pushed on without minding questions, or unable to answer them, but treating the company with double entendres or witticisms on various subjects of natural history, in a style of vulgarity and impudence which I should not have expected to have met in this place and in this country' (David Murray, *Museums: Their History and Use* (Glasgow, publisher not stated, 1904), n. p.212. Given that tickets to the museum were much sought after and the number of visitors restricted, having to rush through the collection must have been frustrating; but what is particularly interesting here is that the visitor appears to have heard some of the stories about curious objects without being amused by them.

11. Arthur MacGregor, 'Collectors and Collections of Rarities in the Sixteenth and Seventeenth Centuries', in Arthur MacGregor (ed.), *Tradescant's Rarities: Essays on the Foundation of the Ashmolean Museum, 1683* (Oxford, Clarendon Press, 1983), p.74.

12. *Ibid.*, p.78.

13. *Ibid.*, p.82.

14. *Ibid.*, p.88.

15. *Ibid.*, pp.91–2.

16. *Ibid.*, p.93.

17. My point supplements, rather than counters, Svetlana Alpers's argument that early modern collecting focused on objects 'judged to be of visual interest' rather than judged to have interesting stories attached to them. See Svetlana Alpers, 'The Museum as a Way of Seeing', in I. Karp and Stephen D. Lavine, *Exhibiting Cultures: The Poetics and Politics of Museum Display* (Washington D.C., Smithsonian Institution Press, 1991), pp.25–32, p.26. Art historical objects underwent similar re-evaluations in the historical transition from cabinet to museum; while the history of art museums is necessarily integrated into that of the modern museum as a whole, disciplinary distinctions have tended to segregate types of museums (natural historical, art historical, ethnographic, historical) in ways which overlook potential similarities of development.

18. Gustav Klemm, *Zur Geschichte der Sammlungen für Wissenschaft und Kunst in Deutschland* (Berbst, G.A. Kummer, 1837), p.152.

19. This interpretive style lives on in many modern histories of the museum. To cite one example, Edward Alexander writes of Sir Hans Sloane, one of the founding fathers of the British Museum, that, 'Not only did Sloane collect widely and well. He also *understood the need* of a museum to put its holdings in order and provide a proper record for each specimen or object' [my italics]. Indeed Sloane used very similar words: 'The putting into some kind of Order my Curiosities ... was necessary in Order to their Preservation and Uses.' But Alexander's presumption of the 'need' which Sloane 'understood' implies a retroactive participation in modern collecting practices, rather than simply stating that Sloane in fact was developing new strategies for his collecting in opposition to a larger trend, the assembly of curiosities. Edward Alexander, *Museum Masters: Their Museums and Their Influence* (Nashville, American Association for State and Local History, 1983), p.29.

20. Klemm, *Zur Geschichte der Sammlungen*, p.146.

21. *Ibid.*, pp.238–9.

22. E.H. Toelken, *Erklärendes Verzeichniss der antiken Denkmäler im Antiquarium des königlichen Museums zu Berlin* (Berlin, publisher not stated, 1835), p.xxi.

23. Gudrun Calov, 'Museen und Sammler des 19 Jahrhunderts in Deutschland', *Museumskunde* 38 (Berlin, Verlag Walter de Gruyter, 1969), p.54.

24. *Ibid.*, p.59.

25. Reinhard Fuchs, 'Zur Geschichte der Sammlungen des rheinischen Landesmuseums Bonn', in R. Fuchs (ed.), *Rheinisches Landesmuseum Bonn: 150 Jahre Sammlungen, 1820–1970* (Düsseldorf, Rheinland-Verlag, 1971), p.6.

26. *Ibid.*, p.4.

27. *Ibid.*, p.16.

28. *Ibid.*, p.17.

29. See also Eugenio Donato, 'The Museums' Furnace: Notes Toward a Contextual Reading of *Bouvard and Pecuchet*', in J. Harari (ed.), *Textual Strategies: Perspectives in Post-Structuralist Criticism* (Ithaca, Cornell University Press, 1979), pp.213–38.

30. Quoted in Christian Altgraf zu Salm, 'Lassberg als Kunstsammler', in K.S. Bader (ed.), *Joseph von Lassberg: Mittler und Sammler* (Stuttgart, Vorwerk, 1955), pp.65–87, p.75.

31. From a letter to the Swiss historian J.A. Pupikofer, 20 November 1830, printed in 'Briefwechsel Lassberg mit J.A. Pupikofer', *Alemania* 15 (1887), pp.231–83, p.266.

32. Arnaldo Momigliano, 'The Rise of Antiquarian Research', in *Classical Foundations of Modern Historiography* (Berkeley, University of California Press, 1990), p.54.

33. *Ibid.*

34. Thomas Nipperdey, 'Vereine als soziale Struktur in Deutschland im späten 18. und frühen 19. Jahrhundert', in Thomas Nipperdey, *Gesellschaft, Kultur, Theorie* (Göttingen, Vandenhoeck und Ruprecht, 1976), pp.175–205.

35. Thüringen-Sächsischen Vereins Für Erforschung des vaterländischen Alterthums, '2er Jahresbericht', *Deutsche Alterthümer*, 2:1 (1826), p.78.

36. The following account of Aufsess's career has been adapted from my earlier publication, Susan Crane, '(Not) Writing History: Rethinking the Intersections of Personal History and Collective Memory with Hans von Aufsess', *History and Memory* 8:1 (1996), pp.5-29.

11.1   Nicolas Salm, Ferdinand Franz Wallraf sitting among his collection like a dragon
in his lair (*c*.1820), chalk drawing

11.2   Hans von Aufsess lived in and amidst his collection of medieval artefacts

11.3   Wilhelm von Kaulbach 'The Knight', Hans von Aufsess, does battle with the foes of historical preservation, pen and ink (1865)

Select secondary literature

Alpers, Svetlana. 'The Museum as a Way of Seeing', in I. Karp and Stephen D. Levine, *Exhibiting Cultures: The Poetics and Politics of Museum Display* (Washington D.C., Smithsonian Institution Press, 1991), pp.25–32.

Baines, Paul. ' "Our Annius": Antiquaries and fraud in the eighteenth century', *British Journal of Eighteenth-Century Studies*, 20 (1997), pp.33–51.

Balsinger, Barbara Jean. 'The Kunst- und Wunderkammern: A Catalogue Raisonné of Collecting in Germany, France and England 1565–1750', PhD thesis, University of Pittsburgh, 1970.

Bender, Barbara. 'The Politics of Vision and the Archaeologies of Landscape', in *Landscape: Politics and Perspectives*, ed. Barbara Bender (Oxford, Berg, 1993), pp.19–48.

Bermingham, Ann. *Landscape and Ideology. The English Rustic Tradition, 1740–1860* (Berkeley and Los Angeles, University of California Press, 1987).

Charlesworth, Michael. 'Sacred Landscape: Signs of Religion in the Eighteenth-century Garden', *Journal of Garden History* 13 (1993), pp.56–68.

Clayton, Timothy. *The English Print, 1688–1802* (New Haven and London, Yale University Press, 1997).

Cleal, Rosamund, Walker, K.E., Montague, R. *et al.*, *Stonehenge in its Landscape: Twentieth-century Excavations*, English Heritage Archaeological Report 10 (London, English Heritage, 1995).

Coffin, David R. *The English Garden: Meditation and Memorial* (Princeton University Press, 1994).

Colley, Linda. *Britons: Forging the Nation 1707–1837* (New Haven and London, Yale University Press, 1992).

Daniels, Stephen. 'Goodly Prospects: English Estate Portraiture, 1670–1730', in Nicholas Alfrey and Stephen Daniels (eds), *Mapping the Landscape: Essays on Art and Cartography*, exhibition catalogue (Nottingham University Art Gallery, 1990).

Dugaw, Dianne. 'The Popular Marketing of "Old Ballads": The Ballad Revival and Eighteenth Century Antiquarianism Reconsidered', *Eighteenth-Century Studies*, 21:1 (1987), pp.71–90.

Evans, Joan. *A History of the Society of Antiquaries* (Oxford, The Society of Antiquaries, 1956).

Findlen, Paula. *Possessing Nature: Museums, Collecting and Scientific Culture* (Berkeley, University of California Press, 1994).

Griffiths, Antony. *Landmarks in Print Collecting, Connoisseurs and Donors at the British Museum since 1753* (London, British Museum Press, 1996).

Harris, R.W. *Reason and Nature in the Eighteenth Century* (London, Blandford Press, 1968).

Harwood, Edward. 'Personal Identity and the Eighteenth-century English Landscape Garden', *Journal of Garden History* 13 (1993), pp.36–48.

Hooper-Greenhill, Eileen. *Museums and the Shaping of Knowledge* (London, Routledge, 1992).

Hunt, John Dixon. 'Emblem and Expressionism in the Eighteenth-century Landscape Garden', *Eighteenth-Century Studies*, 3 (1971), pp.294–317.

—— *The Figure in the Landscape: Poetry, Painting, and Gardening during the Eighteenth century* (London, The MIT Press, 1976).

—— *Garden and Grove: The Italian Renaissance Garden and the English Imagination, 1600–1750* (London, J.M. Dent, 1986).

—— *Gardens and the Picturesque: Studies in the History of Landscape Architecture* (Cambridge, Mass, The MIT Press, 1992).

Hunt, John Dixon and Willis, Peter. *The Genius of the Place: The English Landscape Garden, 1620–1820* (London, The MIT Press, 1988).

Impey, O.R. and MacGregor, A. *The Origins of Museums: The Cabinet of Curiosities in 16th–17th Century Europe* (London, Oxford University Press, 1985).

Karp I. and Lavine, Stephen D. *Exhibiting Cultures: The Poetics and Politics of Museum Display* (Washington D.C., Smithsonian Institution Press, 1991).

Langford, Paul. *A Polite and Commercial People: England 1727–1783* (Oxford University Press, 1992).

—— *Public Life and Propertied Englishmen 1689–1798* (Oxford, Clarendon Press, 1991).

Levesque, Catherine. *Journey Through Landscape in Seventeenth-Century Holland: The Haarlem Print Series and Dutch Identity* (Pennsylvania University Press, 1994).

Levine, Joseph M. *Dr. Woodward's Shield: History, Science, and Satire in Augustan England* (Berkeley and London, University of California Press, 1977).

Levine, Phillipa. *The Amateur and the Professional. Antiquarians, Historians and Archaeologists in Victorian England, 1838–1886* (Cambridge University Press, 1986).

Lipking, Lawrence. *The Ordering of the Arts in Eighteenth-Century England* (Princeton University Press, 1970).

Lippincott, Louise. *Selling Art in Georgian London: The Rise of Arthur Pond* (New Haven and London, Yale University Press, 1983).

MacGregor, Arthur. 'Collectors and Collections of Rarities in the Sixteenth and Seventeenth Centuries', in Arthur MacGregor (ed.), *Tradescant's Rarities: Essays on the Foundation of the Ashmolean Museum, 1683* (Oxford, Clarendon Press, 1983).

McCarthy, Michael. *The Origins of the Gothic Revival* (New Haven and London, Yale University Press, 1987).

McKendrick, Neil, Brewer, John and Plumb, J.H. *The Birth of a Consumer Society: The Commercialization of Eighteenth-Century England* (London, Hutchinson & Co., 1982).

Momigliano, Arnaldo. 'Ancient History and the Antiquarian', *Journal of the Warburg and Courtauld Institutes*, 13 (1950), pp.285–315. [See also Arnaldo Momigliano, 'Ancient History and the Antiquarian', in *Studies in Historiography* (London, Weidenfeld & Nicolson, 1966), pp.1–39.]

—— *Classical Foundations of Modern Historiography* (Berkeley, University of California Press, 1990).

—— 'The Rise of Antiquarian Research', in *The Classical Foundations of Modern Historiography* (Berkeley and Oxford, University of California Press, 1990), pp.54–79.

—— *Studies in Historiography* (London, Weidenfeld & Nicolson, 1966).

Piggott, Stuart. *Ancient Britons and the Antiquarian Imagination* (London, Thames and Hudson, 1989), p.15.

—— *Approach to Archaeology* (London, Black, 1959).

—— *The Druids*, 2nd edn (London, Thames and Hudson, 1975).

—— *Ruins in A Landscape* (Edinburgh University Press, 1976).

—— *William Stukeley: an Eighteenth-Century Antiquary*, 2nd edn (London, Thames and Hudson, 1985).

Pocock, J.G.A. *Virtue, Commerce and History: Essays on Political Thought and History, Chiefly in the Eighteenth Century* (Cambridge University Press, 1985).

Pomian, Krzysztof. *Collectors and Curiosities: Paris and Venice, 1500–1800*, trans. Elizabeth Wiles-Portier (London, Polity Press, 1990).

Rule, John. *Albion's People: English Society 1714–1815* (London, Longman, 1992).

Schulz, Max F. 'The Circuit Walk of the Eighteenth-century Landscape Garden and the Pilgrim's Circuitous Progress', *Eighteenth-Century Studies*, 15 (1981), pp.1–25.

Smiles, Sam. *The Image of Antiquity: Ancient Britain and the Romantic Imagination* (New Haven and London, Yale University Press, 1994).

Ucko, Peter, Hunter, Michael, Clark, Alan and David, Andrew. *Avebury Reconsidered: From the 1660s to the 1990s* (London, Unwin Hyman, 1991).

Wainwright, Clive. *The Romantic Interior: The British Collector at Home, 1750–1850* (New Haven, Yale University Press, 1989).

Index

References to illustrations are given in *italics*.

academic specialization, 8, 27, 169, 172–8
Addison, Joseph, 69, 74
Aikin, John, 84–5
Aislabie, John, 75
Albrecht V, Duke of Bavaria, 190
Allan, George, 117
amateurism, 3, 86–8, 95, 169, 196
antiquarian(s)
  aesthetics, 4, 21–7, 84, 90–91, 169
  and art, 15
  and narrative, 190–91
  and taste, 6, 15, 22–7, 55–6, 89–91
  collecting habits of, 84–7, 194–5
  compared with historians, 4–5, 15, 27, 187
  difference between antiquarian and artist, 16, 143
  draughtsmanship, 97, 98, 100, 105, 123–4
  publishing, 3, 55–6, 117
  reading, 116
  research, 3, 7
    empirical, 16, 117
    fieldwork, 3, 20, 68
    lack of first-hand, 3, 117
    reliance on non-literary evidence, 15, 21, 56, 61–3, 100, 117, 124
  satires of, 2, 3, 15, 187, *130*
  satirized for their
    blind admiration for the past, 23–5
    impotence, 118–20
    obsession with detail, 7, 118–19
    pedantry, 119, 154
  self-perception of, 118
  social propriety of 2, 21, 84–7, 118–19, 195
antiquarianism
  and amateurism, 3, 86–8, 95, 169, 171, 196
  and consumerism, 83–92
  and gentility, 3, 89–92, 135–6
  and national identity
    in England, 87, 90–92
    in Germany, 95, 101–2, 103, 195–8
  and patriotism, 1, 3, 90–92, 126–7
  and poetry, 26, 96, 101, 141
  and politics, 90–91

and preservation, 17–19, 20–27, 100, 105, 195–8
and the exotic, 103
and the spiritual, xx, 101–5
and 'theoretical history', 171
and scientific methods, xx, 4, 137, 171–7, 188–9
as an intellectual pursuit, 24, 56, 96, 169
as entertainment, 56, 83–5, 115–18, 121–5
changing face of, 169
classical, 5, 6, 21, 102
criticisms of, 3, 21, 83–6, 117–20, 169, 172
marginalization of, 4, 88
misguided conclusions of, 86, 118–20, 172
popularization of, 3, 8, 96, 117, 170
women and, 8, 86, 135–44
Archaeologia (see under Society of Antiquaries (London))
Archaeological Institute, 172
archaeology, 173
  classical, xxii, 95
  of modern life, 157–8
architecture
  Bath, 77
  Classical, 170
  Gothic, 101, 170, 171, 174, 176–7
    derision of, 105
    German, plundered for building materials, 101
  history of, 172
  medieval, 169, 171
    reconstruction of, 174
  origins of, rustic, 170
  Palladian, 68
  styles of, 176
Arkona, 104
Arndt, Ernst Moritz, 96
Arntner, Maria Therese von, 141 (48n)
Aubrey, John, 17, 24 (48n), 174
Aufsess, Hans von, xxii, 196–8, *202–3*
autobiography, 135, 138–44
Avebury, 70–77, *80*
Ayloffe, Joseph, 1 (4n)

Bacon, Francis, 40, 120 (22n), 138, 173, 174